Sexual Feelings in Psychotherapy

Sexual Feelings in Psychotherapy

EXPLORATIONS FOR THERAPISTS AND THERAPISTS-IN-TRAINING

Kenneth S. Pope, Janet L. Sonne, Jean Holroyd

 # 27729283
DLC

11-30-94

RC
480.8
P659
1993

c.1

First printing April 1993
Second printing September 1993
Third printing March 1994

Published by the
American Psychological Association
750 First Street, NE
Washington, DC 20002

Copies may be ordered from
APA Order Department
P.O. Box 2710
Hyattsville, MD 20784

In the United Kingdom and Europe, copies may be ordered from
American Psychological Association
3 Henrietta Street
Covent Garden, London
WC2E 8LU England

Printer: Princeton Academic Press, Inc., Lawrenceville, NJ
Typesetter: Techna Type, Inc., York, PA
Cover designer: Berg Design, Albany, NY
Technical/Production editors: Peggy Schlegel and Valerie Montenegro

Library of Congress Cataloging-in-Publication Data
Pope, Kenneth S.
  Sexual feelings in psychotherapy: Explorations for therapists and therapists-in-training / Kenneth S. Pope, Janet L. Sonne, Jean Holroyd.
      p.   cm.
  Includes bibliographical references and index.
  ISBN 1-55798-201-5 (acid-free paper)
  1. Psychotherapists—Sexual behavior.   2. Psychotherapy patients—Sexual behavior.   3. Psychotherapist and patient.
4. Psychotherapists—Professional ethics.   I. Sonne, Janet L.
II. Holroyd, Jean.   III. Title.
  [DNLM: 1. Psychotherapy.   2. Professional–Patient Relations
3. Sex.   4. Sex Behavior   5. Ethics, Profes.   WM 62 P825sa   1993]
RC480.8.P659   1993
616.89´14—dc20
DNLM/DLC
Library of Congress

93-7139
CIP

British Library Cataloguing in Publication Data
A CIP record is available from the British Library.

Printed in the United States of America

Contents

Foreword

In the mental health professions, we have seen the number of ethical complaints continue to increase over the past decade, an increase driven in large part by therapists sexually exploiting their clients. As the research reviewed in appendix C suggests, as many as 10% of male therapists and 2 to 3% of female therapists have reported engaging in sex with current or former clients. Sex with clients continues to be a problem despite the fact that the prohibition against sex with clients has been the clearest and probably the most publicized explicit proscription in all ethical codes of the mental health professions.

Evidence exists that society feels that we have not done enough to monitor our own mental health professions. Because the professions have failed to address this problem adequately, the legal system has stepped in. Civil courts are awarding monetary damages to victims of sexual exploitation by therapists. Such exploitation is so damaging that it is being criminalized. As I write this foreword, sex with clients is already a felony in slightly over a half dozen states, with offenders sometimes incurring stiff fines and prison terms of up to 10 years.

The outrage that many feel about this abuse and the professions' inadequate response to it was reflected in Ann Landers's column "Not All Psychiatrists Are Bad; This One Was."[1] Landers devoted her entire Sunday column to the book *You Must Be Dreaming*.[2] The book described how one of its authors, Barbara Noel, was injected with Amytal, a barbiturate, and raped by psychiatrist Jules H. Masserman, a past president of the American Psychiatric Association and the American Academy of Psychoanalysis. Landers's rage was based in part on the

---

[1]Landers, A. (1992, September 13). Not all psychiatrists are bad; this one was. *Austin American Statesman*, p. E2.

[2]Noel, B., & Watterson, K. (1992). *You must be dreaming*. New York: Poseidon.

perception that the psychiatric community protected Masserman by allowing him to relinquish quietly his license to practice and by declining to expel him from the American Psychiatric Association. At the time of her column, Masserman still sat on the American Psychiatric Association's Board of Trustees. Landers stated, "The psychiatric community does indeed take care of its own, but Ann Landers takes care of HER own, too, and this column will be read by 90 million people"[3]. Approximately one month later, a letter from the current president of the American Psychiatric Association was published in an Ann Landers column mistitled by my local paper as "Psychologist's (sic) Abuse of Patient Strikes Chord."[4] Dr. Joseph English applauded Landers's efforts to protect patients from exploitation, reiterated that doctor–patient sex is always wrong, acknowledged how important it is to publicize these violations more widely, and asserted that his Association had taken action to do so.

This kind of public outcry can help our mental health professions to consider how we can fulfill more adequately our responsibilities to restrict and prevent the damaging behavior of sex with clients. And that is why *Sexual Feelings in Psychotherapy: Explorations for Therapists and Therapists-in-Training* is a landmark contribution. It presents an opportunity for therapists and trainees to explore their reactions to sexual feelings in order to better understand assumptions, behaviors, and approaches to clients and to the process of counseling and psychotherapy.

Most of us do not have sex with our clients. However, in our practice, we are presented with an almost infinite number of situations and circumstances in which we have the power to exploit, abuse, and hurt our clients. The unique approach presented in this book allows us to sensitize ourselves to many ethical and therapeutic issues. Most important, it provides us with the opportunity to improve our ability to reason about sexual issues. The book does so in part by presenting a variety of scenarios and passages that can be discussed with others

---

[3]See note 1 above.

[4]Landers, A. (1992, October 11). Psychologist's (sic) abuse of patient strikes chord. *Austin American Statesman*, p. F2.

regarding optimal ways of handling the situations. The passages and scenarios are meant to call the reader's attention to situations, behaviors, or feelings that may seem taboo and that tend to make many professionals and professionals-in-training uncomfortable. The book encourages acknowledgment and exploration of feelings and reactions elicited by the passages and scenarios as well as by the clinical situations we encounter daily.

Several important assumptions of the authors warrant special emphasis. One is that most therapists have experienced sexual attraction to clients and that this attraction tends to make therapists uncomfortable. Although these attractions and subsequent discomfort are common, the therapist often feels alone in this experience. Therefore, much of the process of exploration and discovery of the therapist's feelings and reactions is best done in the company of others. The process of open discussion of feelings and reactions can help us to emerge from discomfort, shame, and guilt and to move toward ethically and clinically sound problem solving. It is crucial to find appropriate ways to acknowledge and accept sexual feelings in therapy and the complex cognitive, affective, and physical responses to these feelings.

A major theme of the book is that there is no lockstep process or absolute formula for handling such situations. The issues raised are intended to provide an opportunity for self-exploration and discovery. There are no absolutes for how to handle uncomfortable situations that arise in the therapeutic situation, save the most fundamental rule: The authors emphasize that under no circumstances should a therapist ever have sex with a client, and under no circumstances should a therapist ever communicate, either explicitly or implicitly, that sexual intimacies with a client are a possibility. It is solely the therapist's responsibility to ensure that no sexual intimacies occur with a patient. Yet there are no clear or easy answers as to what to do if one experiences sexual feelings for a patient. No "cookbook" approach exists to guide the therapist. Yet one can go through the helpful process of clarifying values, styles, and preferences in managing responses. One chapter of this book, for example, offers valuable insights into the contextual factors that may influence therapists' sexual feelings and responses, including religion, sexual orientation, gender, age, ethnicity, social class, disability, client diagnosis, client physical attractiveness, and therapist orientation. And the appendixes, as another example, offer several articles that provide important research findings about therapist–client sexual issues.

Readers of this text are encouraged to avoid judging behaviors described in the passages and scenarios as right or wrong, sound or unsound, appropriate or inappropriate, but to attend to their own unique cognitive and emotional reactions. This approach fosters readers' emotional learning and professional development. For experienced therapists, the passages and scenarios will indeed stir memories of situations in which they have found themselves and provide opportunities to reflect on what they did at the time and what they might do differently now. For therapists-in-training, the passages and scenarios provide vivid images from the wide range of situations in which they will inevitably find themselves during the course of a career.

This book is a contribution that is long overdue. Training programs are often at a loss as to how to foster therapists' sense of responsibility for ethical behavior in their relationships with clients. One of the key strategies in the prevention of therapist–client sexual contact is trainees' understanding of the many issues raised in this book. The passages and scenarios will evoke and serve as the focus of rich and valuable discussions that will promote self-awareness and knowledge in such areas as attraction to clients, the role of touch in therapy, vulnerabilities, boundaries, and many other vital aspects of counseling and therapy. Knowledge and understanding that come as a result of these discussions can help sensitize trainees to the potential impact of their behavior with clients. They can help lead, for example, to increased awareness of how therapists may at times unwittingly sexualize relationships with clients.

Few of us in the mental health professions take our work lightly, and most of us are highly motivated to behave ethically in all of our work. When we do commit ethical errors, we often do so out of ignorance and from not ever having been exposed to the complex and difficult situations in which we find ourselves. This book is a tremendous contribution to increasing skills in managing the tremendous anxiety and uncertainty about our decisions and behaviors that affect so deeply the lives of our clients. We have an ethical responsibility to develop the abilities to monitor ourselves, our colleagues, and our profession. This book will go far in providing a means to promote those abilities.

The authors are distinguished and outstanding psychologists with international reputations for their rigorous, innovative work in the area of ethics and clinical standards of practice and especially for their pioneering, landmark contributions to our understanding of sexual issues in counseling and psychotherapy. Kenneth S. Pope, Janet L. Sonne, and Jean C. Holroyd have all dedicated much time and energy to the promotion of professionals' responsibility in their behavior with clients. All have served on ethics committees or task forces to develop codes and standards for psychologists. There could be no more appropriate people to write this valuable resource.

MELBA J. T. VASQUEZ, PHD
Diplomate in Counseling Psychology
Former Chair, APA Board for the Advancement of Psychology
    in the Public Interest
Former Member, APA Ethics Committee

Acknowledgments

The authors are deeply indebted to Theodore J. Baroody, Julia Frank-McNeil, Peggy Schlegel, Valerie Montenegro, Olin J. Nettles, and Susan Bedford of APA Books; Gary R. VandenBos of Publications and Communications; and Devona Marinich of Marketing Services for their encouragement, guidance, hard work, and much needed help in bringing this book about.

We appreciate the kindness of Jossey-Bass Inc., Publishers, for allowing an extended quotation from Seymour B. Sarason's *Caring and Compassion in Clinical Practice: Issues in the Selection, Training, and Behavior of Helping Professionals.* Copyright 1985 by Jossey-Bass Inc., Publishers.

We would like to thank the American Psychological Association, Patricia Keith-Spiegel, and Barbara Tabachnick for their kind permission to reprint "Sexual Attraction to Clients: The Human Therapist and the (Sometimes) Inhuman Training System" as appendix A. This article was published in Volume 41 (pp. 147–158) of the journal *American Psychologist.* Copyright 1986 by the American Psychological Association.

We would also like to thank the Division of Psychotherapy (Division 29) of the American Psychological Association and Donald Freedheim, editor of *Psychotherapy,* for their kind permission to reprint "Treating Victims of Therapist–Patient Sexual Involvement" as appendix B. This article was published in Volume 28 (pp. 174-187) of the journal *Psychotherapy.* Copyright 1991 by Division 29 of the American Psychological Association.

Finally, we would like to thank Pergamon Press for their kind permission to reprint "Therapist–Patient Sexual Involvement: A Review of the Research" as appendix C. This article was published in Volume 10 (pp. 477–490) of *Clinical Psychology Review,* the official journal of the Division of Clinical Psychology (Division 12) of the American Psychological Association, edited by Alan S. Bellack and Michel Hersen. Copyright 1990 by Pergamon Press.

I

Fundamentals of Exploration and Discovery

Purpose and Plan of This Book

This is a book of exploration and discovery. It was created to help therapists and therapists-in-training explore their erotic responses to clients, their reactions to their clients' sexual feelings and behavior, their sense of themselves and their clients as physical beings, and the influences that help shape and shade their responses.

Exploration of therapists' sexual feelings tends to be difficult not only because of the profession's long neglect of this area but also because of the tendency to confuse feelings with behavior (see chapter 2). Understanding therapists' sexual feelings must, to some extent, occur in the context of understanding therapists' sexual behavior with clients. Despite the fact that all major mental health disciplines explicitly state that therapist–client sexual intimacies are unethical, some therapists engage in this exploitive behavior. The first national study of therapist–patient sexual intimacies (Holroyd & Brodsky, 1977),[1] for ex-

---

[1]The survey was sent to 1,000 members of the American Psychological Association and obtained a 70% return rate. The article reported that 12.1% of the male and 2.6% of the female participants reported having engaged in erotic contact (whether or not it included intercourse) with at least one opposite-sex patient; that about 4% of the male and 1% of the female participants reported engaging in erotic contact with at least one same-sex patient; and that 7.2% of the male and 0.6% of the female participants reported that they

ample, found that 12.1% of the male and 2.6% of the female participants acknowledged, on an anonymous survey, having engaged in erotic contact with an opposite-sex patient and that about 4% of the male and 1% of the female participants reported having engaged in erotic contact with a same-sex patient. A study published 2 years later, which was also based on a national sample of psychologists, found roughly similar results: About 12% of the men and 3% of the women "reported sexual contact as psychotherapists with their clients" (Pope, Levenson, & Schover, 1979, p. 682). Half of the respondents in a recent national survey reported that they had assessed or treated at least one patient who had been sexually intimate with a previous therapist (Pope & Vetter, 1991).[2] Formal research as well as clinical case studies have vividly described the devastating harm that can occur as a result of these intimacies (see appendixes B and C). Information about therapists who form sexual relationships with their clients has emerged from a variety of sources, including licensing disciplinary actions (Pope, in press).

Although knowledge about therapist–patient sexual behavior is an important part of the context for the explorations in this book, the horror at harm done to the patient, shame that some in the profession victimize those who come for help, and other powerful reactions to therapist–client sexual intimacies (i.e., *behavior*) can make therapists turn away from their own sexual *feelings* as "too dangerous," as reflecting an abusive or pathological nature, or as a temptation to be blotted out of existence and awareness. Thus, the small, atypical group of therapists who have violated the prohibition against therapist–client sex-

---

had "had intercourse with a patient within three months after terminating therapy" (p. 846).

[2]Of the 958 patients who were reported to have engaged in sexual intimacy with a previous therapist, 5% were minors at the time of the intimacies, 32% were victims of child abuse, 10% had experienced rape prior to the intimacies with the therapist, 11% required hospitalization considered to be at least partially due to the intimacies, 14% attempted suicide, and 1% committed suicide. When sexual intimacies began during the course of therapy, harm was reported for 95% of the female and 80% of the male patients. When sexual intimacies began only after termination of the therapy, harm was reported for 80% of the female and 86% of the male patients.

ual intimacies have not only exploited their clients but also helped to create an atmosphere in which acknowledging, accepting, and learning about sexual feelings seem dangerous and daunting for the vast majority of therapists who, whatever their sexual feelings toward patients, would never seriously consider violating the prohibition and placing their patients at risk for great and lasting harm.

The first three of this book's seven fundamental premises are (a) exploration of therapists' sexual feelings and reactions is an important aspect of graduate and medical school training, internships, and continuing professional development; (b) these feelings must be clearly distinguished from sexual intimacies with clients; and (c) *no therapist must ever sexually exploit a client*. The other four basic premises are discussed in the following sections.

Discomfort With Sexual Feelings

The fourth basic premise is that, as the research presented in appendix A suggests, most therapists have experienced sexual attraction to or arousal with a client and that this experience tends to make therapists uncomfortable (i.e., anxious, guilty, or confused). Consider, for example, whatever feelings may be evoked by the following five scenarios:

> During the second year of therapy, a patient remains silent much of the session and seems to have difficulty speaking. Finally the patient says, "There's something I just have to know. Do you think I'm good looking and are you attracted to me?"

> You are teaching a client how to use techniques of progressive relaxation (Jacobson, 1938). The client reclines on the couch, and you direct attention systematically to each part of the body, encouraging relaxation of those muscles. As the focus of attention moves toward and through the hips and buttocks, you notice that the client seems to have become sexually aroused.

> You look at your appointment book and see that at three o'clock that afternoon you have an intake appointment.

Promptly at three, you go to the waiting room, and there is the answer to all the dreams and fantasies you have ever had. You become an instant believer in a concept you had often ridiculed: love at first sight.

You invite the person into your office and, during the interview, begin to feel even more intensely that this is the one and only person with whom you want to spend the rest of your life. You think to yourself, "I have to interrupt. I have to tell this person that I can't start a therapeutic relationship. I have to see if we can have some coffee or something. We have to talk, but not as therapist and patient. If not now, then soon. I'll give this patient some referrals to other therapists."

Doing play therapy with a young child, you find that the child likes to sit on your lap. During one session, you find that as the child moves around on your lap, you are becoming sexually aroused.

You are being intimate with your partner. You whisper something especially sweet and romantic. However, instead of using your partner's name, as you had intended, you accidentally use the name of one of your patients.

This book assumes that the reader who feels some discomfort in taking the role of therapist in these scenarios is by no means alone. But it also assumes that many readers are likely to *feel* alone in experiencing sexual feelings about patients and the anxiety, guilt, confusion, and other uncomfortable reactions that sexual feelings often evoke.

When readers look to the published research, they find few studies about sexual attraction to patients. When they look to their graduate training programs, they tend—at least according to two studies that have addressed training in this area (Pope, Keith-Spiegel, & Tabachnick, 1986; Pope & Tabachnick, 1993)— to find that the issues are ignored, discounted, or dealt with inadequately. They may not hear their colleagues discussing personal experiences in this area; many therapists seem to avoid discussing sexual feelings about patients with others, even their supervisors or consultants (see appendix A).

Chapter 2 discusses the profession's difficulties in addressing therapists' experience of and response to sexual feelings, and explores possible reasons that the topic has been avoided. By candidly confronting the sources of possible resistance to the topic, the profession can better carry out its responsibility to help prepare therapists to acknowledge, accept, and explore sexual feelings that occur in therapy.

The historical information in chapter 2 may seem, at least on a superficial level, disheartening. It shows moments when the profession was not at its best. A profession that from the time of Freud has invited patients to speak with courage and candor about their most private sexual feelings, fantasies, and impulses, has sometimes, by contrast, shied away from confronting sexual feelings, fantasies, and impulses as experienced by the therapists who work with those patients. Acknowledging, understanding, and attending to this history of reluctance and resistance can, however, serve as a source of enlightenment and empowerment.

The information in chapter 2 can serve at least three major purposes. First, remembering its own past in regard to acknowledgment of sexual issues can help the profession to avoid repeating mistakes of the past. The information in chapter 2 serves as a reminder of the strength of professional resistance to this topic historically and of the ways in which acknowledgment and inquiry can be discouraged.

Second, it provides a historical context for understanding the sexual issues presented in this book. Just as chapter 5 presents social, cultural, and demographic factors (e.g., gender, ethnicity, age, and socioeconomic status) that form important aspects of the context in which sexual feelings occur, chapter 2 presents significant aspects of the historical context for understanding sexual feelings in therapy.

Third, the events and factors discussed in chapter 2 may be helpful to learning groups using this text as they reflect on the learning process. At times, learning-group participants may become aware that some issue is making its presence felt but remains unacknowledged in group discussion, that members of the group seem blocked or stalled in their attempts to explore one of the passages or scenarios, or that some baffling group process seems to be occurring. At such times, reflection on the profession's history of difficulty in addressing therapists' sexual feelings may help the group to determine whether some version of the historical events described in chapter 2 are reflected or reenacted, however unintentionally, in the group dynamics.

Avoiding Avoidance

This book's fifth premise is that, where sexual attraction to patients and other sexual feelings are concerned, it is crucial to avoid avoidance. Acknowledging and accepting not only the therapist's sexual feelings but also the complex cognitive (e.g., confusion), affective (e.g., anxiety), and physical (e.g., genital arousal) responses to those feelings are an important part of professional development and functioning. Sexual feelings and responses may be powerful and influential in and of themselves. They may also provide important information for the therapist about him- or herself, about the patient, or about important aspects of the therapeutic situation.

When therapists attempt to avoid acknowledging and accepting their own feelings and responses, they make it more likely that their understanding of their own motivations, intentions, and behavior will be—at best—unnecessarily limited and incomplete. Efforts at avoidance may also make it more likely that these feelings and responses will affect the therapy and patient in ways that are counterproductive or even harmful.

Acknowledging and accepting these feelings and responses, although important to the development and functioning of the individual therapist, also has significance for the profession as a whole. The vast majority of therapists do *not* express sexual attraction to a patient by engaging in therapist–patient sexual intimacies, but a small percentage of therapists do violate the prohibition against such intimacies (see appendix C). The tendency to avoid the topic of sexual attraction to patients has hampered the profession's ability to understand, prevent, and respond to violations of the prohibition against sexual intimacies with patients.

Creating Conditions for Learning

This book's sixth premise is that a significant portion of the process of exploration and discovery is best done with others in a safe, nonjudgmental, and supportive context. This volume was designed for use in a variety of settings, such as graduate and medical school courses, seminars, internships, continuing education programs, peer consultation or support groups (in which several clinicians meet to discuss their work), hospital or clinic in-service training programs, and the office of the individual clinician who seeks to continue his or her professional development in partnership with a trusted colleague, consultant, or supervisor.

This book does not attempt to guide the reader toward any particular understanding or resolution. It attempts to call attention to certain situations, events, behaviors, and contexts that can serve as points of departure for the reader's exploration and discovery. No two readers are likely to experience exactly the same reactions to the passages and scenarios or to reach exactly the same conclusions about how such phenomena are best understood. Because of these differences, the give-and-take among different individuals with different perspectives, values, and personal histories can provide a rich environment for exploration and discovery.

As discussed in a subsequent section, different psychotherapeutic schools or orientations will tend to deal with the material in different ways. A seminar in cognitive–behavior modification, for example, will likely explore these issues using different frameworks, emphases, and approaches than continuing education courses in family systems, feminist, gestalt, psychodynamic, or rational–emotive therapy. Moreover, within each school or orientation, each person will have his or her own sets of reactions, values, goals, and perspectives.

This book also assumes that not only the teacher, supervisor, or group leader—if any—but also the participants share responsibility for creating suitable conditions for learning. Especially in light of the personal nature of the feelings and responses, the uncomfortable reactions (e.g., anxiety, guilt, and confusion) that sexual feelings and responses often evoke, the shared (though sometimes unequal) vulnerability of the participants and identified leader or facilitator, and crucial issues of privacy, everyone involved must work to maintain a safe, supportive structure and environment for the learning process. Chapter 3 notes some of the important issues for learning groups to consider in creating such settings.

Exploration and Discovery

Once therapists and therapists-in-training decide to embark on a course of exploration and discovery in the area of sexual feelings and responses, and have created safe and supportive conditions for learning, another important task is to become more aware of the point of departure. Chapter 4 provides therapists with an opportunity to assess the degree to which they can acknowledge and accept sexual feelings and responses to those feelings. It may also help identify some of the personal attitudes, beliefs, and assumptions that tend to influence those feelings and responses. After completing the course of exploration and discovery provided by this book, readers may want to return to chapter 4 to see if and how their feelings, responses, and views have changed.

Finally, before embarking, therapists and therapists-in-training may renew their awareness of at least three sets of information that may be especially helpful. First, there are contextual factors such as age, race, and gender. The ways in which the society or culture tends to react to these factors may significantly influence whether and how sexual feelings and responses emerge in a particular therapeutic relationship, as well as the subsequent thoughts and feelings a therapist may experience in regard to sexual issues. Chapter 5 highlights a few of these contextual factors. Second, as chapter 6 notes, sexual feelings in therapy can evoke diverse reactions; not only anxiety, guilt, and confusion but also a variety of other responses are not uncommon. Third, as surveyed in chapter 7, clues to unacknowledged sexual feelings in therapy are abundantly available to the therapist.

Although the factors, reactions, and clues introduced in chapters 5, 6, and 7 are by no means exhaustive, attending to each of these three areas may be helpful in the exploration and discovery of therapists' sexual feelings and responses. This book's seventh premise, however, is that even if one could somehow specify all contextual factors, secondary reactions, and revealing clues, there can be no "cookbook" approach to the nature, meaning, and implications of individual sexual feelings and responses. Although helpful if not crucial, knowledge about theory, research, and objective information can take the therapist only so far. Nothing can spare the therapist from the personal, complex, and often unpredictable process of exploration and discovery. As Shapiro (1965) wrote about a different topic,

> The same mental content or behavior will have different significance to different individuals, and different contents will have closely similar significance. Without this understanding, we run the risk. . .of seeing only textbook meanings, possibly correct but far removed from the sense and tone of an individual's experience. (p. 18)

Here is the story of one therapist's reactions to the powerful feelings that the therapeutic situation can evoke:

> The therapist is treating a young woman of keen intellect. He becomes fascinated by her. He begins to make time in his schedule to see her on an almost daily basis. She is surprised to discover that as she talks about the hardships of her life, she feels better. It is as if just being in the presence of the therapist and expressing her feelings of sadness, pain, and frustration are therapeutic.
>
> The therapist begins to extend the sessions, some of them lasting several hours. The treatment is working.
>
> As a year passes, the therapist becomes increasingly intrigued by this woman. He begins to talk with his wife about this very special patient. His wife questions him about his

feelings for her, but he is aware only of a professional therapist–patient relationship that seems to be remarkably helpful. He continues to talk about the young woman, and his
wife begins to feel jealous.

During the second year of therapy it dawns on him: There
is some sort of erotic tone to the relationship. He grows
nervous. He decides that the woman, having made such
strides toward recovery, is ready for termination. He tells
her that it is best that their sessions come to an end, noting
that she has benefited from the therapy, has achieved a remarkable recovery, and can continue on her own.

Soon, however, the therapist receives an urgent call. The
patient has relapsed and is acting very strangely. He discovers that she is acting as if she were giving birth to a child,
though she is not pregnant. The therapist administers a form
of crisis therapy. As soon as possible, he rushes away from
her in a chilled sweat. She is soon hospitalized.

Rushing home, the therapist joins his wife and both leave
promptly on a trip out of the country. This trip serves as a
second honeymoon, and the couple conceive a daughter.

The patient continues to suffer for several years. When
she recovers, she becomes a social worker, a political organ-
izer, and a scholar, translating Mary Wollstonecraft's treatise
on women's rights.

The therapist in this story is Josef Breuer (1842–1925), one of
Freud's (1856–1939) early collaborators. The patient is Bertha
Pappenheim (1859–1936)—given the pseudonym "Anna O." in
Breuer's and Freud's writings—who sought help from Breuer
in 1880. This account of this therapy is drawn mainly from Jones
(1961) as well as from Breuer and Freud (1895/1957); for additional information and perspectives, see Ellenberger (1972), Kavaler-Adler (1991), Pollock (1973), and Schonbar and Beatus
(1990).

Breuer, Freud, and Pappenheim each seemed to respond
differently to the sexual feelings and other issues that emerged
in this therapy. During the therapy, Breuer seemed unaware
of the sexual nature of the patient's behavior and of the possible
meanings of the extended time he spent with her. When he
became aware of her sexual feelings, they seemed to frighten
him. He quickly terminated the therapy and took a long journey

with his wife. Interestingly, when he reflected on the experience, he focused on himself and his own behavior. He searched for what he might have said or done to the patient that would have elicited her sexual feelings.

Freud, on the other hand, sought to understand the patient's sexual feelings not as a reaction to the individual therapist or to his specific characteristics or behaviors but rather as a natural response of a female patient to a male therapist. "He had come up against something that is never absent—his patient's transference on to her physician, and he had not grasped the impersonal nature of the process" (1925/1961a, p. 280). Freud began to develop the concept of transference.

One can only speculate on Pappenheim's response on the basis of her subsequent activities. It seems possible that she came to understand the causes of her distress and the resources for recovery in light of larger cultural forces (e.g., the role of women in society) rather than through focusing on the role of therapist or patient.

> The mute hysteric who had invented "the talking cure" found her voice, and her sanity, in the women's liberation movement . . . . Under her own name, Bertha Pappenheim became a prominent feminist social worker, intellectual, and organizer. In the course of a long and fruitful career she directed an orphanage for girls, founded a feminist organization for Jewish women, and traveled throughout Europe and the Middle East to campaign against the sexual exploitation of women and children . . . . In the words of a colleague, "A volcano lived in this woman. . . . Her fight against the abuse of women and children was almost a physically felt pain for her." (Herman, 1992, p. 19)

Each focus—the behaviors of the therapist, the naturally occurring transference, and gender-related cultural forces—draws attention to different sets of organizing principles for understanding the sexual aspects of this therapy. Each focus changes the array of likely causes and meanings, and brings with it numerous assumptions about human behavior and experience (see, e.g., Hare-Mustin, 1992).

What does it mean when sexual feelings emerge in therapy? Do they imply that something is amiss in the therapy? That there is a new and healthy component to the relationship between therapist and patient? That the therapist has unresolved personal conflicts or issues? That the therapist is more open to personal feelings about the patient? That the patient has become more healthy and integrated? That the therapist is distorting or avoiding other feelings about the patient? That the therapist has an unfulfilling sex life and is looking to the patient for sexual gratification? That larger cultural forces or dynamics are gaining expression in the therapy? That the patient is covertly building up the therapist's ego? That the therapist is at risk for engaging in sex with the patient? That the patient is using sexual behavior on an unconscious level as a sort of "code" to communicate something important to the therapist? That the therapist is influenced by sex role stereotypes? That the therapist and patient are assuming roles and relationships that reflect their own family structure? That the patient has acted seductively? That the therapist is experiencing countertransference? That the therapy needs to address sexual issues? These are but some of the almost countless possibilities, none of them mutually exclusive.

Passages and Scenarios

Part II of this book presents readers with passages and scenarios that can be used to explore and learn about their sexual feelings and responses. Each passage or scenario is followed by questions intended to help this exploratory process. *There is no attempt to supply possible answers to these questions or otherwise to impose interpretations of the material, because the process is necessarily a unique pursuit for each individual.*

It is important to note that material presented in this book is meant to be helpful in calling the reader's attention to various situations, behaviors, or feelings that may seem taboo and that tend to make many professionals and professionals-in-training uncomfortable; but this material is hardly exhaustive or comprehensive. Many vignettes will likely come to mind suggesting issues that are not represented in this book. Similarly, the reader will be able to formulate questions about a given passage or scenario that are much more relevant to his or her unique reactions than those that are provided in this book. The more extensively the reader is able to explore those original vignettes and personal questions, the more likely he or she will accomplish this book's intended goals. The issues raised and the questions set forth in the text are meant to help initiate, lend structure to, and foster—rather than determine in a lockstep fashion—a process of self-exploration and discovery.

Each reader is encouraged to attend carefully to his or her spontaneous responses to the passages and scenarios, and to follow the paths of exploration and discovery that seem most important in light of his or her own values, interests, theoretical orientation, and personal history and experience. As Stricker (1991) wrote in another context,

> There are no general rules other than the need to attend to the specifics of each situation. This recognition of lack of generalizations leads to one important generalization: any attempt to impose our predetermined structure on a situation runs the risk of failing dismally. It is only through recognizing how little we know that we can make effective use of how much we know. (pp. 211–212)

In some instances, the reader may be tempted to critique or condemn some behavior illustrated in the passages or scenarios of the following chapters. Such critiques would likely be unfair and counterproductive.

A judgmental approach would be unfair because the material was chosen to illustrate and evoke the types of feelings that are the focus of this book rather than to describe in adequate detail a specific therapist's orientation, interventions, and rationales. To critique a therapist's work on the basis of an abbreviated bit of material would be unfair because the passages and scenarios present only an isolated episode or statement, without the context. This caution goes beyond the obvious observation that an intervention that is based on the principles of behavior therapy may seem misguided to the psychoanalytic observer, and vice versa. It is likely that none of us would want others to judge the appropriateness of our work solely on the basis of a brief description of one isolated behavior or event in therapy; we would want to be able to describe in adequate detail our theoretical orientation, what we know about the individual client, what we sought to accomplish through therapy, the obvious and subtle therapeutic process as it was unfolding, the context of our work, and many other factors without which an individual behavior or event in therapy cannot be understood. These passages and scenarios are presented without those contextual details because, standing by themselves, they seem to point to or illustrate the kind of behaviors and events relevant to the topic of this book. They are intended to serve an evocative purpose for the reader, whatever the reader's theoretical orientation, values, or beliefs.

To critique the behaviors presented in this book would be not only unfair but also counterproductive. This book will be most productive if it enables the reader to identify, accept, understand, and make therapeutic use of his or her own feelings. To critique someone else's feelings, attitudes, or behaviors is a good way to avoid examining one's own reactions. It shifts the focus in a way that is at odds with the purpose of this book.

There are, of course, ethical and legal standards of practice, ways of evaluating clinically sound and unsound practices within various theoretical orientations, and interventions that may seem clearly appropriate or inappropriate for a given client in a given situation. Such factors are crucial and are discussed in detail in many other publications. But the necessary attention to such factors—namely, focusing on mandated, appropriate, or sound practices—can sometimes serve, by default, as an inadequate substitute for an exploration of the therapist's genuine emotional and cognitive responses. Moreover, an exclusive emphasis on "right" and "wrong" (or "sound" and "unsound," "appropriate" and "inappropriate," etc.) practices can sometimes actively inhibit the emotional learning and professional development of the therapist. If discussion of therapist–patient sexual intimacy is limited to the ethical and legal prohibitions and to the devastating effects that clients might suffer, a trainee may be mortified to discover that he or she is fantasizing about a social or sexual relationship with a client. If focus on clients' sexual attraction to therapists is limited almost exclusively to admonitions that therapists must respond with sensitivity, respect, appropriate limit setting, and most of all acceptance to such attraction, a therapist may find it difficult to tell anyone else that he or she is terrified of a certain client's sexual intensity and behavior.

Beyond standards of practice, it is important that therapists and therapists-in-training acquaint themselves with the research and theory about sexual feelings that occur in therapeutic relationships. But again, as with the standards of practice, an almost exclusive preoccupation with research data and theoretical developments can, however unintentionally, serve as an inappropriate substitute for a careful exploration of the therapist's psychological and bodily reactions to the client and to the therapeutic process. The purpose of this book is to focus direct attention on those reactions. As previously noted, research data about *feelings* (e.g., sexual attraction to patients) and clinical and research data about *behavior* (e.g., the occurrence and consequences of therapist–patient sex or the treatment approaches to help victimized patients) provide an important context for the explorations in this book; three appendixes provide relevant information. Readers will likely find it more beneficial to consult these appendixes *after*, rather than before, completing the rest of the book.

Considering the Questionable Act: Confronting an Impasse

This book's final chapter concerns what to do when "stuck." Examination of sexual feelings and other factors may lead the therapist to contemplate a particular action or intervention, yet the therapist remains uncertain whether the contemplated course of action is wise or foolish, insightful or self-deceptive, helpful or hurtful. The therapist wants to be of help to the patient and adheres to the ironclad commitment to avoid sexual intimacies with the patient but cannot decide whether a certain intervention makes good clinical sense. In light of the uniqueness of each situation (which includes the uniqueness of the therapist, the patient, and their unfolding relationship), the vast differences in the implications of competing theoretical orientations, and the diversity of treatment paths and goals, there can no more be lists of universally "correct" specific behaviors than there can be lists of universally "correct" meanings and implications of the sexual feelings that therapists experience. However, there are questions that therapists may use in exploring or contemplating specific behaviors in this context. The final chapter presents ten considerations that therapists may find useful when they reach an impasse.

A Note on Terminology

First, this book uses such terms as *therapist, counselor,* and *clinician* interchangeably. Similarly, the terms *client* and *patient* are used interchangeably.

Second, although sexual *behavior* (i.e., therapist–patient sex) is, as previously discussed, different from sexual *feelings,* understanding the dynamics, effects, and implications of therapist–patient sexual intimacy is part of the crucial context of the work that is the focus of this book. This book rests on a fundamental premise that sexual intimacies with clients must be avoided. We provide a chapter ("Confronting an Impasse") examining ways in which particularly challenging feelings, fantasies, and impulses can be thought through in order to avoid behaviors that constitute or lead to such intimacies; an appendix (C) reviewing some of the published research (including research on the harm that can occur for clients who are sexually exploited) on therapist–client sexual intimacies; and an appendix (B) on providing help to clients who have been sexually involved with their therapists.[3] It is important to note that *sexual intimacies,* as a term, does not refer exclusively to sexual intercourse. For example, the California Business and Professions

---

[3]Extensive discussion of fundamental issues in the psychological assessment of both patients and therapists who have been involved in therapist–patient sexual intimacies is presented in a special section of Pope, Butcher, and Seelen (1993, pp. 165–186).

Code states that any kind of *sexual contact, asking for sexual contact,* or *sexual misconduct* by a therapist with a client is illegal and unethical, and a cause for disciplinary action (sections 726 and 4982k). The Code states that *sexual contact* refers to touching an intimate part (e.g., sexual organ, anus, buttocks, groin, or breast) of someone else. *Touching,* according to the Code, refers to physical contact with someone else *either* directly on the person's skin or through the person's clothing. Thus, sexual contact can include a much broader range of behavior than simply intercourse.

In some cases, sexual intimacies may not involve direct touch or contact, as noted in the following: "Sexual misconduct covers an even broader range, such as nudity, kissing, spanking, and sexual suggestions or innuendos. This kind of sexual behavior by a therapist with a client is sexual exploitation. It is unethical, unprofessional, and illegal" (California Department of Consumer Affairs, 1990, p. 2). The diversity of behaviors that fall within the domain of the term *sexual intimacies* and have led to disciplinary actions is suggested by a summary provided by Thomas O'Connor, Executive Officer of the California Board of Psychology:

> Sexual abuse cases have involved an amazing range of people, circumstances, and behaviors. Most involve a male therapist and a female patient, but there have been pairings of female therapists with male patients, female therapists with female patients, and male therapists with male patients. Although such therapists generally have sex with only one patient at a time, we've seen instances in which therapists involved patients in group sex. Instances of sexual misconduct have included a therapist seeing a couple for marital therapy who had intercourse with the wife while the husband sat in the waiting room unsuspecting; a therapist becoming sexually involved with a client who was a ten year old girl; a male therapist directing a female patient to suck on the therapist's finger while she masturbated; a therapist sexually abusing developmentally disabled teenagers; a therapist using vibrators and other sexual aids on female clients who had been victims of incest as children; a female therapist who had a five year sexual relationship with a female client;

a therapist giving a client herpes; a therapist subjecting a patient to forcible anal rape; a therapist engaging in sexual acts including kissing, caressing, photo taking, spanking, group sex and masturbation with several clients, including a 65 year old nun; and a therapist directing a client to stand on her head in what was supposed to be a yoga position without any clothes on. (Personal communication, December 1992)[4]

Ethical codes (e.g., American Psychological Association [APA], 1992) have wisely avoided attempting to define *sexual intimacies* through an exhaustive listing of anatomical couplings or specific behaviors. When activities in therapy (or between therapist and client) do not involve intercourse or more direct forms of sexual contact, the context and the specifics of the situation must be taken into account to determine whether the behaviors constitute unethical sexual intimacies. For example, imagine that a male therapist ends a therapy session by putting his arms around a female patient and giving her a tight and lingering hug. Is this behavior unethical? Does it constitute a form of sexual exploitation?

In our opinion, the answer is, it depends. One possible scenario involves a theoretical orientation that permits nonsexual physical contact, a relationship between therapist and client grounded in trust and safety, and a use of a hug to offer comfort and support to a distraught patient who has recently lost her husband. In this scenario, there might be no erotic transference or countertransference. The therapist believes that the hug can play an important role in helping the woman through a difficult period of grieving and has been trained in the use of nonsexual, therapeutic touch. Neither therapist nor patient feels that there is a sexual component to the hug. Both believe that it is valuable, as does the therapist's supervisor. In this case, assuming that all the relevant facts have been given, it would appear that no sexual intimacies or exploitation occurred.

---

[4]Other examples of the diverse ways in which therapist–patient sexual intimacy occurs are presented in the section, Disbelief and Denial, in appendix B.

Another possible scenario involves a therapist and patient who have felt, but not discussed, intense sexual attraction to each other. Both are aware of the erotic feelings, but the topic is never mentioned. During the session, the therapist has invited the patient to describe her sexual fantasies. During the session, both therapist and patient become extremely aroused and remain aroused during the course of the session. Though they have never had physical contact of any type before, they impulsively hug at the end of the hour. The brief contact of the tight hug leads both, in their states of prolonged sexual excitement, to experience orgasm. In this case, it appears clear that sexual intimacies have occurred.

When considering whether to act on the basis of the types of feelings explored in this book (and, if so, how), the context and the specifics will often be crucial in determining whether a proposed activity or intervention constitutes or is likely to lead to unethical sexual intimacies. One critical aspect of understanding the context and specifics is the therapist's willingness and ability to recognize and explore his or her own sexual feelings in therapy.

Attempts to recognize and explore sexual feelings in therapy are more likely to succeed if they are guided by awareness of the barriers to recognition and exploration. Chapter 2 examines these barriers.

2

The Topic That Isn't There

Why is it so hard to acknowledge—let alone explore and talk about—sexual attraction to patients? Research suggests that attraction to patients makes most therapists feel guilty, anxious, or confused (see appendix A). But we lack studies helping us understand *why* it makes us uncomfortable or why we tend to avoid addressing the topic.

In light of the multitude of books in the areas of human sexuality, sexual dynamics, sex therapies, unethical therapist–patient sexual contact, management of the therapist's or patient's sexual behaviors, and so on, it is curious that sexual attraction to patients per se has not served as the primary focus of a wide range of texts. The professor, supervisor, or librarian seeking books that turn their *primary* attention to exploring the therapist's *feelings* in this regard would be hard pressed to assemble a selection from which to choose an appropriate course text. If someone unfamiliar with psychotherapy were to judge the prevalence and significance of therapists' sexual feelings on the basis of the books that focus exclusively on that topic, he or she might conclude that the phenomenon is neither widespread nor important.

Pope et al. (1986) reported research suggesting that many graduate training programs and internships tend to stop short of addressing this issue directly and adequately (see appendix A). A majority of the participants in this research reported that their graduate training and internships provided *no coverage whatsoever* about this topic. Less than 10% reported that their graduate and internship training covered this topic adequately. More recent research has found that a majority characterize their graduate training about therapists' feelings of sexual excitement as poor or virtually nonexistent (Pope & Tabachnick, 1993).

What is it about the therapist's sexual attraction to a patient that inspires such profound avoidance? Reviewing the profession's response to the issue of therapist–patient sex suggests possible reasons that the profession continues to avoid openly and adequately addressing the topic of sexual attraction to patients.

Guilt by Association

Sexual attraction to a patient, of course, is *not* the equivalent of sexual intimacies with a patient. However, the profession historically has demonstrated great resistance to acknowledging the problem of therapist–patient sexual intimacies. The veil that has covered the problem of sexual behavior with patients has fallen also over the topic of sexual feelings about patients. An elaborate "Catch 22" evolves: The more sexual feelings about a patient are identified with therapist–patient sex, the less anyone wants to acknowledge the feelings or discuss the topic in a personal context; the less sexual attraction is acknowledged and discussed as a topic distinct from therapist–patient sex, the more attraction becomes identified—by default—with therapist–patient sex.

The prohibition against therapist–patient sexual intimacies is by no means recent, having been affirmed by Freud. The prohibition against physician–patient sexual intimacies is even older, having been codified even before the Hippocratic oath (see Brodsky, 1989). However, it is only since the 1970s that the profession, prompted in part by the findings of Masters and Johnson described in appendix C, has begun to acknowledge openly violations of the prohibition, to study the incidence and effects of those violations (see appendix C), and to develop ways to help victims (see appendix B).

Attempts to raise and address this topic seemed to reveal professional resistance to publicly acknowledging that violations of the prohibition were occurring. Psychiatrist Clay Dahlberg (1970), for example, who was finally able to publish his article "Sexual Contact Between Patient and Therapist," described the string of editorial rejections that met his attempts to find a publication outlet: "I have had trouble getting this paper accepted. . . .I was told that it was too controversial. What a word for a profession which talked about infantile sexuality and incest in Victorian times" (p. 107).

Seven years later, there still had been so little published on the topic that Davidson (1977) referred, in the title of her article, to the "problem with no name." Even relatively recently, Gechtman (1989) has explored evidence that resistance to publishing information about social workers who become sexually involved with their clients remains strong among prominent social work associations.

Published accounts suggest that there were at least two attempts to gather and make public incidence data on violation of the prohibition before Dahlberg's 1970 article. Rather strong resistance met both attempts.

Shepard (1971) described psychologist Harold Greenwald's suggestion, at a meeting of a clinical psychological association, that the association support research into the occurrence of sexual intimacies between therapists and their patients. Greenwald described what happened to him as a result of making this suggestion in the 1960s:

> I just raised the questions. . .intending, as a clinical psychologist, that it be studied like any other phenomenon. And just for raising the question, some members circulated a petition that I should be expelled from the Psychological Association. (Greenwald, as quoted by Shepard, p. 2)

Some have questioned whether Greenwald ever made such a statement. Masson (1988), for example, wrote, "However, this information comes from Martin Shepard. . .[who] advocates sexual contact with some patients, so it must be taken with a grain of salt" (p. 178). Although Masson's skepticism is not unreasonable, the authors of this book have verified with Greenwald his account:

> Understand that I was only suggesting that we conduct some research, perhaps a survey, on the subject. All I asked was that we take a look at the topic, that we get some data. But there was talk among some members of expelling me. And they cancelled a radio interview. Because I had been scheduled to speak at the convention, those in charge had arranged for one of the radio stations to interview me at the end of the convention. But when they heard what I said, they told me that they had cancelled my interview, that I would not be one of those invited to the scheduled interviews. It was all very strange, but you could see what a nerve this had touched. There was considerable resistance to airing this topic in public. (H. Greenwald, personal communication, October 1992)

Another psychologist, Bertram Forer, also attempted to encourage study of therapist–patient sexual intimacies in the late 1960s. Obtaining the approval of the Los Angeles County Psychological Association (LACPA) to conduct a formal survey of their memberships, Forer started the first systematic research into the rates or frequency with which therapists engage in sex with their patients. Unfortunately, his findings indicated a higher rate of sexual intimacies than the research sponsorship had anticipated. On October 28, 1968, the LACPA Board of Directors, after discussing the research data with the Association's leadership, resolved to prohibit presentation of the findings in any public forum (i.e., convention presentation, journal publication, etc.), because it was "not in the best interests of psychology to present it publicly" (B. Forer, personal communication, January 27, 1993; see also Forer, 1980; Pope, 1990).

Although the Forer data were not permitted to be presented publicly for many years, only a few years later the profession's first psychology journal article addressing therapist–patient "sexual improprieties" on the basis of systematically collected empirical data was published. This *American Psychologist* article

(Brownfain, 1971) presented an analysis and discussion of 10 years' data about professional liability lawsuits filed against psychologists. The database was the records maintained by the insurance carrier that provided liability insurance to APA members. Interestingly, this article made no mention of any valid complaint involving a psychologist who had actually engaged in sexual intimacies with a patient. Instead, the insurance data were used as the basis for the conclusion

> that the greatest number of [all malpractice] actions are brought by women who lead lives of very quiet desperation, who form close attachments to their therapists, who feel rejected or spurned when they discover that relations are maintained on a formal and professional level, and who then react with allegations of sexual improprieties. (Brownfain, 1971, p. 651)

This period extending to the early 1970s suggests that there may have been considerable resistance in the profession to openly acknowledging and studying violations of the prohibition against therapist–patient sexual involvement. It was not until 1973 that the first survey providing evidence—based on anonymous self-reports of professionals—of sexual contact between therapist and patient was published (Kardener, Fuller, & Mensh, 1973). It was not until 1983 and 1984 that the first studies focusing on sexually exploited patients and analyzing evidence of the harm that can result from those violations (Bouhoutsos, Holroyd, Lerman, Forer, & Greenberg, 1983; Feldman-Summers & Jones, 1984) were published.

Perhaps some of this resistance was based on therapists' shame and embarrassment for the profession that such violations occurred. The therapy profession professes to seek to help people. It invites the trust of the general public and of the specific people who come—as patients—for help. Many therapists may find it acutely uncomfortable for it to be made public that some members of the profession are exploiting that trust and those patients. Public reports of research or other evidence that some therapists sexually exploit their patients have been described occasionally as giving the profession "a black eye."

A second source of resistance may be that therapists personally experience discomfort with the topic of sexual intimacies with patients. When professor Nanette Gartrell, who at that time was at Harvard University, and her colleagues planned an anonymous survey of the membership of the American Psychiatric Association to gather information about psychiatrists' attitudes, beliefs, and behavior in regard to sexual intimacies with patients, the Association refused to support the research. There appeared to be a stark contrast between the detailed interest taken in eliciting information from and about patients in this area—about victimized patients' possible "promiscuity," sexual history, predisposing clinical conditions, problems setting limits, and so on—and the American Psychiatric Association's lack of support for an *anonymous* survey of its own membership. As the [then] chair of the Ethics Committee of the American Psychiatric Association explained, the association does not believe in asking members for "sensitive information about themselves" (Bass, 1989, p. 28). Feeling that one's privacy has been invaded—that the spotlight has shifted from the disorders, distress, and actions of the patient to include unflattering characteristics and exploitive behaviors of the therapist—may make many therapists uncomfortable.

The resistance may also have been based on fear of being sued. Research exploring the occurrence and consequences of therapist–patient sex drew the public's attention to the topic and might have been seen as inviting unwarranted malpractice suits. Practitioners may feel less than invulnerable to false charges by a greedy patient. One chair of the American Psychological Association Insurance Trust wrote that some "consumers recognize the vulnerability of the provider and are attempting to exploit that vulnerability for economic gain" (Wright, 1985, p. 114).

Yet another source of resistance may have been a more general concern about economic loss in the form of drastically increased professional liability insurance premiums. Increased publication of research on therapist–patient sexual intimacy was positively correlated (which, of course, may or may not reflect causation) with an increase in the malpractice suits filed against therapists. During the late 1980s, costs associated with therapist–patient sex claims accounted for about half of all monies paid for claims against psychologists covered by the APA insurance carrier, according to the president of the company (R. Imbert, personal communication, 1990). Faced with such actual and potential economic losses, it would not be surprising if therapists were uncomfortable with the topic and ambivalent toward continuing publication of research data that drew increasing public attention to the topic. Although the economic concerns may have potentially affected virtually any therapist, they may have been especially acute for members of the American Psychiatric Association, whose organization had a more direct link to the carrier. Alan Stone (1990), professor of psychiatry and law at Harvard University and a former president of the American Psychiatric Association, emphasized that "we should all realize that there is a serious conflict of interest between APA's [American Psychiatric Association's] professional concerns for the victims of sexual exploitation in therapy and its financial concerns when the association's economic interests are at serious risk" (p. 26). He noted that actions taken to eliminate or cap the coverage for sex claims in professional liability policies seemed to violate the profession's commitment for the welfare of its patients.

> Each of us contributes by paying liability insurance to a fund that has two functions: to protect us and to compensate those who are unfortunate victims of our negligence. With this in mind, the policy decision to exclude victims of sexual exploitation, who are typically women, from participation in our victim compensation fund is difficult to defend. If we are concerned about them, why should they be "victimized" by the exclusion? (Stone, 1990, p. 25)[5]

---

[5]Although historically the American Psychiatric Association may have had a more direct investment in such economic concerns, research published in peer-reviewed scientific and professional journals does *not* show that the major mental health professions engage in therapist–patient sex at different rates. The only national study to use the same survey form at the same time with the three major disciplines (i.e., psychiatry, psychology, and social work) found—on the basis of a 49% return rate for the 4,800 therapists surveyed—

Another form of economic loss that may be feared by therapists is that the loss of public trust in the profession would cause a decrease in the number of people seeking therapy.

Other Possible Sources of Denial and Avoidance

To the extent that sexual attraction to patients is not a topic with its own distinct research and theory identity (i.e., not inherently linked or equivalent to sexual intimacy with a patient), the factors that prompted the profession to deny or avoid exploring the area of therapist–patient sexual intimacy may have generalized to the topic of therapists' sexual feelings about patients. The profoundly and understandably negative professional reaction to sexual exploitation of patients may have become associated with all sexual feelings about patients.

But the reluctance may have been even stronger for the general area of sexual attraction to patients than it has been for sexual contact with patients: Anonymous survey research focusing on sex with patients was not published until 1973; anon-

---

that these disciplines "did not differ among themselves in terms of. . .sexual intimacies with clients before or after termination" (Borys & Pope, 1989, p. 283). It is interesting to compare the 1.0% of male psychologists and 0.4% of female psychologists who reported having engaged in sex with a current client in this 1989 study with (a) the 3.6% of male psychologists and 0.4% of female psychologists who reported "engaging in sexual contact with a client" (p. 996) in a study published two years earlier (Pope et al., 1987) and (b) the 12.1% of male psychologists and 2.6% of female psychologists who reported having engaged in erotic contact with at least one opposite-sex patient and the 4% of male psychologists and 1% of female psychologists who reported having engaged in erotic contact with at least one same-sex patient in the Holroyd and Brodsky (1977) study, conducted over a decade earlier, discussed previously in footnote 1. Similarly, the more recent study's finding that 10.5% of the male psychologists and 2.0% of the female psychologists reported engaging "in sexual activity with a client after termination" (p. 288) may be compared with (a) the 1987 study's finding that 14% of the male and 4.7% of the female psychologists reported "becoming sexually involved with a former client" (p. 996) and (b) the 1977 study's finding that 7.2% of the male and 0.6% of the female psychologists reported engaging in intercourse with a patient within 3 months after termination.

ymous survey research focusing on sexual attraction to patients was not published until 1986. What other factors may account for the profession's seeming reluctance to engage in research on this topic?

Perhaps the first additional factor is that sexual attraction to patients is a topic closer to each therapist's personal experience and, thus, is more threatening and immediate. According to the research (see appendix A), sexual attraction to patients is widespread, whereas only a relatively few professionals engage in therapist–patient sex (see appendix C). The overwhelming majority of therapists can honestly assure themselves that they are not among those who have violated the prohibition against sexually exploiting patients. Most, however, have felt sexual attraction toward a patient, even if they would *never* seriously consider acting on this attraction in a way that constitutes sexual intimacies with the patient. Thus, the topic of therapist–patient sexual contact may have less personal immediacy than the topic of feeling attracted toward a patient. The research suggests that, statistically speaking, sexual intimacy with a patient tends to involve someone else; sexual attraction to a patient tends to involve oneself.

Second, the topic of sexual feelings about patients calls the public's attention to aspects of the therapist that may seem discordant with the persona of the therapist as a caring provider of help to those who are in need. Therapists may feel legitimate pride in their altruism and in the services that they provide to those who are hurting. The idea that this altruistic helper may become sexually aroused in the presence of a vulnerable patient may be alarming to the therapist, the patient, and the general public.

Third, therapists may be apprehensive that published research on attraction to patients may elicit or invite a patient's questions about the therapist's feelings. Some therapists may feel anxiety at the prospect of a patient asking them, point blank: Do you find me attractive? Do you ever think about having sex with me? Do you like it when I flirt with you?

Fourth, therapists may fear that openly acknowledging and publishing works on sexual attraction to patients may somehow increase the likelihood that therapists will engage in sex with patients. The ideas and material are viewed as potentially dangerous—to the therapist, to the patient, and to the profession. It is a very human response to attempt to deal with taboo wishes and dangerous temptations by trying to keep them out of awareness. The premise seems to be that if one begins thinking about the forbidden attraction, it will take root, gain force, and thrive, perhaps achieving an uncontrollable life of its own and eventual expression through action. To counter this threat, attempts are made to drive the impulse from awareness, to deny it a foothold in one's thoughts and daydreams, and to distract attention from it. But the assumption that trying to ignore and block feelings of attraction will produce the best results for therapists, patients, or the profession is likely no more sound than the discredited fallacy that one should never talk about suicide with a patient because bringing up the topic may "plant the seed" in the person who was not previously suicidal and may overwhelm the suicidal patient, thus increasing the risk that he or she will commit suicide.

Fifth, therapists may be concerned that material on therapists' sexual feelings may be misused or misconstrued, especially by those who would take it out of context. Such misuse as well as the fear of misuse of sexual material would certainly not be without ample precedent. Adolescents and adults have been known to use anatomy and other medical textbooks not only to satisfy sexual curiosity but also as a source of sexual excitement. Critics have blocked national surveys of child and adolescent sexuality that were to have been undertaken by the U.S. government; citing survey items out of context, critics emphasized their fear that the governmental study of such issues would create the appearance that the government condoned some of the behaviors that were topics of survey items. Whether adherents or critics of the Freudian tradition, therapists familiar with the history of psychotherapy are aware of the flood of misunderstanding, distortions, and resistance that Freud's attempts to discuss sexual material in the context of psychotherapy encountered not only among many members of the public but also among many of his professional colleagues. Jones (1961) quoted Freud's dismayed reaction when he attempted to discuss his sexual theories at a meeting of the Vienna Neurological Society.

> I treated my discoveries as ordinary contributions to science and hoped to be met in the same spirit. But the silence with which my addresses were received, the void which formed itself about me, the insinuations that found their way to me, caused me gradually to realize that one cannot count upon views about the part played by sexuality. . . meeting with the same reception as other communications. . .I could not reckon upon objectivity and tolerance. (p. 177)

The reaction to Freud's ideas about sexuality stands as such a vivid scene in the history of psychotherapy that it may be difficult to escape entirely lingering fears that some versions of the scene may be repeated whenever new areas of sexual exploration are opened up.

Sixth, therapists may feel conflicted about the topic of sexual attraction to patients becoming generally recognized as an important part of training programs. As noted in the opening section of this chapter, research suggests that historically the topic has been ignored in most graduate schools and internships. It is not uncommon for therapists-in-training to feel uncomfortable about self-disclosure because they are afraid that they will be criticized or that their disclosures will be viewed as signs of inadequacy as therapists. The prospect that sexual feelings about patients may become a focus of discussion in classrooms and supervision may intensify that discomfort. Even so senior and prominent a clinician as Harold Searles (1959) emphasized the difficulty he had writing about his own sexual reactions to patients. Discussing such reactions, he confessed, "I reacted to such feelings with considerable anxiety, guilt, and embarrassment" (p. 183).

Seventh, the topic of sexual feelings about patients may be much more frustratingly complex, uncertain, variable, unpredictable, ambiguous, and elusive than that of therapist–patient sexual intimacies. Exploring sexual feelings about patients may not be as likely to lead to a clear sense of closure, conclusion, or confidence about what will follow as examining the issue of therapist–patient sexual contact. One fundamental difference is this: A therapist's engaging in sexual activity with a patient is a voluntary behavior on the part of the therapist. As a voluntary behavior, it is something that the therapist can control. By contrast, few would argue that feelings are always or even generally susceptible to voluntary control. That the therapist may at any time be vulnerable to a flow of spontaneous, surprising, and "uncontrolled" feelings may make the topic of such feelings much more difficult to address with certainty or confidence.

A second fundamental difference is this: The profession has reached a consensus view regarding sexual intimacies with patients. That view is, "Don't do it. No matter what." There is a clear prohibition against the behavior. Engaging in sex with patients is wrong under any circumstances, it is unethical, and it places patients at risk for harm. On the other hand, the profession does not quite know how to respond to therapists' sexual feelings about their patients. What should a therapist experiencing such feelings do? Aside from redundantly restating the prohibition against sexual contact with patients, there is no consensus about how to respond to such feelings. It would probably make no sense to encourage or discourage them; they occur, at least for most therapists. Declining even to subject such feelings to research until the mid-1980s, the profession knows relatively little about the topic.

A third fundamental difference—related to the second—is this: There is no concrete set of guidelines by which therapists can understand the meaning and implications of feeling sexually attracted to a patient. Any sexual intimacies with patients are a violation of the prohibition. The accumulated research has enabled the profession to learn something about the frequency of such unethical behavior, the conditions under which it occurs, common characteristics of perpetrators, and possible effects for patients (see appendixes B and C). This research has enhanced the profession's understanding of the negative implications of therapist–patient sex for the therapy. But as emphasized in chapter 1, there can be no understanding of the meaning and implications of sexual feelings apart from their relation to the individual therapist and the unique situation. Even once the topic is comprehensively researched, it is unlikely that there could ever be a valid "cookbook" that would spell out what sexual feelings mean across different therapeutic situations. The nature, meanings, and implications of sexual feelings about a patient can never be adequately understood apart from the individual therapist, the individual patient, the unique therapeutic situation, and the history and context.

The impossibility of a cookbook approach and the necessity to attend carefully to the shifting undercurrents of the therapist's feelings create the need for special learning conditions in which the process of exploration and discovery can occur safely, sensitively, and constructively. The next chapter discusses the creation of these conditions.

Chapter

3

Creating Conditions for Learning

It may be awhile before the standard curriculum includes Therapists' Sexual Feelings 101, yet the profession must at least try to prepare new professionals better than we have in the past. It is hard to imagine a similarly significant area in psychology in which teaching has been so weak. Even minimally adequate training programs assure that their nascent professionals know how to manage suicidal or homicidal patients in quite specific ways. Few psychologists begin practice without having learned how to administer, score, and understand some of the basic standardized tests such as the MMPI (Minnesota Multiphasic Personality Inventory) and the WAIS-R (Wechsler Adult Intelligence Scale—Revised). Appropriate interventions are drilled into the professional repertoire for dramatic and subtle symptoms or problems, such as child abuse, requests for fee reductions, and so on. Topics with less import and less intrinsic interest are readily included in workshops and graduate seminars.

We believe that fear of unknown (or fantasied) consequences fuels the professional resistance that has impeded progress in helping therapists and therapists-in-training to explore their feelings about patients in sexualized situations. The first step in creating relevant, realistic educational strategies is to deal with this fear of consequences.

Fear of the consequences of teaching about therapists' sexual feelings and sexualized interactions in therapy is amplified by not knowing much about what the consequences might be. One is reminded of 14th-century Europeans' fears of sailing out too far on the ocean. The psychological literature is rich with comparisons of sexuality and intimate feelings to water, particularly the ocean (e.g., Freud, 1900/1950, 1901/1961b; Reich, 1942). Acknowledging our debt to those who have developed this analogy, we draw on it to illustrate the fears and anxieties that the anticipation of exploring sexual feelings may evoke. Imagine the southern California beaches crowded with people who cannot or will not enter the water because they can't see into its depths. They don't know if the waves will overwhelm them or the undertow will draw them where they don't want to go. They see no one else in the water to support them should they become afraid, flail about, or even flounder and sink.

This chapter is intended to provide some safety, support, and guidance for swimming in strange waters. Realizing that reducing fear of the unknown must precede discovery of what is unknown, we wish to underscore the factors that can make the exploration of therapists' sexual feelings safe.

One of the fundamentals of ocean swimming is to go with a partner or group. That is one of the principal recommendations we make about the use of this book: Exploration of sexual feelings about patients is best done with the help, support, encouragement, and reassurance of other people. A variety of formal training and employment settings can provide structured opportunities for this kind of exploration. Practica, pre- and postdoctoral internships, and postdoctoral peer supervision groups seem especially appropriate because of the immediacy and relevance imparted by continuing patient contact.

Making these training situations safe for learning about therapists' sexual thoughts and feelings is an absolute prerequisite for useful learning to occur. Although the conditions for safe and productive exploration are akin in some ways to those for safe and productive psychotherapy, this is *not* psychotherapy. The goals are quite different. The explorations promoted by this book are not psychotherapy supervision either. We would like people to become aware of and explore the waters—the shallows, the tides, the swells, and the depths.

Even if you are confident and feel safe venturing out into the ocean with the people who share your part of the beach, we recommend an active review and discussion of the following checklist of what we consider to be requisite aspects of your learning setting, a kind of ocean-exploration checklist:

- Safety
- Understanding the task
- Respect
- Openness
- Encouragement
- Appropriate privacy
- Acceptance
- Sensitivity
- Frankness
- Support

Discussing these conditions—the degree to which they are present, lingering doubts about them, ways they might be improved in a specific situation, and additional conditions that enable participants to feel safe during the process of exploration—may be a useful way for participants to begin a study group, to get to know each other, to develop trust, and to create appropriate boundaries and ground rules for their own learning.

Safety

Nothing is more important than each participant's sense of safety and basic trust in the learning process. Not only the teacher, supervisor, or group leader—if there is one—but all participants must take responsibility for creating, maintaining, and ensuring the security of the process. Exploration of personal feelings, particularly when sexuality is involved, usually requires some degree of actual or perceived risk. Exploring their reactions to a hypothetical client or situation, participants run the risk of discovering surprises, some of them unpleasant or frightening. They may find themselves thinking the unthinkable or feeling the forbidden. Not only the discovery of such responses but also the choice to disclose them to others (or *not* to disclose them to others) may require considerable courage.

Such risk taking must be done within a safe and secure environment. For example, participants must believe that what they say will not be used against them, either personally or professionally. It is helpful for a teacher, supervisor, or group leader to give overt reassurances that no adverse consequences will follow, but verbal pronouncements must be supported by moment-to-moment modeling of acceptance of content that emerges. Issues of confidentiality should be discussed at the outset. Whether new members can join the study group once the participants have done the work of establishing a safe context should be addressed early. The concerns surrounding dual roles—when the person who initiates the training is an employer, an internship director, a university instructor assigning a grade, or a supervisor who may be called on to write a letter of recommendation—should be carefully and explicitly considered.

Understanding the Task

The model of learning that this book promotes may differ from what participants might have experienced in some parts of their preprofessional and professional training. Participants will not be told or guided to specific answers. The model is not an assemblage of prescribed behaviors and prohibitory rules.

The model of learning promoted here exposes therapists to a wide variety of evocative situations, encourages them to tune in to their own feelings and response tendencies, and invites discussion in the relative "comfort and security of their own homes." Understanding that the imaginary and fantasy rehearsal of scenarios—playing them out in different directions—is directed at making them both more comfortable and more broadly prepared and is the first prerequisite for learning.

Respect

Valuing both the person and his or her contribution is easily threatened in this type of learning situation, because a principal goal is to explore uncharted waters. People reveal a lot about themselves, even when discussing hypothetical cases. The possibility that differences in attitudes, feelings, and experience may be perceived as sexual or psychological deviance can be discussed before learning exercises are undertaken. Using one of the passages in Part II (e.g., those by Searles or Lewis) for discussion of respect for the self-disclosing person might be helpful. Although respect for disclosing participants is a prerequisite for learning in this area, it is likely that this learning process will also strengthen participants' inclination to respect peers for exploration of their feelings about other taboo subjects.

Openness

The ability of students—whether new therapists-in-training or seasoned therapists—to be open in receiving information from others and in disclosing information about themselves is fundamental, because the content of each learning session derives from individual personal awareness. To paraphrase Pogo, "We have met the sexual contact problem and it is us." Because of wide individual differences in how therapists experience sexuality in the context of their work or in how they respond to the passages and scenarios in Part II, one could expect that groups would generate more material than dyads. This assumes that the members remain open to hear as well as to disclose personal feelings. Note that this requirement for openness serves a different function from that served by openness in personal psychotherapy. In the case of psychotherapy, openness facilitates personal growth and the resolution of problems. In this case, it is important to have representative material in order for the group to be able to discuss and explore the many ramifications of sexuality in therapy. The material that each learning group will explore is the variety of feelings evoked by reading the passages and scenarios in Part II, as well as the questions following each segment.

Encouragement

It can be expected that people in the study group will vary in the amount of encouragement required to enter into this learning activity. It will not be obvious to everybody that the more they participate, the better prepared they will be in the office, clinic, or hospital. If participants were learning to ride a bike or to speak a foreign language, they would intuitively understand that participation increases skill and knowledge. When it comes to understanding the therapist's sexual feelings toward patients, many would like to sit back and learn vicariously. But exploration of the deep currents of feeling cannot be a passive or secondhand experience. It is not something that can be reasoned out from reading basic texts on theory or pieced together from research data.

Learning groups and their leaders must confront honestly the issue of motivation and encouragement to participate in the learning process. We have found that some therapists can be motivated by desire for excellence in performance, some by the need to talk about powerful aspects of therapy that were previously treated as unspeakable, some by a recognition that the ability to help others most effectively is inconsistent with attempts to avoid understanding oneself, and some by the inherent fascination of previously taboo inner experience. Others may find it useful to be reminded that they could lose everything they own or may *ever* own if they do not understand at a fairly deep level what is going on in themselves and their clients.

Some teachers or students may not have made a voluntary choice to enter the group. Participation may be required by the graduate training program, internship, or employing agency providing in-service training. Some faculty members may have been "volunteered" for the course by the departmental chair. All participants must confront honestly the reasons that led to their membership in the learning group and the ways in which the setting, the participants, and the process can best offer nonintrusive, gentle encouragement of a safe and useful learning experience.

Appropriate Privacy

Participants need to know that they are the arbiters of what they will or won't disclose, without pressure to bare their souls more than would be comfortable or manageable. Unlike sensitivity groups, in learning groups the goal is *not* to teach people to be less defensive with peers. In addition to explicit statements about people's rights not to reveal personal material, the structure of the learning experience can be used to reduce implicit pressure for self-disclosure. For example, participants may be given the opportunity to deal with some, but not all, of the passages and scenarios in Part II. All participants and group leaders must be sensitive to the fact that what one person at one time may feel as encouragement (as discussed in the previous section), another person (or the same person at another time) may feel as pressure.

Acceptance

To be able to discuss the ramifications of different kinds of therapist responses to different kinds of sexualized patient–therapist situations, it is necessary to promote discussion and understanding of a wide variety of feelings, attitudes, and behaviors. In Part II, this book has presented to the reader, in uncritical fashion, a sampling of first-person anecdotes that are bound to stir emotions and both observable and covert reactions. Many of the readers' reactions probably would not by the wildest stretch of the imagination be considered acceptance of what some therapists in the anecdotes are described as experiencing or doing. However, participants must learn to attend carefully to these immediate feelings (e.g., fear, anxiety, anger, confusion, or disgust) and to work toward understanding them in order for the group discussion to be productive. There must be receptivity to encountering and exploring content that at times provokes negative or rejecting reactions and an ability to handle the attendant emotion so that productive learning can occur. The same would hold true, and even more so, for material presented from the participants' own experiences.

There are two caveats that apply to learning the acceptance-of-content process, one obvious and one subtle. Obviously, acceptance or receptivity to someone's attitudes, feelings, thoughts, and fantasies does *not* imply that one would eventually decide to act along the lines of those feelings. For example, acceptance (receptivity) toward someone who suggests that rocking and stroking an affection-deprived patient is therapeutic does not imply that one would eventually include that in one's repertoire, but it does imply that one can discuss the pros and cons openly and attempt to explore and understand the meanings of this intervention. Another example, this one from a different context, may be useful. A client may confront a therapist with suicidal feelings, intent, and plans. Rather than reflexively rejecting the client's feelings and stated goal (i.e., to commit suicide), the therapist may explore this frightening, final, and "unacceptable" option with the client. The client may discuss in detail the pain and confusion that led to this choice, the client's methods for ending his or her life, anticipations or fantasies about what it would be like to die and to be dead, ideas about how the act might affect others, the relief and other positive feelings the client may experience when thinking about ending all suffering and problems, and the deeply textured meanings of bringing one's life to an end. The therapist's careful attention to and acceptance of the client's feelings, intentions, and fantasies, and the exploration and discovery that therapist and client conduct together, does *not* mean that the therapist believes that suicide is the best or even an acceptable alternative. In some cases, such exploration and discovery may be the most effective way to reduce the risk that the client will commit suicide. *Acceptance,* as used in this section, refers to the acknowledgment of and willingness to explore areas of human experience that may evoke anxiety, fear, guilt, disgust, outrage, and an almost infinite variety of other human reactions. It refers to the acknowledgment of and willingness to explore these areas in oneself as well as in others.

Less obviously, there is a tendency for psychotherapists to intellectualize or objectify in extreme degree their feelings in this area, in order to avoid the emotional work attendant on acknowledging, exploring, and understanding associated issues. If participants resort to cool rationality in dealing with this material too quickly or too exclusively, we believe they will be less prepared to deal with their own feelings in real-life situations later.

Sensitivity

In addition to being receptive toward reading or hearing about sexualized interactions between therapists and patients, participants will need to fine tune their perceptive and expressive skills. This is where those well-established ideal therapist qualities of empathy and accurate perception come in. If a patient says, "I really want to go to bed with you," what are the many dimensions of this communication? Can we listen with the third ear or read between the lines? If a group participant confesses, "That patient's statement would make me feel [powerful, sad, envious]," can the participants in this situation hear the communication with the same sensitive attention to nuances of meaning that hopefully they provide for their patients?

The same attention to sensitivity must occur when group members address each other with clarifying statements, questions, and so on. From the start, participants must take responsibility for not offending, embarrassing, or threatening other group members in the way they talk with them. This is a distinct departure from the more free-flowing group therapy situation in which confrontation and even abrasiveness among group members are simply more grist for the mill. Again, the goal is not to learn to manage the tension arising from interpersonal interactions, but to learn about the breadth, depth, and variety of one's own unique and evolving responses to sexual issues in therapy.

Frankness

A sensitive way of expressing one's thoughts, observations, and feelings should not interfere with clear and honest communication. Frank communication probably emerges from several other items on this list of prerequisites of the learning situation—respect, openness, and acceptance in particular. Occasionally, a study group may be so concerned with protecting the welfare of its members that it doesn't permit open discussion of potentially disruptive material. Periodically (e.g., every

15 or 30 minutes) asking the members to attend to what is *not* being said or acknowledged by themselves or other members may be helpful. There may be, for example, a powerful, central issue that seems to influence or even dominate the discussion, yet participants may be acting as if the issue did not exist. Or participants may be discussing an issue using euphemisms, jargon, or other language that works more to conceal, obscure, and distort than to communicate. Setting a model of thanking people for their frank, honest expression is not surprisingly very reinforcing of that behavior.

Support

Finally, a supportive attitude on the part of the leader, if there is a leader, and on the part of each member facilitates the learning process in this model. The nature of the material often provokes anxiety, and discussions entail real or perceived risks for the participants. To repeat once again, in yet a different context, the goals are distinctly different from psychotherapy. Support is not intended in this case to reduce guilt, to indicate acceptance of someone with low self-esteem, or to promote specific behaviors. In helping therapists and therapists-in-training to learn about the feelings that sexual issues in therapy can evoke, support is useful for reducing tension and a sense of risk in self-disclosure, thereby assuring that a sufficiently rich database is available for consideration and discussion. If personal growth occurs as a result of the ensuing discussion, that is incidental.

Anyone who grew up with less than total confidence in the safety of the world and new experiences and who was not instantly at home in the water may remember a certain hesitancy about approaching the ocean or any other large body of water. (Some of us may, in our earliest years, have had a distinct mistrust of the bathtub with its mysterious and somewhat threatening drain.) Picture, for example, the person who walks out to the shoreline but feels somewhat threatened by the thought of entering the water. Or a person who walks out on a pier and considers jumping, for the first time, into the ocean. The authors of this book are not strangers to similar discomfort at the prospect of encountering and exploring the feelings that are the focus of this book. We have felt it personally during our own training and professional evolution. We have also found it to be not uncommon among those with whom we—in our roles as classroom teachers, clinical supervisors, workshop leaders, and consultants—have worked in a variety of graduate training programs, internships, professional institutes, continuing education courses, and so on.

If preparing to explore the undercurrents of feelings evoked by sexual issues in psychotherapy has at least some similarity to standing at the shoreline of a forbidding ocean or on the edge of a diving pier, remembering or imagining what it is like to be caught in the grip of apprehension, fear, and uncertainty can help us to intuit or decide what is and is not helpful in such circumstances. Anything that even hints at a sudden push, an authoritative command to jump, ridicule at the indecision, stern pressure to hurry up, or a discounting of the individual's feelings is not only likely to be unhelpful but also to spoil the experience. Blocking out, suppressing, overriding, or otherwise turning away from those feelings is likely to be counterproductive. Acknowledgment of, acceptance of, and attempts to understand the impulse or inclination to avoid the process of exploration and discovery are essential points of departure as well as part of the learning process suggested in this book. The process involves looking inward, attending closely to personal feelings, and exploring the self. To help initiate this journey, the next chapter provides an opportunity for self-assessment.

4

Self-Assessment

The process of exploration, discovery, and learning about sexual feelings in psychotherapy is recursive, requiring us to look inward, then outward to others in our profession—both our psychotherapeutic forebears and our contemporary colleagues—then inward again. We start with questions created to help the reader conduct an introspective survey of personal attitudes and beliefs relevant to sexuality in psychotherapy. These include sexual feelings about clients, reactions to clients' sexual feelings and behavior, the sense of both clients and oneself as physical beings, the physical and other boundaries between therapist and client, and the social and other influences that affect a therapist's attitudes, beliefs, feelings, and responses.

Our hope is that the reader will begin, with this small exercise, the process of addressing previously taboo issues with thoughtfulness, frankness, and sensitivity, while avoiding censoring ideas, quashing feelings, or rushing through the questions in this chapter without thinking *and* feeling. To reflect meaningfully on the issues, it may sometimes be useful to close one's eyes and engage in imagery or to run through an imaginary scenario with several diverse clients in one's practice.

The reader might consider that the questions are those of a kind, gentle, and completely accepting interviewer whose principal concern is that the reader know him- or herself. Within that framework, we invite the reader to respond to the questions that follow.

Can you remember a time during a therapy session that you became privately but intensely aware of your own body? What seemed to lead to this awareness?

Can you remember a time during a therapy session when your bodily processes (e.g., a burp or a stomach rumble) became obvious not only to you but also to your client? How did you respond?

During a therapy session, have you ever had the impulse to get up and move about (e.g., to stretch, to relieve the tension in your arms and legs, or to help you "wake up")? How did you respond to this impulse?

Can you remember a time during a therapy session that you became intensely aware of the client's body? What seemed to lead to this awareness? Did the client seem to notice? Did you discuss it with the client?

During a therapy session, has a client ever made a move that startled or frightened you? Why were you startled or frightened?

Under what circumstances would you hold a client's hand?

Under what circumstances would you put your arm around a client?

Under what circumstances would you cradle a client's head in your lap?

Under what circumstances would you hug a client?

Have you ever hugged a client or been hugged by a client in such a way that seemed to have sexual overtones for you or the client? What did you feel? What did you do?

Has a client ever initiated a hug or kiss that was unwanted by you? What feelings did it evoke? How did you handle the situation?

Under what circumstances would you kiss a client on the cheek or forehead?

Under what circumstances would you kiss a client on the mouth?

Under what circumstances would you have dinner with a client?

Under what circumstances would you go to a client's home?

Under what circumstances would you enter a client's bedroom?

Has a client ever dressed in a way that made you uncomfortable? What was the nature of your discomfort? How did you respond to feelings of discomfort?

Have you ever imagined what a client's body would look like if he or she were not wearing any clothes? What feelings did this imaginary scene evoke in you? Do you think the client was ever aware that you were creating this imaginary scene? If he or she had been aware, what feelings do you think it might have evoked in him or her?

Do you believe that a client has ever imagined what your body would look like if you were not wearing any clothes? What feelings does this evoke in you?

Has a client ever touched his or her genitals in your presence? What feelings did this evoke in you?

What is the most private part of a client's body that you have seen? How did your viewing this part of their body come about? Has a private part of a client's body ever been exposed to you through apparent accident (e.g., a man's gym shorts shift to reveal he is not wearing underwear; a woman's low-cut blouse slides down)? Was it apparent to the client that a private part of his or her anatomy was exposed? Was it apparent to the client that you noticed? Did either you or the client mention the incident? What feelings did it seem to evoke in the client? What feelings did it evoke in you?

Has a client ever talked about his or her sexual experiences or fantasies in a way that you found exceptionally enjoyable? What feelings did they evoke in you? Do you think that the client was aware of your enjoyment? If so, how do you think this awareness might have affected or influenced the client?

Have you ever had an erotic dream about a client? Did you pay any particular attention to the dream once you awoke?

Have you ever been so upset over something that has happened in therapy or so concerned about a patient that it interfered with your sex life?

Have you ever become aware of a client's body odor? What feelings did this evoke in you? How did you respond to those feelings?

Have you ever blushed in the presence of a client? What was the cause of your blushing? Did the client notice? Did you discuss the incident with the client?

During a therapy session, have you ever become sexually aroused? Do you think the client noticed? Did you make any effort to conceal your arousal from the client? Did you make any effort to reveal your arousal to the client?

Have you ever fantasized about a client while you masturbated or had sex with someone else (who was not your client)? Did you reflect on the fantasy later? Did your awareness of the fantasy affect the therapy or your relationship with the client? Did you have any positive reactions to your fantasy (e.g., excitement, pride, or curiosity)? Did you have any negative reactions to your fantasy (e.g., anxiety, guilt, fear, or uncomfortable confusion)?

Have you ever had a sexual fantasy or daydream during a therapy session? Did it involve the client? Did it seem to have any meaning for the therapy or for your relationship to the client?

Has a client ever seemed to become sexually aroused or excited in your presence? What seemed to cue you to your client's arousal? What feelings did that evoke in you?

Has a client ever told you that he or she was sexually attracted to you? What feelings did that evoke in you?

Try to remember a client who told you that he or she was sexually attracted to you but whom you did not find yourself attracted to, and another client who told you he or she was sexually attracted to you and to whom you were attracted. (If you have not experienced both situations, try to create the situations in your imagination.) Does whether you're attracted make any difference at all in how you respond to the two clients? Do you believe that either of the two clients could intuit whether you were attracted to him or her?

When you were in graduate school, were there any sexual issues that you felt were "off limits" or that you did not feel comfortable discussing with your clinical supervisors?

During a counseling session with a client, have you ever had feelings of which you were ashamed? How did you respond to those feelings? Have you ever experienced a reaction to a client that you were too ashamed to tell to anyone else?

Does a client's sexual orientation evoke any particular feelings in you? Does it affect how you respond to a client's discussion of sexual attraction to you?

Does your sexual orientation affect your responses to clients' physical attributes? Does it affect your responses to clients' discussions of sexual feelings or behaviors? If so, how?

Have you ever compared your own physical attractiveness with that of a client?

Have you ever compared your own sexual behaviors or experiences with those of a client?

Have you ever reacted to a client's sexual talk or behavior with anger?

Have you ever reacted to a client's sexual talk or behavior with fear?

Have you ever reacted to a client's sexual talk or behavior with anxiety?

Have you ever reacted to a client's sexual talk or behavior with guilt?

Have you ever reacted to a client's sexual talk or behavior with embarrassment?

Have you ever reacted to a client's sexual talk or behavior with intense curiosity?

Have you ever been concerned that a client might file a false complaint against you for sexual misconduct? What led you to become concerned? How did this concern affect the way you conducted therapy? How did this concern affect the way you felt about the client?

Do you talk about sexual issues more with your male clients, your female clients, or both about equally?

Have you ever daydreamed about being married to one of your clients?

Do you touch your male clients more, your female clients more, or both about equally?

What are the proportions of men and women among your clientele? Is that due to chance, to the general distribution of male and female clients in your geographic area (or clinic), or to other factors? Do you wish you had more male clients or more female clients?

Do you generally find yourself more sexually attracted to people of a certain race (or races)? If so, what implications might this have for the way to conduct therapy?

Under what conditions would you discuss your own sexual fantasies with a client?

Under what conditions would you show a client how to put on a condom?

Under what conditions would you show a client how to insert a tampax?

Under what conditions would you examine a female client's chest and nipples?

Under what conditions would you examine a male client's chest and nipples?

Under what conditions would you allow a client to disrobe partially during a session?

Under what conditions would you allow a client to disrobe completely during a session?

Under what conditions would you partially disrobe during a session?

Under what conditions would you completely disrobe during a session?

Do you ever cry or "tear up" during therapy sessions? If so, does this seem to happen more with male clients, more with female clients, or about equally with male and female clients?

With what client have you felt most intimate? How did you express the intimacy?

In graduate school, did you ever do anything with a client that you were reluctant to mention to your supervisor? Did you ultimately reveal or refrain from revealing this matter to the supervisor? What were your reasons for making this choice?

In graduate school, did you ever find that the sexual feelings in the therapy you conducted were reflected in some way in your relationship to your supervisor?

At what time while you were doing psychotherapy did you feel the most emotional intensity? Would you describe it as a positive or negative emotional experience? What evoked this intensity? How did you respond to it?

In providing therapy to a survivor of some form of abuse (e.g., incest or rape), have you ever found yourself sexually attracted to your client? How did you respond to this attraction?

Considering the time you devote to them in therapy and the degree to which you believe they are significant in the therapy, do you believe that sexual issues are over- or underrepresented in your chart notes?

Under what circumstances do you avoid recording sexual material in a client's chart?

Have you ever told a sexual partner about one of your clients? Did this include talking about sexual material? Do you believe that the client was aware of the possibility that you might be discussing him or her with your sexual partner? How do you believe the client would feel were he or she to know that you had had such discussions with your sexual partner?

If you could be given an absolute assurance that you yourself would suffer no negative consequences (e.g., no one else would ever know; there would be no complaint to a licensing board, ethics committee, civil court, or criminal court), would you ever consider entering into a sexual relationship with one of your clients? What factors would you take into account in your considerations? What would you decide?

If your clients could, beginning right now, read your mind—including, but not limited to, all the thoughts and feelings you've had about them—what thought or feeling would be most surprising to them?

If your clinical supervisors in graduate school could, beginning right now, read your mind—including, but not limited to, all the thoughts and feelings you've had about them—what thought or feeling would be most surprising to them?

What comment could a client make about your looks, sexuality, or other personal aspects that you would find most hurtful?

Do you believe that it is possible that you may have acted seductively toward a client without your being aware of it?

Have you ever felt jealous of a client's life partner, sexual partner, or dating partner?

Have you ever felt jealous of a client for other reasons?

5

Awareness of Context

Therapists do not conduct their work in a social vacuum, nor do they experience sexual feelings toward patients in a vacuum. Each episode of therapy occurs in the context of a multitude of factors that make a significant difference. Beutler, Crago, and Arizmendi (1986) observed that therapists differ in not only externally observed characteristics (e.g., gender, age, race, and social class) but also internally inferred characteristics (e.g., religious attitudes and values, sociocultural beliefs and values, sexual orientation, and theoretical orientation). Similarly, clients vary along external as well as internal dimensions. The evolving interaction of these many deeply layered contexts colors the experience of sexuality in therapy. Buckley, Karasu, Charles, and Stein (1979; see also Strupp, 1980) concluded that although therapists may hold value-free therapy as an ideal, they invariably bring their personal beliefs and values into the treatment situation.

The purpose of this chapter is to highlight a few of the contextual factors that subtly shape the therapy interaction as well as the feelings that are the focus of this book. The presentation does not attempt an exhaustive review of all pertinent literature. Rather, the examples are intended to serve as springboards for readers to consider how such factors may influence their own thoughts, feelings, and behavior. Some factors (e.g., gender) have been the subject of much more research than others (e.g., age or religion). Readers seeking more detailed information are referred to such excellent reviews as those provided by Garfield and Bergin (1978, 1986), Gurman and Razin (1977), and Beutler and Crago (1991).

Age Factors

A common premise in the practice of psychotherapy is that touch is at least permissible in working with children (e.g., Bosanquet, 1970) and perhaps essential in work with children who have suffered a developmental arrest of the attachment process (e.g., Hopkins, 1987; Mitchum, 1987). Palombo (1985) noted that the literature exploring the therapist's reactions to the child client (including sexual feelings) or the child's experience or demonstration of sexual feelings is nearly nonexistent. A notable exception is Kohrman, Fineberg, Gelman, and Weiss (1971) who wrote, "Younger children who feel free to touch the analyst, crawl on his lap, jump on him from heights, kiss him, can create intense reactions regardless of their sex" (p. 496).

At the other end of the age spectrum, again touch is acknowledged as important and therapeutic in the treatment of the elderly (e.g., Baldwin, 1986; Weisberg & Haberman, 1989). However, therapists may have difficulty acknowledging and processing sexual feelings and behaviors that arise in work with the elderly client. Poggi and Berland (1985) described their feeling as if they were "boys" to very elderly women and recognized that they tended to focus on the provision of medical treatment, avoiding complex (and, at times, sexual) concerns. Goodstein (1982) noted that many therapists seem to treat discussion of sex with older clients as if it were taboo. Okun (1989) has suggested that discussion of sexual issues and feelings with an older couple can lead therapists to feel that they are intruding on their own parents' sex life. Genevay (1990; see also Kimmel, 1988) poignantly described how the sexual expressions of the elderly are often experienced as meaningless to those who treat them. She wrote, "We are participants in an ageist North American culture which devalues older people. Among the strongest mandate of young-and-beauty worship is our denigration of people who are wrinkled, fat, bald, skinny, gray, old-looking, or disabled when they act like sexual beings" (p. 152).

Religious Factors

Bergin and Jensen (1990; see also Jensen & Bergin, 1988) conducted a national survey of therapists regarding their religious and mental health values. A total of 425 clinical psychologists, clinical social workers, marriage and family therapists, and psychiatrists provided usable returns. The most frequently endorsed religious affiliation was Protestant (38%), followed by Jewish (18%) and Catholic (15%). About 20% reported that they were "not religious in any traditional sense (e.g., atheist, agnostic, humanist, and 'none')" (Jensen & Bergin, 1988, p. 292). Comparing their survey data to a 1985 Gallup poll, *Religion in America* (1985), Bergin and Jensen (1990) found that

> 91% of the public show a religious preference, which is somewhat higher than our professional sample (80%); but . . . professionals . . . have levels of religious attendance and life-style commitment that are surprisingly similar to the lay public's profile. In our survey, 41% of the therapists attend services regularly compared with 40% of the public. (p. 5)

In some instances, religious variables were related to beliefs about sexuality. For example, "Christian adherents generally agreed significantly more than Jews, agnostics, and atheists with items related to regulated sexual behavior. . . ." (Jensen & Bergin, 1988, p. 294).

A study by Borenzweig (1983) suggested that religious values bear directly on the therapist's use of bodily contact with the client. He found that overall, whereas 83% of the California clinical social workers surveyed indicated a positive attitude toward touching, only 50% indicated that they touched their clients in actual practice. Protestant social workers scored highest on both positive attitudes and touching. In contrast, 100% of the Catholic social workers ($n = 10$) avoided actual touching because it could be perceived as sexually stimulating.

Clients' religious beliefs and values may significantly influence their sexual attitudes, fantasies, behavior, and experience. For example, in a study exploring the effects of religiosity, race, and gender, among other variables, on sexual fantasies, attitudes, and behavior, Robinson and Calhoun (1982–1983) found that "those people low on religiosity reported more liberality concerning the behaviors acceptable for males to fantasize about, attitudes about female and personal behavior, and actual sexual behavior than those high on religiosity" (p. 287).

The religious and spiritual values of both therapist and client form an important context for understanding the sexual feelings that can arise in therapy. The research and clinical literature in this area provides an important resource (see, e.g., Bergin, 1983, 1988, 1991; Bergin & Payne, 1991; Bullis & Harrigan, 1992; McMinn, 1991; Galanter, Larson, & Rubenstone, 1991). As Bergin and Jensen (1990) suggest,

> When discussing religion and psychotherapy, it is helpful to recall the axiom that "every therapeutic relationship is a cross-cultural experience" . . . . Such is the case, on a collective level, as our . . . field addresses in a newly rigorous way the world of the religious client. This cross-cultural gap begs to be bridged, for in their deepest moments of self-comprehension and change, many clients see, feel, and act in spiritual terms. (p. 3)

Sexual Orientation Factors

In a previously cited study, Jensen and Bergin (1988) concluded that mental health professionals responded with greater divergence among themselves to items tapping their values regarding a "healthy" sexual life-style; responses in this area did not reflect the consensus that characterized reported values in many of the other areas surveyed. Fifty-seven percent of the professionals agreed that preference for a heterosexual relationship was important for a positive, mentally healthy life-style. A national survey of psychologists found that over one in five therapists treated homosexuality *per se* as pathological

(Pope et al., 1987). Stein (1988) wrote, "The monolithic antagonism to homosexuality within psychotherapy has only begun to change in response to research findings" (p. 80), with resistance to change bolstered by formidable sociocultural homophobic bias (see also Baer, 1981; Gartrell, 1981b; Malyon 1986a, 1986b; Morin & Rothblum, 1991).

Such bias can undermine, block, and distort the therapeutic process and relationship. For example, it may disrupt the therapist's empathy with the gay client and foster the view that a gay client is manifesting a "homosexual defense" against the fear of women (Martin, 1991). Bias may also result in inappropriate focus on sexual orientation. The APA Task Force on Bias in Psychotherapy With Lesbians and Gay Men, for example, reported a case in which a person who had become unemployed and was depressed sought therapy. The therapist stipulated that the therapy must focus on changing the client's sexual orientation (Garnets, Hancock, Cochran, Goodchilds, & Peplau, 1991). In some instances, the very mention of a particular sexual orientation may evoke strong feelings in the therapist. The Task Force also reported an instance in which a university student developed a transference toward his male psychologist. When the client disclosed his feelings of affection for the psychologist and remarked on his surprise at loving feelings for a man, the "psychologist became angry [and] immediately terminated the session and all therapy" (Garnets et al., 1991, p. 967).

Bias related to sexual orientation may cause a therapist to discount the sexual meaning of certain behaviors (L.S. Brown, personal communication, November 1992) or lead to the inappropriate sexualization of therapy. Urging greater awareness and education of the therapist, Brown (1985; see also Brown, 1989) emphasized that the sexuality of women is not only experienced genitally. She suggested that the therapist be sensitive to the presence of sexual dynamics in nurturing, holding, and hugging the female client. Brown's emphasis on therapist education is consistent with the view of Kus (1990) that not all problems with services for gays and lesbians are due solely to homophobia. In many instances, according to Kus, "poor quality care given to gay and lesbian clients is the result of a lack of knowledge on the part of the helping professional, rather than of any deep-seated homophobia. I assume most helping professionals truly wish to be helpful and would be if they had sufficient knowledge" (p. 7). Similarly, the APA Task Force on Bias in Psychotherapy With Lesbians and Gay Men, on the basis of a study involving 2,544 survey participants, concluded that

> psychologists, regardless of their own sexual orientation, can provide appropriate and sensitive care to lesbians and gay men. The beneficial practices identified in this survey suggest issues and strategies that may help therapists provide ethical and competent care and that may point the way toward the development of lesbian- and gay-affirmative practice. (Garnets et al., 1991, p. 970)

Whatever the therapist's sexual orientation, he or she must be informed and aware of the diverse ways in which factors related to sexual orientation (e.g., not only the sexual orientation per se of the therapist and client but also the sociocultural contexts in which both have grown up and now live) can affect the occurrence, experience, and meaning of sexual feelings in therapy (e.g., Garnets, Herek, & Levy, 1990; Gartrell, 1981a; Gonsiorek, 1988; Herek, 1990; Malyon, 1981–1982, 1982).

Gender Factors

For decades, creative research paradigms have provided evidence that women have historically been evaluated and treated—in the general as well as the clinical sense of those terms—differently than men and that this difference has often been based on sex role stereotypes (e.g., Feldman-Summers & Kiesler, 1974; Fidell, 1970; for reviews and commentary, see, e.g., Mednick, 1989; Tavris, 1992; Unger, 1979; Unger & Crawford, 1992).

Henley (1973, 1977) found that touch in social and professional situations was highly correlated with gender: Men were more likely to touch women than vice versa. She also found that men were more likely to return or reciprocate a touch initiated by a woman than women were likely to reciprocate a touch initiated by a man. Henley proposed that touching communicated power and social status: Those who are more powerful and maintain a higher social status are more likely to initiate touch and to reciprocate touch. By contrast, those with less power and of lower social status are more likely to be touched and less likely to reciprocate a touch. Holroyd and Brodsky's (1980) investigation of the use of touch in psychotherapy found evidence of sex bias when they identified a subgroup of male therapists who differentially engaged in *nonerotic* hugging, kissing, and touching of opposite-sex clients but not of same-sex clients.

Research also tends to support the notion that men may frequently perceive women's behavior as sexually motivated. Johnson, Stockdale, and Saal (1991), for example, presented brief videotaped scenes in which a man and a woman interacted. Several factors, including the behavior of the woman, were systematically varied. They found that male participants in the study consistently perceived the woman in the videotaped scene "as behaving in a 'sexier' manner regardless" of the other factors that were varied (p. 463). The male participants misinterpreted the videotaped woman's (nonsexually) friendly behaviors as sexual in a variety of interpersonal encounters.

Holroyd (1983) cited sex bias as the source of the clear gender differences in therapist–patient sexual intimacies. Even when the proportions of male and female therapists and male and female patients are taken into account, male therapists tend to engage in erotic contact with their patients at significantly higher rates than do female therapists, and female patients are much more likely than male patients to be sexually exploited by a therapist (see appendix C). Holroyd noted, "Sexual contact between therapist and patient is perhaps the quintessence of sex-biased therapeutic practice. . . . Women patients have had sexual contact with their therapists in part because of social attitudes and expectancies about gender-related role behavior, and in part because of psychopathology in therapists" (p. 285).

Several other investigators have suggested that female therapists and male therapists experience their clients' sexual material differently. Brodsky (1977) found that for a male therapist, a client stating that she was in love with the therapist raised the dilemma of rejecting the client versus seducing her. For a female therapist, concerns were raised for the therapist's safety should the client lose control and sexually attack her or try to pursue her outside of the therapy situation. Braude (1984) reported a similar finding that female psychiatrists were more likely than male psychiatrists to experience sexual approaches by patients as frightening or threatening. Schlachet (1984) suggested that an eroticized transference may be more threatening to a woman analyst when coming from a male patient

> when her experience with unsolicited male sexuality has trained her to react defensively, be wary of physical danger that can be all too real, and be sure that in some way she's not "asking for it". . . . Since the analyst is always "asking for it". . . , this becomes quite dissonant with the woman analyst's gender-role training. (p. 63)

Schover's (1981) analogue study produced somewhat different findings. Twelve male and 12 female therapists were presented with a description of either a male or female client, a photograph, and an audiotape of the client. On the tape, the client discussed either a mild sexual dysfunction or sexual attraction to the therapist. Assessments of the therapists' affective reactions, verbal responses, and clinical judgments suggested that female therapists tended to feel more comfortable with client sexual material. Male therapists with conservative sexual attitudes were sexually aroused by the female client describing dysfunction but reacted with anxiety and avoided talking about the material. Male therapists with liberal sexual attitudes were sexually aroused by the female client who expressed sexual attraction to the therapist; they spoke words of encouragement.

Howard, Orlinsky, and Hill (1969) conducted a complex factor analytic investigation of therapists' and their female clients' feelings in the therapeutic process. After each therapy session, both therapists and patients completed questionnaires designed to assess the therapeutic experience. The dimensions of therapist experience included Sexual Arousal, Feeling Good, and Uneasy Intimacy. One dimension of the female patient reaction was labeled Erotic Transference Resistance (i.e., blocking and embarrassing sexual arousal). The female patients' experience of Erotic Transference Resistance was significantly correlated with male therapists' experience of Sexual Arousal and *not* Feeling Good. In contrast, the female patients' experience of Erotic Transference Resistance was significantly correlated with the female therapists' feelings of Uneasy Intimacy. The authors concluded that the patients' erotic transference tended to impair both male and female therapists' sense of effectiveness. The authors added that the congruence in feeling between the male therapist and female client was not indicated in verbal transactions. "Each seemed to be saying, 'What's wrong with me? I shouldn't be having these thoughts and feelings.' Some process of nonverbal communication must be posited as operative in effecting their affective congruence" (p. 92).

Regarding client gender as a differential factor, Person (1985) discussed the different qualities of erotic transference (a reaction characterized by an intense sexual feeling toward the therapist) in male clients versus female clients. She suggested that, in general, female clients are more likely to experience erotic transference serving as resistance, whereas male clients are more likely to experience resistance to the awareness of erotic transference. For women in psychotherapy with male therapists, erotic transference more often tends to be overt, consciously experienced, intense, long lived, and directed toward the therapist, with the focus more on love than on sex. Male clients in therapy with female therapists, on the other hand, more often tend to experience an erotic transference in a less intense, seldom conscious, and relatively short-lived manner. According to Person, the transference appears indirectly in dreams, preoccupations with triangular relationships, and displacements onto women outside of the therapeutic relationship. The focus is more sexual than a longing for love.

Gender differences in experiencing sexual feelings and fantasies in therapy may reflect gender or sex role biases. Shor and Sanville (1974) suggested that a male therapist is likely to share the gender-specific fantasy with other men in society that he may free a female client from unhappiness through "the gift" of his virility. They suggested that a female therapist, on the other hand, may share the gender-specific fantasy that she may help a male client by mothering him. The "mother fantasy" may tend to block recognition, discussion, and understanding of sexual issues in a female therapist–male client relationship.

Similarly, Guttman (1984) and Zicherman (1984; see also Lester, 1985) explored potential difficulties that cultural sex roles can pose for female therapist–male client dyads. Socialized sex roles may tend not only to make male clients reluctant to talk about their sexual fantasies and dreams but also to make it difficult for female therapists to focus on and explore male clients' sexual thoughts, feelings, and wishes.

Abramowitz et al. (1976) examined therapist responses to case materials regarding a male or female confederate outpatient. The case presentation highlighted sexual performance conflicts and hostile–dependent dynamics. The authors failed to support their hypothesis that gender-related differences would occur in time spent in sessions with the client. The authors had expected therapist behavior to reflect or reveal a countertransference based on sex roles: Male therapists would prolong a situation likely to arouse sexual curiosity, and female therapists would avoid such a situation. The investigators did find, however, that female therapists were less likely to use an overtly directive response (e.g., clarification or confrontation) but more likely to use specific theory-based responses (e.g., psychodynamic interpretation) and nonobvious controlling responses (e.g., subtle guidance).

Pope et al. (1987) examined responses of 456 psychologists (231 men and 225 women), who reported the degree to which they believed each of 83 behaviors to be ethical in psychotherapy and the degree to which they had engaged in these behaviors. Significant gender differences for engaging in these behaviors emerged in regard to only about 7% of the 86 behaviors; however, of the behaviors for which there were gender differences, about 67% pertained to the therapists' sexual feelings and behaviors and the use of physical contact. Female therapists were more likely to hug a client than were male therapists. Male therapists were more likely to tell a client, "I'm sexually attracted to you"; to treat homosexuality per se as pathological; and to engage in sexual fantasy about a client.

Finally, a 1986 study by Pope, Keith-Spiegel, and Tabachnick (see appendix A) asked participants to describe the characteristics or qualities of patients to whom the therapists experienced sexual attraction. As Table 4 in appendix A shows, participants named 997 descriptive characteristics that were sorted into 19 content categories. With two exceptions, male and female therapists did not differ in the frequency with which they named characteristics in each category. However, male therapists (209 times) far more often than female therapists (87 times) mentioned "physical attractiveness"; female therapists (27 times) significantly more often than male therapists (6 times) mentioned "successful."

Ethnicity Factors

Compared with research on gender factors, there is a relative dearth of studies addressing the relationship of sexual and ethnic factors in psychotherapy. This may reflect a texture of interwoven taboos about sexual attraction and physical closeness to patients in the context of ethnic and racial stereotypes.

Geller (1988) conducted research exploring the potential role of racial bias in clinicians' evaluations of patients and in the desire to be close to or to avoid certain patients. White psychiatric residents and younger faculty psychiatrists read one of three versions of an intake summary for a 25-year-old male patient living on a low income. The three-page summaries varied *only* in regard to the race and IQ of the patient. In one version, the client was White, with an IQ of 120 (reported as a WAIS score). In the second version, the client was Black, with an IQ of 120. And in the third version, the client was White, with an IQ of 85. The clinicians described the Black patient as significantly less responsive and warm and "significantly more impulsive, intolerant of frustration, in need of immediate gratification, and intolerant of successful treatment" (pp. 125–126) than either of the White patients. As Geller summarized, the clinicians indicated a lack of desire to get close to the Black patient.

An analogue study lends detail to Geller's finding that race was related to the "desire to get close." Word, Zanna, and Cooper (1974) found that during interviews, White interviewers spent more time with and maintained less physical distance from White interviewees than from Black interviewees. Research of this sort suggests that discomfort with other races may serve as a barrier to the recognition and exploration of sexual feelings in the therapy.

Communication styles and use of language may affect the ways in which ethnicity influences therapeutic discussions of intimate issues. Russell (1988), for example, cited a case in which a Black professional couple in their early 30s began marital therapy with a White therapist. The couple remained reserved as all communicated in standard English. Only when the therapist used some moderate forms of Black nonstandard English with informal standard English did the couple relax and begin exploration of more intimate issues. Sue (1981) observed that American Indians and Mexican Americans share intimate aspects of their lives only with close friends. These examples elucidate the early findings of Carkhuff and Pierce (1967) that "patients most similar to the race and social class of the counselor involved tended to explore themselves most, while patients most dissimilar tended to explore themselves least" (p. 634).

Useful recognition of racial, ethnic, cultural, and similar factors that can ground and inform or block and distort the therapeutic process involves something different from a therapist's mentally reviewing relevant research studies on ethnicity whenever a minority client walks into the consulting room. The therapist must be aware of the complex attitudes, beliefs, customs, histories, stereotypes, and biases about ethnicity and race that weave their way through our society and *all* our individual lives. Ethnic or racial stereotyping is not something that affects only minority clients. As Munoz (1985) wrote,

> Feelings of racism and being stereotyped are experienced not only by minorities, but also by white persons when they

interact with minorities. The more unlike the minority person they themselves are, especially in terms of education and income, the greater the feelings of discomfort they experience. Thus, a special effort must be made to desensitize professionals-in-training from working with patients who are different from themselves. (p. 181)

Desensitizing therapists to the discomforts of difference (i.e., enabling them to be more comfortable with difference), however, is only one of the necessary steps in addressing issues of ethnicity and race. Espin and Gawelek (1992) noted the complexity of addressing authentically and usefully the issues of ethnicity and race, especially as they are related to other factors. Discussing the psychology of women, they wrote,

In developing [an] approach to the psychology of women, it is clear that the experiences of women of color must be incorporated. But to "add women of color and stir" will not produce an integrated theory. Moreover, the endless groups of women and their experiences that would need to be "stirred in" would condemn this approach to failure. . . . The psychological impact of either social privilege or oppression because of factors other than gender, the impact of insidious trauma, the processes involved in the development of ethnic identity, the emotional implications of language use, the variety of cultural messages concerning sexuality, and other factors will be incorporated into the theory as constituting the experiences of all women. (p. 104)

Addressing ethnic or racial diversity is not only a matter of content (i.e., of learning as much as possible about other ethnic groups and races and of how other factors interact with race and ethnicity) but also of process. It means more than trying to learn about the "other" from our own perspective; it also means trying to imagine accurately and understand empathetically the other person's perspective. As Ballou (1990) wrote, "The demand of diversity is not merely gaining information about other races, cultures, classes, and ethnicities, to know them in 'our' terms. It is considering diversities through 'their' own realities and modes of knowing" (p. 33). Or, as

Pedersen, Dragguns, Lonner, and Trimble (1989) emphasized, "Multicultural counseling is not an exotic topic that applies to remote regions, but is the heart and core of good counseling with any client" (p. 1). The challenge, then, is for clinicians to seek a useful understanding not only of the sexual feelings of both therapist and client but also of both therapist's and client's "modes of knowing" and "modes of responding" to those feelings in the relevant contexts of ethnicity, race, and culture.

Social Class Factors

Like race and ethnicity, social class appears to influence the quality of the psychotherapeutic interaction. In their book *Social Class and Mental Illness*, sociologist Augustus Hollingshead and psychiatrist Fritz Redlich (1958; see also Redlich & Kellert, 1978, for a 25-year follow-up study) reported the results of an intensive, block-by-block study of the residents of New Haven, Connecticut. They found that, when generally matched on other relevant characteristics, those of lower socioeconomic status tended to be diagnosed as suffering from more serious forms of psychopathology. What might be termed *crazy* for a person with few social and economic resources might be termed *eccentric* for a person of higher socioeconomic status. They also found that when providing mental health services, the mental health system tended to discriminate against people of lower socioeconomic status. The significant limitations of psychological services provided to people characterized as the lower socioeconomic classes has been well documented (e.g., Knesper, Pagnucco, & Wheeler, 1985; Korchin, 1976; Redlich & Pope, 1980; Srole et al., 1977).

What remains to be studied is how socioeconomic factors influence sexual issues and feelings in psychotherapy. The research findings of Nash et al., (1965) provide an initial clue. Socioeconomic status was positively related to therapists' rating of client attractiveness, ease of establishing rapport, and prognosis, each of which, in turn, was positively related to continuation in therapy. Given that it is likely that discussion of topics of sexual intimacy between therapist and client is dependent on the positive, ongoing relationship between the two, social class bias may play an influential role.

Disability Factors

Physical disability or special physical needs of either therapist or client may affect the exploration of sexual topics in psychotherapy. Etnyre (1990), for example, presented a vivid case study of a young client for whom an ostomy was conducted in response to long-term ulcerative colitis. The ultimately successful psychotherapy addressed his strong feelings that sexual relations with others were now precluded. The man was certain

> that no one would ever want him for a lover. Getting a job as a freak in a circus sideshow entered his mind. He was sure he'd smell bad and have to wear a bag down to his knees. A sex life was out of the question. . . . He even contemplated suicide. (p. 51)

However, again the research and clinical literature focusing on this topic is relatively sparse. In one of the few examples, Zwerner (1982) pointed to the paucity of therapeutic expertise in dealing effectively with the sexual issues of women who have suffered spinal cord injury (SCI). She cited a prevailing attitude that sexual identity and behavior readjustment for the woman with SCI were not as traumatic as for the man with SCI, "due to continued fertility, pretrauma attitudes towards sexuality, and a more passive role in sexual relations" (p. 158). An interesting finding from Zwerner's questioning of 68 women with SCI was that among those involved in therapy with a psychiatrist, psychologist, or social worker, the client's sexuality *was not* discussed nearly as often as it *was* discussed. In those instances in which the client's sexuality was discussed, it was more often the client than the mental health professional who raised the topic. It was as if therapists tended to assume that sexual issues were not much of a problem for women with SCI. One woman with SCI, quoted by Zwerner, stated that a woman with SCI is more often viewed as "a helpless victim or someone to be taken care of" (p. 165) than as a sexual woman.

Macdougall and Morin (1979), on the basis of their research, emphasized the need for "reorientation. . .toward recognizing and accepting the emotional and sexual needs of disabled persons" (p. 189). Part of the reorientation involves learning about not only how special physical needs can affect sexuality (e.g., Cochran, Hacker, Wellisch, & Berek, 1987) but also how socio-cultural "misconceptions and prejudicial responses to the client's disability [or physical changes]" (Gill, 1985, p. 424) can affect client, therapist, and therapy.

Client Diagnosis Factors

The use of touch in therapy with psychotic patients, particularly those suffering from schizophrenia, has a long tradition (see, e.g., Geller, 1978; Sechehaye, 1951). Bowers, Banquer, and Bloomfield (1974) described the rationale: "The chronic psychotic patient has difficulty in distinguishing real from fantasized feeling and using abstract verbal communications. . .(N)onverbal exercises allow the patient to concretize his feelings, learning to trust them, and then expressing them more freely and appropriately" (p. 14). The authors described their own use of nonverbal exercises with schizophrenic patients and noted the positive effects. However, they noted, "Nonverbal exercises seem to be harder for the therapist than the patient to use: Will the patient respond? Will he think I'm silly? Will I think I'm silly?. . .Will my patient lose control?" (p. 23).

The use of body awareness and contact exercises is central to several therapeutic interventions for clients with sexual dysfunction, gender dysphoria, and paraphilia. Examples of such exercises include didactic discussion of sexual functioning, exploratory discussion of object choice and sexual fantasies, self-exploration of the body, sensate focusing, and guided masturbation. Schover (1989) discussed several issues surrounding the sex therapists' likely attraction to their patients (sometimes accompanied by sexual arousal), including acknowledgment of the elements specific to behavioral sex therapy methods mitigating against the therapists acting out.

The literature on helping patients who have suffered sexual abuse has highlighted the issue of male therapists' sexual reaction to female clients. Briere (1989) suggested that a "sexualization dynamic" is inherent in the male therapist's treatment of the female sexual abuse survivor. He described how men are socialized to view most emotionally intimate relationships as potentially sexual ones—a response that may be intensified in psychotherapy with the sexual abuse survivor.

Herman (1981) also discussed the possibility that male therapists may react sexually to a female client's description of incest. She cautioned that such reactions can evoke the client's original feelings of shame, guilt, and disappointment experienced as a result of the incest experience. Mann (1989) emphasized that the male therapist must recognize and contain his reactions to allow the client to experience a nonsexual emotionally intimate relationship with a man.[6]

Client Physical Attractiveness

Physical attractiveness can play a powerful role in therapist–client relationships, as suggested by a study conducted by Walster, Aronson, Abrahams, and Rottman (1966). Invited to a dance in which participants were supposedly matched by computer on such variables as physical attractiveness, intelligence, social skills, and personality, college students were actually paired randomly, though each of the variables was assessed. After the dance, the researchers studied the degree to which the participants said that they liked their "computer-assigned" partners, stated that they wanted to see their "dates" again, and actually attempted to contact the partners again. It would

---

[6]For additional discussion of therapists' voyeuristic and other sexual reactions to incest survivors, see Ganzarain and Buchele (1986, 1988) and Courtois (1988); for discussion of therapists' voyeuristic reactions to victims of torture, see Pope and Garcia-Peltoniemi (1991); for discussion of therapists' sexual arousal or attraction to patients who have been sexually intimate with a previous therapist, see the section, Sexual Reactions to the Victim, in appendix B.

be nice to believe that personality, intelligence, or social skills had at least *some* relationship to the three dependent variables, but they did not, at least in this study. Whether participants said that they liked their partners, wanted to see them again, or tried to arrange follow-up meetings was statistically associated only with the partner's physical attractiveness.

Sprecher and Hatfield (1985), having reviewed the research about the effects of physical attractiveness, discussed some of the possible explanations for the influence of this variable.

> It may simply be that people have an innate preference for what is aesthetically pleasing (Valentine, 1962). What is aesthetically pleasing, however, seems to be greatly influenced by cultural standards. Attractive persons may also be preferred because it is assumed that beauty is *more* than skin-deep. Much experimental evidence exists to support the physical attractiveness stereotype, "What is beautiful is good." People assume that those who are physically attractive possess many other desirable qualities as well (Dion, Berscheid, & Walster, 1972; Miller, 1970). Attractive people may be preferred for yet another reason, namely, that people hope that their physical attractiveness will rub off. Many years ago, Waller (1937) stated that there is a prestige value in being seen with attractive people. This has more recently been verified by an experiment demonstrating that men are most likely to be rated positively by outsiders when they are accompanied by a good-looking woman, and most likely to be rated negatively when they are accompanied by an unattractive woman (Sigall & Landy, 1973). (p. 183)

In addition to the general research on attractiveness, research has focused directly on how client attractiveness influences therapists' responses and behavior in psychotherapy. For instance, Schwartz and Abramowitz (1978) examined the effects of a female client's physical attractiveness on male psychotherapy trainees' clinical judgments. The results failed to show a significant pattern of prejudice against the relatively unattractive client. However, male therapists rated the unattractive client as more likely to terminate therapy prematurely and delivered fewer relationship-building responses to her than to the physically attractive (but otherwise identical) client. It is not much of an intuitive leap to propose that the likelihood of the processing of sexual feelings in therapy would decline with the therapist's expectation that the relationship would not extend over much time or be of much depth.

Therapist Orientation Factors

Undoubtedly, therapist orientation is one of the factors with the greatest power in differentiating the psychotherapeutic situations that focus on the awareness and use of the body and the processing of sexual feelings and behaviors from those that do not. Freud implored psychoanalysts to maintain absolute abstinence from erotic touch. Burton and Heller (1964) reiterated the cautions against touching. They wrote, "The combination of unanalyzed or unanalyzable residuals in the psychotherapist coupled with the legalistic definitions of touching behavior, make it extremely difficult to be free and spontaneous in this area of treatment" (p. 132).

Mintz (1969) challenged the taboo against touching. She stated, "Even [a]. . .cursory glance at various attitudes toward touch may suggest that they are determined less by the patient's individual needs than by the predetermined bias of the therapist" (p. 370). More recently, other psychoanalysts have argued that touching particular clients for particular reasons (namely for personality growth rather than for its pleasure value) may be an essential aspect of psychotherapy (see, e.g., Fuchs, 1975; Geller, 1978; Spotnitz, 1972).

McKneely (1987) suggested from a Jungian perspective that touch in the therapy context can defuse sexual acting out by bringing the therapist and client to an awareness of underlying pre-Oedipal conflicts. The author did caution, however, that the therapist who uses touch must have a thorough training analysis in body awareness.

At the other end of the orientation spectrum, the more experiential therapies are at least partially based on the premise that life energy becomes trapped in and by the body. The goal is to increase bodily awareness and unblock the energy. Such therapies often use direct physical contact between therapist and client in the form of massage and body manipulation (see, e.g., Leland, 1976; Rappaport, 1975).

Holroyd and Brodsky's (1977) national survey (see chapter 1) yielded information about different theoretical orientations. They found that 68% of psychodynamic therapists and less than 20% of humanistic therapists thought *non*erotic contact (affectionate, nonsexual hugging, kissing, and touching) would rarely or never benefit clients of the same or the opposite sex (a statistically significant difference). Furthermore, the majority of psychodynamic therapists believed that such behavior might be misunderstood by the client (same- and opposite-sex) frequently or always, whereas the majority of the humanistic therapists thought that would be the case rarely or never (a statistically significant difference).

Theoretical orientation may influence the degree to which therapists introduce not only nonerotic touch but also a social or quasi-social component in their work and relationships with patients. A national survey of psychiatrists, psychologists, and social workers, for example, found that humanistic therapists reported significantly more social involvements (e.g., inviting clients to a party or social event; going out to eat with a client after a session) than did behavioral therapists or psychodynamically oriented therapists (Borys & Pope, 1989). The degree to which a theoretical orientation allows or encourages such involvements forms an important part of the context in which the therapist or client may experience sexual feelings.

This chapter presented material illustrating some of the contextual factors (e.g., age, gender, and ethnicity) that can influence therapists' sexual feelings and responses. It is important to emphasize that we have presented only a few of the many factors to which therapists must be alert and, for each factor, only a few of the relevant clinical discussions and research findings from the published literature. Awareness of these factors—as well as of the multitude of theoretical, clinical, and research studies addressing these factors—can inform, deepen, and enrich the process of exploring therapists' sexual feelings.

However, attending *only* to such factors can serve to block therapists' openness to their own feelings. In light of the taboo nature of therapists' sexual feelings and the discomfort that they can provoke, it may seem much safer and less threatening to stay on an intellectual level, using the kind of research and concepts presented in this chapter as a substitute for exploring feelings. However, focusing exclusively on such factors can block therapists' openness to a client as a unique human being and *not* merely the sum of a list of "factors."

In addition to providing a context for therapists' sexual feelings in therapy, these factors also provide a context for therapists' frequent reactions to sexual feelings in therapy, the topic of the next chapter.

6

Frequent Reactions to Sexual Feelings in Therapy

The historic tendency to treat sexual feelings as if they were taboo has made it difficult for therapists to recognize, acknowledge, and accept the attraction or arousal they may experience (see chapters 1 and 2). The lack of adequate research, training, theory, and opportunity to discuss such feelings has created a context in which the occurrence of these feelings may evoke other responses that are difficult for therapists to identify, explore, and understand. The whole area having remained virtually unacknowledged and unexplored, the taboo nature of the content provides an unfamiliar, somewhat sinister context for the therapist's experience of sexual attraction, arousal, or desire.

In light of this history and context, it may be useful for therapists to become aware of some of the frequent reactions to sexual feelings in therapy. Among the most typical reactions to sexual feelings in therapy are the following:

- Surprise, startle, and shock
- Guilt
- Anxiety about unresolved personal issues
- Fear of losing control
- Fear of being criticized
- Frustration at not being able to speak openly
- Frustration at not being able to make sexual contact
- Confusion about tasks

- Confusion about boundaries and roles
- Confusion about actions
- Anger at the patient's sexuality
- Fear or discomfort at frustrating the patient's demands

The intent in providing such a list, however necessarily incomplete, is to make it easier to recognize patterns of feelings and reactions. Learning that various reactions frequently accompany sexual feelings may also make it easier for therapists to accept both the feelings and the accompanying reactions. Knowing that many others have experienced these feelings and reactions may help the individual therapist to feel less alone and less likely to think that these reactions reflect some pathological or evil process and must be kept secret.

The list, then, is meant to provide help and reassurance: help in recognizing and accepting (as frequently occurring) reactions to sexual feelings in therapy and reassurance that *many* others have experienced these reactions. We have assembled this list from our own experiences as therapists-in-training and therapists as well as from our experiences teaching, supervising, and consulting in a variety of settings.

There are at least two pitfalls with such a list that require it to be approached with great care. First, the list includes only some of the most frequently experienced reactions. There are *many* that are not included. Unless approached carefully, the list may be misperceived as a normative, defining, comprehensive chart of *the* common reactions. Any reaction that is not on the list may be experienced as weird, abnormal (not only in that term's statistical sense but also with its negative and pejorative connotations), or somehow off-limits. This list only provides some examples of frequent reactions. That certain reactions do not appear on the list does *not* mean that they are astonishingly rare or that there is anything wrong with them.

The second pitfall is that sexual feelings and the reactions they evoke can be so uncomfortable for therapists that it becomes easier to attend to the list than to their actual experience. Just as the research findings noted in the previous chapter can occlude and obscure rather than clarify and provide context, the terms on the preceding list can unfortunately become the focus, distracting and detracting from the immediacy of first-person human experience. Thinking and talking about such words and concepts become a substitute for thinking and talking about what is felt and experienced. *It is crucial that readers' feelings and reactions form the primary focus, the raw data, and the subject matter for exploration and discovery.* The principal goal of the learning process for which this book was created is attending to and finding out about oneself and one's experience of and reaction to sexual feelings in therapy, *not* to concentrate principally on a list compiled by the authors.

Surprise, Startle, and Shock at Sexual Feelings

One of the most frequent reactions to sexual feelings in therapy, at least in our experience, is surprise or even shock. This reaction seems understandable in light of the historic tendency of graduate training programs, residencies, internships, and the profession more generally to deny, discount, distort, or downplay the occurrence of such feelings. If formal education and the professional literature have failed to alert a therapist to the possibility that sexual feelings may arise, it is no wonder that such feelings may catch the therapist off guard and cause something like a startle reaction. As with many of the other frequent reactions, the shock of experiencing attraction, arousal, or other sexual feelings may be so profound, and there may be so few apparent internal and external resources for understanding what is going on, that the therapist "freezes" and is shocked into paralysis. In such instances, it may be very difficult for the therapist to take steps or even to consider steps that are usually taken when the therapist feels the need for help (e.g., asking for consultation).

In other instances, the adrenaline of shock seems to evoke a form of the "fight or flight" syndrome. Denigrating the patient to whom one is sexually attracted or in whose presence one becomes sexually aroused is perhaps one way to "blame" the patient for the therapist's feelings. It may also be part of an effort—that the therapist becomes aware of only later, on reflection—to drive the patient out of therapy. The therapist gets rid of the person who seems to evoke shocking feelings rather than addresses the feelings more directly in an exploratory manner. In some rare instances, the therapist may begin fighting with the patient literally and physically. One therapist, for example, suggested that he and the patient needed to "wrestle" as part of the therapy. During the wrestling, he became increasingly aroused and finally began grabbing the patient's breasts. She was offended, outraged, and told him so. He replied that he could not help himself because she was so attractive.

Perhaps the clearest versions of the "flight" reaction involve the therapist who begins escaping or avoiding therapy situations in which he or she encounters sexual feelings. Some therapists may begin missing appointments, writing down incorrect session dates and times, or "calling in sick." Some may discover what seem to be clearly valid, compelling, and irrefutable reasons to terminate or transfer a patient. More subtle versions involve therapists who continue to work with the patient but who become more emotionally distant, less engaged, and less open to the patient. They seem to function more as disembodied computers, to run "on automatic pilot," and to give superficial, pro forma interventions. Patients are generally aware of such sudden shifts in a therapist's involvement in therapy, and some may ask the therapist why he or she is acting differently. Some therapists may remain unaware of the change in (or reasons for) their behavior and some, unwilling to discuss uncomfortable feelings with the patient, may deny that they are feeling or behaving any differently with the patient. The resulting discrepancy between what the patient feels *is* different and what the patient is told *is not* different can be, at best, quite confusing for the patient.

Certain clinical situations may intensify the surprise, startle, or shock that the therapist experiences when becoming aware of sexual feelings. The therapist may believe that these situations are such that any sexual feelings about the patient are especially inappropriate, inexplicable, or even abhorrent. For example, the therapist may be working with a young child and may never before have experienced any sexual feelings in regard to a minor. The therapist may be working with an adult survivor of incest, rape, or torture, and may find the accounts of the abuse sexually stimulating (see the section, Client Diagnosis Factors, in chapter 5). The therapist may be conducting family therapy and discover intense sexual attraction toward one of the parents. In each of these situations, the apparent extreme discordance between the situation and the sexual feelings can intensify the therapist's astonishment or bewilderment at the occurrence of sexual feelings about a patient.

Guilt at Feeling Sexual About a Patient

Research suggests that most therapists who experience sexual attraction to a patient react to the attraction with guilt (see appendix A). In our culture, of course, it is not uncommon for people to experience some form of guilt in regard to—depending on the individual's personality and background—at least a few sexual issues. But it is likely that a far more prevalent and powerful source of the guilt that may accompany therapists' sexual feelings in psychotherapy is the historical tendency of the profession to treat therapists' sexual feelings as taboo (see chapter 2). This taboo has contributed to a proverbial vicious circle: When the profession tends to deny, discount, and dismiss the topic of therapists' sexual feelings, individual therapists tend to receive little or no training in the area, find virtually no mention of it in research, and might infer from the almost studied silence on the topic that there is something threatening or wrong with the feelings. Consequently, individual therapists may react with guilt when they encounter these taboo feelings in therapy. To complete the vicious circle, the guilt experienced by individual therapists may strengthen the profession's tendency to avoid such an uncomfortable and personally immediate topic.

Each individual therapist helps to interrupt this destructive and disruptive cycle of increasing guilt when he or she acknowledges, accepts, and attempts to understand the nature and sources of his or her own guilty reactions to sexual feelings in therapy. The therapist, by going beyond an assumption that a therapist's sexual feelings per se are wrong and thus an appropriate source of guilt, probably will discover that guilt accompanying sexual feelings can have a variety of meanings. For example, the therapist may, by courageously reviewing his or her behavior with the patient, uncover inappropriate actions that serve as the source of guilt. The therapist may have acted— perhaps without being aware of it—in a seductive manner with the patient or may have indirectly encouraged the patient to dress, act, or talk in a sexually exciting (for the therapist) manner. In other cases, a therapist—again, perhaps without being aware of it at the time—may have reacted insensitively, clumsily, or punitively to a patient's discussion of sexual attraction to the therapist. In still other cases, the therapist may be experiencing what in psychodynamic theory might be termed *countertransference*. In still other cases, the therapist may have some personal conflicts—including guilt—about sex that need to be addressed as part of professional development. And, as one last example, the therapist and his or her supervisor may have different and inherently contradictory views of the patient's clinical needs and of the best intervention. If the therapist is subverting his or her best judgment and deferring to the supervisor's approach, the therapist may feel guilty vis-a-vis the patient (i.e., for not implementing what seems to the therapist the best approach to the patient's clinical needs), and this guilt may emerge in regard to sexual issues. If, on the other hand, the therapist is (perhaps covertly) defying the authority of the supervisor and is using interventions that the supervisor believes to be inappropriate, unethical, or harmful, the therapist may feel guilt vis-a-vis the supervisor, and this guilt may emerge as interwoven with sexual issues in the therapy. These are but a few of the virtually countless ways in which guilt can accompany sexual feelings in therapy. What is crucial is that the therapist be open and alert to the possibility of guilty reactions, accept and explore them when they occur, and attempt to understand why they are arising.

Anxiety About Unresolved Personal Issues

Especially for therapists-in-training, who may be insecure and wonder if their "personal problems" will become apparent to clinical supervisors who will consequently invite them to consider other career options for which they "might be better suited," the experience of sexual feelings in therapy may set off the alarm bells of anxiety. Therapists-in-training may recognize almost instantly that their attraction to a certain patient reflects or taps into a long-standing, unresolved issue. Sexual feelings about a patient may prompt the emergence or re-emergence of conflicts (e.g., conflicting feelings about sexual orientation, ambivalence about responsibilities of the therapist's role, questions and worries about marital fidelity, or anger at or rebellion against the "rule-bound" training program) or of unmet emotional needs (e.g., loneliness or childlike dependency). When sexual feelings about a patient are somehow linked to the therapists' unresolved personal issues, any anxiety or discomfort associated with the emerging sexual feelings is likely to be amplified by anxiety about the unresolved personal issue. In a cascading set of consequences, therapists may experience a renewed sense of vulnerability (i.e., that they *have*—contrary to the false stereotype of the inhumanly perfect therapist—unresolved personal issues); then concern that the personal issue may block their effectiveness; and finally ambivalence about seeking appropriate help to address and resolve the issue.

Fear of Losing Control

Perhaps one of the most uncomfortable responses a therapist can have in regard to encountering sexual feelings in therapy is fear of losing control: fear that the therapist will stop providing effective therapy and harm the patient through sexual exploitation. In light of the historical lack of education and training in this area, it is no wonder that therapists and therapists-in-training may feel "on their own" when sexual feelings arise, may feel uncertain about what to do, and may wonder if they are capable—especially in the extreme privacy of the consulting room and the emotional intensity of the therapy relationship—of resisting temptation to take advantage of the patient's vulnerability. As described elsewhere in this book, an uncomfortable reaction such as fear can—if not adequately acknowledged, accepted, and addressed—motivate and mobilize a variety of defensive maneuvers such as denial, avoidance (of the patient, of examination of the therapist's feelings, and of helpful resources); rationalization (e.g., "I'm called by fate to move boldly to the cutting edge of my profession: I'm ready to pioneer a new treatment strategy that, while *seeming* on a very superficial level to focus on sexual interaction with the patient, actually helps the patient"); and deception (e.g., statement to a supervisor: "Oh, I guess I can see how others might find him attractive, but he's not my type. Really. No, *really*. Not in any way at all!").

The fear of losing control, although serving as a signal that the therapist probably needs to seek some consultation or supervision, at the same time can be experienced by the therapist as adding an additional hurdle to seeking that help. The therapist may feel that disclosure is tantamount to saying, "As a therapist, I'm a potential sex abuser!" In more extreme cases, the therapist may feel that "potential" is not a sufficiently strong word, that he or she is a "pre-abuser," someone who has sneaked into the profession by mistake (i.e., through the admission committee's lack of acuity) and for whom it is just a matter of time before the first instance of therapist–patient sex occurs.

It may be helpful for those who are afraid of losing control to be reminded that the growing research literature gives very clear indications that relatively few therapists actually engage in sex with a client (see appendix C). It may also be helpful to be reminded that, as with all the reactions discussed in this chapter, fear of losing control seems to be a frequent experience among therapists and therapists-in-training. The experience of this reaction does not mean that the therapist is a high-risk candidate for violating the prohibition against therapist–patient sexual involvement or that he or she is one of an infinitesimal minority who feel uncertain about controlling their behavior with patients.

What is crucial is that the fear of losing control be adequately acknowledged, accepted, and addressed. The following generality seems to hold: *Fear or concern about losing control with a patient is experienced by many if not most therapists at least at some point in their professional development and career and can only be transformed into a true source of danger if unattended.*

Fear of Being Criticized

Because sexual feelings about patients have historically been taboo and because it is so easy to equate falsely the experience of sexual attraction to a patient with sexual intimacies with a patient (see chapter 2), therapists who encounter their own sexual feelings in therapy may be afraid—almost terrified—to disclose these feelings to anyone else, even the most trusted supervisors, consultants, or colleagues. They may fear that others will react critically, calling into question the therapist's motivation, attitudes, and behavior. The fear may be intensified if the therapist believes that sexual feelings aroused in therapy may increase the chances that a patient might file a false complaint—alleging therapist–patient sexual intimacies—against the therapist. Moreover, the therapist may believe that disclosing such feelings to a supervisor, consultant, or colleague, or documenting sexual issues in the patient's chart may somehow be harmful in the future by providing "evidence" should the patient file a formal complaint.

It may require considerable courage to break the silence within a graduate training program, internship, hospital, or mental health center that has traditionally acted as if such feelings did not exist. The fear of being criticized can be heightened if one considers that a supervisor may have substantial power to affect one's future. If the supervisor or other individual to whom one were to disclose such feelings were to react negatively (e.g., view such feelings as tantamount to unprofessional behavior, as a pathognomonic sign of the therapist's pervasive psychopathology, or as evidence of the therapist's inability to handle countertransference), he or she, of course, might share this negative information with others. It could affect one's chances for a fellowship, an internship placement, or a research assistantship; the data might be provided to a licensing board when the individual applies for licensure; the evaluation might be shared with all future prospective employers.

The fears of criticism and consequences may be heightened still further if the therapist does not feel completely safe discussing sexual matters with the supervisor, consultant, or colleague. The therapist may fear that breaking silence on this topic opens the door to focused and perhaps even intrusive questioning about the therapist's own sexual attitudes, beliefs, development, experiences, orientation, desires, and conflicts.

Again, it may be helpful for therapists experiencing sexual feelings in therapy to recognize that they are not alone, that *many* therapists and therapists-in-training are or have been afraid of the feelings themselves and the prospect of speaking out about them. Especially if there is fear or concern that seeking consultation about sexual feelings puts the therapist at risk for negative consequences, he or she might offer the consultant material such as contained in this book as a framework for the consultation. The consultant's or supervisor's recognition of his or her own responsibilities to provide a safe and supportive environment for such disclosures and of the therapist's courage in telling someone else about these feelings is crucial if the profession is to address this topic adequately, sensitively, and helpfully.

Frustration at Not Being Able to Speak Openly

Sexual attraction, arousal, and desire are such powerful, immediate feelings that it can be frustrating not to share them with the person who evokes them. Session after session, the therapist spends time alone with the patient in the privacy of the consulting room. The patient may speak freely and intensely of intimate matters. In such a context, the therapist may long to be able to give words to his or her sexual feelings, impulses, and longings.

The prohibition against sexual exploitation of patients extends beyond the fundamental rule against sexual contact. It includes the crucial responsibility of never using a patient to gratify the therapist's needs, sexual or otherwise. As discussed previously (see chapter 1), therapists can engage in unethical sexual exploitation of their patients in a variety of ways that do not involve erotic contact. The therapist, for example, may engage in sexual conversations with the patient, not for any clinical rationale, but simply to meet the therapist's needs for sexual stimulation. The therapist may invite or command the patient to engage in erotic conversations about what therapist and patient might do were they to become sexually involved. The therapist may describe his or her erotic reactions and fantasies (sometimes including masturbatory fantasies) about the patient. Such descriptions, when motivated by the therapist's rather than the patient's needs, may nevertheless be introduced in the guise of usual and customary therapy procedures: dynamic self-disclosure, existential authenticity, systematic desensitization of erotic concerns, attempts to improve the patient's self-image, enhancing the patient's ability to "reality test" another individual's reactions to him or her, modeling sexual frankness to enable the patient to escape the strangling grasp of a sexually repressed society, and so on.

As with the other reactions to sexual feelings in therapy, recognition that the frustration at not being able to speak openly to the patient about the therapist's sexual attraction, desire, or arousal is shared by many therapists may be helpful to therapists-in-training as well as seasoned therapists. The frustration leads to questions that all therapists must address: What are the limits to the therapist's appropriate self-disclosure to a patient? What information should remain private? What questions are best left unanswered?

Approaches to addressing this issue are influenced to some degree by theoretical orientation and personal style. A theoretical orientation in which the therapist is conceptualized as a "blank screen" may mandate minimal self-disclosure. Some approaches may focus exclusively on the patient's self-exploration, discouraging or deflecting patient questions about the nature and techniques of therapy, the therapist's credentials, why the therapist makes certain interpretations, and so on, as defenses against the task of self-examination. For example, Glover's (1955) survey of the British Psycho-analytical Society found that one of the "points on which there is (almost) complete agreement" is the "practice of analyzing questions instead of answering them" (p. 345).

Other approaches emphasize the importance of responding to such questions. Sarason (1985), for example, describes his supervision of a therapy session (after which the patient quit therapy).

> A student was presenting to me his first psychotherapeutic session with a man who was fifty-five years old. . . . The student described the patient as overcontrolled, respectful, somewhat imperious in manner, and seemingly uncomfortable about what he should say and when. Early in the hour, he asked the student: "What is psychotherapy?" The student did not answer the question but instead asked: "Why do you ask that question?" The man was obviously dissatisfied with the student but politely said that he had asked the question because he was frankly puzzled about what psychotherapy was and how it worked. To which the student replied: "You will get an understanding as we continue to meet."
> [The student held] a picture of the therapist as someone who passively listens, who nonverbally conveys sincere interest and compassion, who makes wise interpretations every now and then, and who never falls into the "trap" of directly answering a direct question. . . . [The student viewed the question as the patient's] defense against talking about his problems. . . . How, I asked, did you know fifteen minutes into the first hour that this was a defense? And what if it was a defense? Does that mean that you never answer a question that reflects a defensive maneuver? What one should do, the student said, is to interpret, not answer, such questions. What, I asked, would you have done if in this hour, during which you felt that he was quite anxious, he had asked you where the toilet is? Would you have refused to tell him because you were convinced that he wanted time out from you? The student agreed that he would tell him where the toilet is, because he understood from his own experience the relationship between anxiety and urination and defecation. (pp. 152–153)

In some rare cases, it may be clinically useful and appropriate to disclose to the patient one's sexual attraction to the patient (see the final chapter, "Confronting an Impasse"). However, such disclosure is so fraught with potential risks that it should be done only after particularly careful consideration. It is especially important that the disclosure be consistent with the therapist's theoretical orientation (e.g., an existential approach focusing on the honesty and authenticity of the encounter); that it meet an appropriate clinical need of the patient (e.g., that it not represent the therapist's "dumping" on the patient the therapist's own sexual conflicts, needs, or desires rather than responding aptly, ethically, and helpfully to the patient's clinical situation); that it not be hidden as a secret (i.e., that the therapist consult with experienced colleagues about all relevant issues); that the therapist possess current knowledge, skill, and competence in such areas as the therapeutic uses of self-disclosure; that the disclosure not reflect a subtle or incremental process of seduction; that communications be clear; that the patient's possible interpretation of and responses to the information be anticipated and evaluated; and that the therapist ensure that the communication occurs within a safe and trusting context in which the patient is free from risk of sexual exploitation.

Frustration at Not Being Able to Make Sexual Contact

Similar in some ways to the frustration at not being able to disclose sexual attraction, desires, and arousal with a patient is the frustration at not being able to make sexual contact. When a therapist experiences attraction to a patient, it is natural to want to draw closer and make contact and to resent the fact that the therapeutic situation precludes sexual intimacies and contact. When a therapist desires to engage in sex with a patient, it is understandable that resisting the impulse may feel like a troublesome imposition. When a therapist is sexually aroused, it is normal to feel frustrated when avoiding the temptation to sexually exploit the patient in order to enhance and bring the arousal to a climax.

To deny that refraining from sexual intimacies with patients can involve considerable frustration for a therapist is to deny an important dynamic experienced by many therapists in fulfilling their professional responsibilities and avoiding placing their patients at risk for serious and lasting harm. Intellectually, therapists may know that they will never exploit their patients in this way. They may be committed without reservation to ethical practice. And yet inhibiting what may be strong impulses to become sexually intimate with another person who happens to be a patient may require considerable self-knowledge, self-acceptance, and self-control. Avoiding exploitation may create deep disappointment, resentment, and frustration for the therapist. Failure to acknowledge the high emotional costs of ethical behavior may lead a therapist who is at risk for exploiting a patient to underestimate the internal resources that will be necessary to resist an urgent, persistent temptation. In cases in which the therapist is at no risk for sexually exploiting the patient, failure to acknowledge the possible frustrations, resentments, and disappointments involved in refraining from sexual behavior with the patient may lead to the therapist's taking out these feelings on the patient, a supervisor, a colleague, a friend, a life partner, or a lover. Denial of or discounting the feelings resulting from blocked attraction, desire, or arousal can lead to anger, bitterness, hostility, or self-pity that the therapist may find surprising and difficult to understand.

Part of the process of exploration and discovery in the area of sexual feelings in therapy involves learning about the occurrence of frustration—and the growing power of frustration if it remains hidden and unacknowledged—when the therapist refrains from expressing or consummating those sexual feelings through sexual involvement with a patient. For the profession to acknowledge openly the nature and dynamics of this frustration may be exceptionally difficult, for it involves publicly acknowledging the intensity of sexual attraction, arousal, and desire that therapists may experience with their patients. It precludes the stance that therapists are neutral and disinterested helpers, or the manifestation of pure altruism, or superhuman healers and caregivers who leave their sexuality at the door to the consulting room. Only when the nature and forms of frustration are identified, accepted, and explored can professional identity and training rest on a more realistic foundation.

Confusion About Tasks

The legitimate tasks of psychotherapy encompass a vast scope. Therapist and patient working together may attempt to decrease the patient's suffering, help the patient recover from trauma, enrich the patient's self-understanding, help the patient avoid unwanted or dysfunctional behaviors, escape dangerous and harmful environments, participate in more satisfying relationships, find meaning in life, cope with loss, face death imposed by terminal illness, and so on. Tasks specific to a particular therapy are determined in part by the clinical needs, resources, and choices of the individual patient as well as by the skills, resources, and choices of the individual therapist. The therapist's theoretical orientation may also shape these tasks. Some orientations may direct attention to external conditions and the individual's potential to change those conditions, whereas others may focus on the individual's cognitive and emotional reactions to external conditions and the individual's potential to change his or her cognitive and emotional reactions to those conditions.

Whatever the legitimate tasks of a particular therapy as defined or influenced by theoretical orientation, specific circumstances, and the various characteristics, resources, and choices of patient and therapist, the occurrence of sexual feelings may, if not adequately acknowledged, accepted, and addressed, pull the therapy off course toward meeting the sexual (and related) needs of the therapist. The most obvious examples are those in which a therapist begins spending more and more time with a particular patient, sometimes using that time to focus on sexually stimulating material. The therapist may, for example, encourage the patient to describe sexual activities or fantasies in great detail. The therapist may start using—without adequate clinical justification—the techniques of sex therapy, perhaps adapting them to maximize sexual stimulation of the patient or therapist. Less obvious is when the therapist begins to talk about him- or herself or to chat and socialize without regard to the goals of therapy or the clinical needs of the patient.

When the actual therapeutic tasks recede and are replaced by pseudotherapy that has clear sexual components, the confusion of tasks is relatively clear to most clinicians (who may discuss such instances in case conferences or supervision). The emphasis on sexual content is also potentially clear to the therapist him- or herself, if he or she would take a moment to reflect on the dramatic switching of gears.

There are, however, almost countless situations in which the therapist loses sight of the legitimate therapeutic tasks but has not introduced explicitly sexual discussions or tasks. The therapist may have stopped short of focusing on sexually stimulating material because of a failure of the therapist's nerve, fear that the patient would object, indecision about whether to exploit the patient in this way, the wish to avoid malpractice actions, empathy for the patient, or the steadying effects of conscience. Frequently, the confusion about the tasks of therapy is manifested when the therapist begins drifting and losing concentration on the work of therapy. The discussions or other activities (e.g., systematic desensitization, covert rehearsal, biofeedback, or behavioral charting) may fail to reflect and further the aims of the therapeutic tasks but rather may serve as background music and pretext for the therapist to be with the patient. It is not that the tasks move toward explicit sexuality or distinctly sexual themes but rather that the therapeutic discussion and activities drift aimlessly, serving as pretext for the therapist to spend time with someone he or she finds sexually attractive, arousing, or intriguing. In fact, *failure* to discuss explicit sexual material that is relevant to the therapeutic task may be evidence of drifting.

This aimless drifting in therapy tends to avoid any destination in particular, just as someone drifting on a raft in a swimming pool may avoid resting against the side of the pool (generally by sticking out an arm or leg to shove off again more toward the middle of the pool when the raft drifts too near the side). The drifting therapist tends to avoid any task, process, or event that might bring the therapy to a conclusion and thus deprive the therapist of the opportunity to spend time with someone he or she finds sexually alluring. Thus, although otherwise relatively aimless and without a clear sense of task, the therapist may actively (though covertly) sabotage the patient's progress in order to prolong the therapist's enjoyment of the patient's presence. If, for example, a woman has sought therapy because she feels lonely and wants to be able to enter a lasting and fulfilling intimate relationship, the therapist may find fault with any of the potential partners that the patient discusses during "therapy" sessions. The therapist treats any progress or opportunity that move the patient toward termination as a threat.

There is one major exception to the general tendency for therapists who have lost sight of the genuine tasks of therapy to avoid movement toward termination. This exception occurs when the therapist, unable or unwilling to take the risk of engaging in more sexually explicit discussion or intimacies with the patient during therapy, decides to use termination as a means and justification for engaging in a closer relationship with the patient. The therapy sessions having served as a subtle—and sometimes not so subtle—form of courtship and seduction, the therapist devises some form of termination (generally one that will look good or hold up in retrospect should there by any formal complaint) as a prelude to more directly sexual encounters.

Confusion About Boundaries and Roles

The conventional marriage ceremony sometimes refers explicitly to the husband and wife becoming "one." There is something about intense sexual, romantic, or loving feelings that encourages the experience—some would say illusion—of being at one (at least for brief periods of time) with the other person. When a therapist begins to feel intense sexual feelings for a patient, a similar phenomenon can occur.

In some instances, the therapist may become preoccupied with the patient. Thoughts, impulses, and fantasies about the patient frequently seize the therapist's attention. As the therapist becomes more and more "bound"—through thoughts, feelings, fantasies, memories, desires, and so on—to the patient, the sense of clear boundaries separating therapist and patient may become blurred. The therapist may forget him- or herself in the relationship and lose sight of his or her role as an agent of change, as one who is there to help.

The confusion about boundaries may be reflected in the degree to which the content of the therapy sessions focuses on the needs, experiences, and goals of the patient. A shift begins. The focus of therapy moves from the patient and the patient's life to the therapist and the therapist's life. The shift may begin with the therapist making a few more casual comments than usual about current events (inviting a sharing of views on seemingly "safe" topics), what has been happening in the therapist's life, the therapist's plans for the weekend vacation, and so on. The shift gathers momentum as the therapist begins to talk more and more about increasingly personal matters. In advanced stages, a naive observer watching a hypothetical videotape of the session might incorrectly assume that the therapist is the patient. What is described here is *not* therapeutically oriented self-disclosure but rather the therapist's increasing confusion about his or her role in the therapy relationship.

The therapist who experiences sexual feelings for a patient may also behave in other ways that are uncharacteristic for that therapist and that reflect an erosion of boundaries. For example, a therapist who customarily greets a patient at the door of the consulting room and who remains in the consulting room when the patient leaves, may begin to go down the hall to the reception area and escort the patient to the consulting room; after a session, the therapist may walk the patient back down the hall and even, in some cases, to his or her car.

Some therapists may begin erasing almost every conceivable boundary. They may phone the patient to chat between sessions, ask the patient to give them a ride to or from work, suggest that they meet the patient for lunch or dinner, and begin, in essence, dating the patient.

Confusion About Actions

Therapists experiencing sexual attraction, arousal, or stimulation with a patient may become exceptionally confused about actions: the patient's or their own. Changes in the way the patient dresses, in what the patient talks about, or in the patient's posture and movements can be misread to suggest that the patient is attracted to the therapist, desires a sexual relationship with the therapist, or does not really consider him- or herself to be in a "therapy" relationship with the therapist and thus is not off-limits for sexual involvement.

The very fact that an individual is sexually aroused in the presence of another person (who is therefore "accessible") may lead to distortions in perceptions of and attributions about that other person (see, e.g., Stephen, Berscheid, & Walster, 1971; Walster & Walster, 1978). For example, in one component of a complex study of sexual arousal and heterosexual perception (Stephen et al., 1971), men were told that they would be asked their reaction to a woman with whom they had been paired for a date. The men were to be given the woman's picture and some descriptive information about her (e.g., her background). While the first investigator went to get the picture and descriptive information, another investigator asked the men if they would take a few minutes to read a passage describing sexual behavior and to rate the degree to which they found it sexually arousing. Half of the men were given "an article depicting a romantic seduction scene. . . (We hoped that the subjects would find this article sexually arousing.) The other. . .subjects read an article describing the sex life of herring gulls. (We considered this article to be nonarousing.)" (pp. 95–96). The men's ratings, immediately after they read the article and at a later point, indicated that those reading the seduction passage found it arousing, whereas those reading about herring gulls were not aroused.

All participants were actually asked to rate two women (on the basis of a photograph and descriptive information): one with whom they would be spending time on a get-acquainted "date" and who was therefore "accessible" (in the sense that they would be in her presence) and one with whom they would not be spending time and who was therefore "inaccessible" (i.e., they would not have the opportunity to be in her presence at some time in the future). The relevant finding for this component of the experiment was that "subjects in the aroused-accessible condition were more likely to perceive the girl as being sexually receptive than were subjects in the aroused-nonaccessible condition" (p. 99). In other words, the combination of sexual arousal and (anticipated) proximity appeared to lead men to make attributions that they would not otherwise make—solely on the basis of a picture and on information that the woman provided about herself—that a person was sexually receptive.

Such experimental findings are consistent with the notion that therapists who are sexually aroused and in the presence of a patient may misperceive or misinterpret the patient's words and behavior as reflecting or communicating sexual receptivity. In the previously described experiment, the men's inferences of sexual receptivity were based solely on apparently neutral self-descriptions. In therapy sessions, a patient may be receptive to or may actively seek nonsexual caring, nonsexual touch, nonsexual intimacy or a sense of closeness, reassurance about his or her attractiveness, and so on. In each instance, a sexually aroused therapist may be vulnerable to misinterpreting this receptivity or seeking as a clear communication that the patient is sexually aroused, desires sex with the therapist, and is thus not off-limits for sexual involvement.

Sexual feelings in therapy may lead a therapist to misperceive or misattribute not only the patient's behavior but also the therapist's own behavior. For example, the therapist may confuse nonerotic with erotic touching. Finding ample justification to cradle a grieving patient, the therapist may justify the behavior as nonerotic comforting, avoiding acknowledging that rubbing up against the patient is sexually stimulating to both therapist and patient.

Anger at the Patient's Sexuality

Although it occurs frequently, anger as a reaction to the patient's sexuality seems particularly likely to catch the therapist off guard. It is one of the reactions that, if unacknowledged or misunderstood, seems to have the most potential for turning therapy into a process that is not helpful to the patient. Therapists who remain unaware of their anger may take that anger out on the patient in direct and indirect ways. Reiser and Levenson (1984), for example, discuss ways in which clinicians may abuse the borderline diagnosis by assigning it in the absence of clinical justification "to defend against sexual clinical material" (p. 1528).

The anger evoked by the therapist's experience of sexual feelings in therapy may spring from diverse sources and may be directed outward or inward. Therapists may be angry at and disgusted with themselves for their own sexual reactions or for experiencing an attraction that may seem so discordant with the needs of a client who is vulnerable, hurting, and perhaps in crisis. They may feel anger at their own vulnerability and at the patient's ability to evoke sexual arousal or desire. They may respond to sexual attraction, arousal, or desire with anger and even aggression growing out of the frustration that these feelings cannot be physically expressed and consummated, as discussed in a previous section. This pattern of response to sexual feelings is consistent with the well-researched frustration–aggression hypothesis originally described by Dollard, Doob, Miller, Mowrer, and Sears (1939). Conversely, therapists may become irritated and angry at the patient's sexual feelings for the therapist, at the patient's sexual behaviors, and at the patient's comments or questions (e.g., describing why the patient finds the therapist attractive or asking about the therapist's sexual experiences) that the therapist may experience as intrusive and disconcerting. They may become angry at the patient for introducing material that the therapist will find difficult to discuss with the supervisor.

Anger at patients is another taboo feeling that has been relatively neglected in training programs and the research literature. Findings from a recent national study indicated that although over 80% of the therapist-participants had experienced a variety of angry feelings toward their patients (and 31% had experienced "hatred" toward a patient), over one third reported that their graduate training in this area had been either poor or virtually nonexistent (Pope & Tabachnick, 1993).

By recognizing that anger is not an uncommon reaction to sexual feelings in therapy, therapists and therapists-in-training can minimize the likelihood that they will deny or discount this reaction, treat it as abnormal or taboo, or avoid the responsibility of exploring its meaning and implications.

Fear or Discomfort About Frustrating the Patient's Demands

At some point in therapy, a therapist may intuit that *something*—it is not clear exactly what—is going on between therapist and patient. It hovers at the edge of awareness or sounds a vague, persistent undertone. Although it would likely be immediately clear what the something is if it were occurring in any other context (e.g., a party), the therapist may have difficulty recognizing that sexual feelings seem to be bouncing back and forth between therapist and patient. If the therapist were able to view videotapes of the sessions, it might be clear that therapist and patient were subtly flirting with each other, or that each seemed sexually stimulated by the presence of the other, or that the language they were using seemed to carry double meanings, expressing romantic or erotic feelings. Such sexual feelings can be especially difficult for the therapist to identify if the therapist views the therapeutic situation and the occurrence of sexual feelings as mutually exclusive or incompatible.

The therapeutic setting may also make it difficult for the therapist to respond appropriately to a patient's flirtation, invitations, or even sexual demands. If the setting were different (e.g., a first date or a social get-together), the therapist might find it easier to respond, including setting limits to sexual behavior that he or she does not want to occur but that is desired by the other person. But the fact that the therapist may be unprepared to encounter a patient's invitation to sexual intimacy and may, in the role of therapist, be attempting to be responsive to the patient's needs, can tend to make it difficult for the therapist to respond appropriately.

A theme emphasized repeatedly in this volume (see especially chapters 1 and 10) is that, in any and all circumstances, the therapist must *never* engage in sexual intimacies with a patient, and it is the therapist who always bears sole responsibility for ensuring that this fundamental prohibition is never violated. Nevertheless, the therapist may feel uncomfortable or even afraid of the patient's reaction to a refusal to allow sexual intimacies to occur. In some cases, the therapist may be sensitive about disappointing a vulnerable patient who may experience the therapist's careful maintenance of appropriate boundaries as a personal rejection, or a confirmation that the patient is sexually unattractive, worthless, and doomed to meet rejection for the rest of his or her life. In other cases, the therapist may fear the anger or even rage that a patient may direct at a therapist who refuses an invitation or demand for sexual intimacy. In still other cases, the therapist may believe that the patient, frustrated, will engage in some self-destructive act. Eyman and Gabbard (1991), for example, describe therapists who have developed this fear into a rationalization for sexually exploiting the patient. The therapists rationalized that so intent was the patient on having sex with the therapists that the patient would have committed suicide if the therapists had not agreed. In other words, the therapists maintained that having sex with the patient was the only intervention that could prevent the patient from taking her life.

This chapter presented some of the most common therapist reactions to the recognition of sexual feelings in therapy. The reactions include the therapist's experience of surprise, guilt, anxiety, frustration, anger, confusion, and fear. It is important to emphasize again that this chapter listed only a few of the many and diverse reactions that often occur when a therapist encounters sexual feelings in therapy. Extending this list may be a useful project for study groups exploring this issue and may encourage an active alertness to the range of such reactions.

Despite attempts of even the most informed, open, and aware therapists, there may, however, be occasions when sexual feelings remain hidden beneath the surface. Therapists may be able to discover such feelings if they attend to clues to unacknowledged feelings. Chapter 7 reviews some of the most frequent clues that sexual feelings may be present but have not yet emerged into the therapist's awareness.

7

Frequent Clues to Unacknowledged Sexual Feelings

Sexual feelings having been historically a virtually taboo topic in research and training (see chapter 2), it is no wonder that many therapists find it difficult to recognize promptly, identify correctly, and explore fully their sexual feelings in therapy. When such feelings begin to grow toward awareness, they often seem to be gated, distorted, or otherwise blocked from awareness. Each theoretical orientation may have its own assumptions and terminology for understanding why and how this deflection from awareness occurs.

In this chapter, we briefly mention some of the most frequent clues that may help a therapist become aware of unacknowledged sexual feelings:

- Dehumanization of the patient
- Dehumanization of the therapist
- Avoidance
- Obsession
- Interesting slips and meaningful mistakes
- Fantasies during sexual activities
- Undue special treatment
- Isolation of the patient
- Isolation of the therapist
- Creating a secret
- Seeking repeated reassurances from colleagues
- Boredom or drowsiness as protective reactions

The clues are mentioned only briefly not only because there is nothing elaborate or mysterious about how they work but also because they are so blatantly obvious—at least if one is *not* currently experiencing them. They are the kind of experiences that, when presented to a consultant, suggest immediately that something is going on that needs to be attended to. When we look back on our own experiences with such clues, we tend to find them signals of exceptional clarity. . .at least in hindsight. However, it is exceptionally easy to miss these clues if it is *we* who are *currently* experiencing them. For that reason, we provide these examples in the form of a brief list, with minimal discussion. If therapists can hold these constantly in mind and, from time to time, go down this "checklist," it may help them to make prompt and effective use of the clues.

It is important to emphasize that although these clues seem frequently associated with unacknowledged sexual feelings, in many instances they may have nothing whatsoever to do with such feelings. They can also serve as clues to a diversity of other phenomena that may benefit from careful exploration. What is important is to be alert to the occurrence of such clues and, as soon as one occurs, to use it as the basis for careful exploration.

Dehumanization of the Patient

When therapists experience sexual feelings about a patient and find it uncomfortable to acknowledge these feelings, one protective measure is to dehumanize the patient. If, for example, the person about whom the therapist feels sexual can be turned into a diagnosis (e.g., "that schizophrenic" or "the borderline I'm treating"), the person might seemingly be reduced into a few dysfunctions, symptoms, or labels. It may seem that the patient's power to evoke sexual feelings would be diminished. This outcome, however, generally fails to happen, at least in our experience. What does seem to happen frequently is that dehumanizing the patient protects therapists from becoming aware of the feelings (which may intensify and influence therapists' behavior because they are unrecognized). Therapists may be much more likely to become aware of sexual feelings about another *person* than to become aware that they have sexual feelings about a "dyslexic," a "multiple [personality]," or a "worker's comp case."

Dehumanization of the Therapist

A similar approach to blocking sexual feelings from awareness is the dehumanization of the therapist. In this strategy, the therapist attempts to drain away the humanity of the therapist rather than that of the patient. The therapist may begin acting like a wise and distant computer, emitting observations, wisdom, or advice as neutrally as possible. The therapist may begin to use jargon and technical terms to the exclusion of more immediate, everyday words. In supervision or consultation, the therapist may seem to be talking and functioning almost exclusively on an intellectual, rational, or theory-driven level, avoiding all but the most perfunctory and superficial reference to feelings, impulses, or spontaneous reactions. Conceptualizations, terminology, and interventions seem to hold the therapist's feelings at bay (i.e., from the therapist's own awareness) rather than to enable the therapist to respond helpfully to the person who is the patient.

Avoidance

Although avoidance may more commonly indicate fear of or anger at a patient, it often seems to signify—particularly when the therapist remains steadfastly unaware that he or she is avoiding the patient—unacknowledged sexual feelings (see the section, Surprise, Startle, and Shock at Sexual Feelings, in the previous chapter). The therapist reacts to the discomfort or perceived threat of sexual feelings by strategies of avoidance. There may be an abundance of reasons to cancel sessions or to reduce the frequency of regularly scheduled sessions. The therapist may find that miscommunications lead to missed sessions. The therapist may record the wrong time or date for the next appointment or may forget that a session has been scheduled.

The therapist may try to avoid any thoughts of the patient or may mentally cast around to see if there might be a reason to transfer the patient to someone else. If the therapist meets with a supervisor each week to discuss five current clients, the therapist may find that there is only enough time, as the weeks pass, to discuss the other four patients; the avoided patient tends to slip between the cracks, remaining unmentioned or receiving only quick, perfunctory mention at the end of the supervisory session. If the patient talks of termination, the therapist may immediately and without clinical rationale encourage this option, avoiding discussion of reasons, consequences, or meanings. If the patient terminates abruptly and without notice, the therapist may simply write "patient terminated" in the chart and make no real effort to contact the patient.

Obsession

Obsession with a patient is one of the most vivid examples of a situation in which the clue to unacknowledged sexual feelings about a patient can be instantly apparent to those (e.g., a supervisor, consultant, or colleague) to whom the therapist makes the clue known but are difficult to decipher for the therapist who experiences the obsession. As with each of the other clues, obsession may have a variety of meanings (e.g., anger at the patient or fear of the patient) that may be unrelated to sexual feelings. However, like its apparent opposite—avoidance of the patient—obsession seems to be frequently associated with sexual attraction to or other sexual responses to a patient.

Therapists who find that a patient is constantly on their mind, who find their thoughts returning again and again to the patient, who find their daydreams drifting repeatedly to the patient can, if they will only attend to this clue, begin to unravel the meaning of the obsession. The most difficult part, when one obsesses about a patient (it is much less difficult to recognize when it is someone *else* who is obsessing), tends to be recognizing that obsessing is a clue that *something* is going on that warrants attention and exploration.

Interesting Slips and Meaningful Mistakes

This can be one of the most embarrassing clues because, if it occurs in the presence of others (e.g., the patient, a supervisor, or colleagues at a case conference), the others can become aware of the therapist's unacknowledged sexual feelings at the same time as or even before the therapist does. Here are some examples:

> A therapist, not yet aware of the fact that she was strongly attracted to a patient, was using covert rehearsal, self-talk, and a variety of other cognitive–behavioral techniques to help the patient gain self-confidence. Near the end of one session, the therapist was summing up, and, intending to say, "The whole point of this is, you've got to trust yourself!", actually said, "The whole point of this is, you've got to trust your sex!" She was unaware of what she had actually said until the patient, somewhat puzzled, asked her about it. Only then did she realize that there was something that she needed to talk over with her supervisor.

> A senior counselor in a large mental health center was accustomed to offering coffee or tea to his clients. He was smitten by a new client. At the third meeting, he carefully prepared the client's coffee with just the right amount of sugar and cream. As they sat down to begin the counseling session, he was mortified to discover that he had given this client a coffee cup that his wife had given him and that he used *only* when his wife visited him at his office. An extremely raunchy bit of sexual doggerel appeared on one side of the cup.

> A therapist had met an extremely interesting person at a party the previous week and had decided that she would call the person up after work for a date. At the end of a long,

hard day she made the call and was pleased when she heard the familiar voice answer the phone. But when she said the person's name, she quickly discovered that she had not dialed the right phone number. For some reason, she had unintentionally dialed the number of one of her long-term patients who was experiencing an intense erotic transference toward the therapist. After she awkwardly terminated the phone conversation, it took her only a few minutes of reflection to discover that she was experiencing some erotic countertransference to the patient.

A male therapist who had been living with a woman with whom he shared a fulfilling romantic and sexual relationship for the past 5 years, began work with a new patient, a gay male. The therapist scheduled 15 minutes between each therapy session so that he could return phone calls, record notes in the previous patient's chart, review the chart of the next patient, and make a quick trip, if need be, to the bathroom. It was halfway through his sixth session with his new patient that the therapist noticed that, when he had gone to the bathroom right before the current session, he had accidentally forgotten to zip up his fly. He did his best to cover his mistake during the rest of the session and was greatly relieved when the patient left the office. Tending at first to dismiss the event as a simple but meaningless mistake, he found his memory returning to the event repeatedly over the next few days. Exploring his action more deeply, he identified it as a clue to some unresolved personal issues about sexual orientation. He decided to resume his own therapy to explore these issues more deeply.

As noted earlier, such slips and mistakes may have a variety of meanings, some with no relationship to sexual feelings. Moreover, except for those whose theoretical orientation holds that every slip or mistake a therapist makes during therapy has some significance for therapy, it is possible that the slips and mistakes are unrelated to the therapeutic process: They are simply slips and mistakes to which all humans are vulnerable. What is important is to attend to them when they occur and to explore the extent to which they may have significance for the therapist or therapy.

Fantasies During Sexual Activities

When therapists fantasize about a patient while masturbating or engaging in sex with someone else, it is a not-too-subtle clue that there may be unacknowledged sexual feelings in therapy. Because these fantasies may include imaginary scenes of therapist–patient sex, they may be especially prone to evoke feelings of anxiety, guilt, fear of losing control (i.e., of subsequently engaging in sex with the patient), and many of the other reactions listed in the previous chapter. The therapist may therefore find it very difficult to acknowledge and examine the meaning of the fantasy as a potential clue to unacknowledged feelings about the patient.

National research studies suggest that most therapists experience some sort of sexual fantasies about a patient, and a substantial minority have experienced such fantasies while engaging in sex with another person. One national study asked, "While engaging in sexual activity with someone other than a client, have you ever had sexual fantasies about someone who is or was a client?" (see appendix A). Over one fourth (28.7%) answered that they had experienced such fantasies. A national study conducted 1 year later found that almost half (46.3%) of the respondents reported experiencing some sexual fantasy (regardless of the occasion) about a patient on a rare basis, and an additional one fourth (25.5%) reported that they engaged in such fantasies more frequently (Pope et al., 1987; see Pope & Tabachnick, 1993, for survey data about discussion of sexual fantasies with clients).

Recognition that sexual fantasies about a patient—unlike instances of actual therapist–patient sexual intimacies or telling the therapist's sexual fantasies to the patient—occur not infrequently among therapists may help therapists to acknowledge, accept, and explore the imaginary scenes.

Undue Special Treatment

Therapists may find that they are treating a patient in some special way that is different from the treatment offered to most if not all other patients. Obviously, the majority of therapists do this occasionally. Each patient is different, and each has unique needs and circumstances. The patient may be so frightened or insecure that he or she needs special assurance or procedures. The patient's work or child-care schedule may require special hours for therapy sessions. The therapist may try, with appropriate preparation, thoughtfulness, care, and safeguards, an innovative treatment approach not tried with other patients. But in all instances in which a therapist is somehow doing something exceptionally different or differently, it is worth reflecting on the question of whether the patient's clinical needs and "real world" circumstances (e.g., the client's travel schedule requiring special therapy-scheduling considerations) serve as adequate justification for special treatment.

It is always possible that special treatment is a clue that the therapist is experiencing unacknowledged sexual feelings. Some therapists, for example, may give their home phone numbers or addresses to a patient, may send holiday cards to the patient, or may engage in long, nonemergency phone conversations when they would not do these things with any other patient. They may encourage the patient to call the therapist by his or her first name (while asking to be addressed as "Dr. _____" by other patients); tell the patient how much they enjoy meeting with the patient (without discussing such reactions with other patients); or sit next to the patient on the couch (while customarily sitting in a chair with other patients sitting or reclining on the couch).

Isolation of the Patient

Although it may be viewed as an example of the special treatment noted in the previous section, therapists' attempts to isolate a patient—from family and friends or from other people and resources—can be an especially salient clue to unacknowledged sexual feelings. The isolation çan serve many purposes related to therapists' sexual attraction, desires, and arousal. The isolation can make the patient more dependent on the therapist, intensify the feelings that the patient has for the therapist, and make it more likely that the patient will think about the therapist between sessions. Isolation can also serve to allay the therapist's jealous feelings. By attempting to cut the patient off from whatever romantic, sexual, or intimate relationships might occur in his or her life, the therapist eliminates all competition for the patient and leaves no one for the therapist to feel jealous about. As a third example, isolation can make it less likely that the patient will tell anyone—at least contemporaneously—should there be any sexually intimate words or behavior between therapist and patient. Whenever therapists isolate their patients or find themselves daydreaming about, considering, or planning isolation of patients, it is worth asking if the impulse to isolate is a clue that the therapist is experiencing unacknowledged sexual feelings about the patient.

Isolation of the Therapist

The converse of isolating patients is isolating therapists. Without recognizing their sexual feelings for a patient and the immediate reactions to those feelings (e.g., anxiety, guilt, or fear), therapists may begin moving away from their colleagues and perhaps even their friends. In some instances, therapists may be trying to reduce the "stimulus overload," to give themselves a less stressful environment in which to handle the stress of feelings that they are aware of only indirectly (perhaps through chronic fatigue, somatic complaints such as headaches or upset stomachs, or difficulty sleeping or concentrating). They may reduce the number of appointments they have with their other patients, decline to accept new patients, or fail to return any phone calls. (As with the other clues mentioned in this chapter, sexual feelings about a patient are but one of many possible causes of such isolative behavior.) They intuitively view colleagues as threatening or stressful rather than as potentially accepting, understanding, and helpful. (Part of the purpose of this book is to enable therapists not only to acknowledge, accept, and understand their own sexual feelings but also— through exploration and discovery with others in classes, seminars, workshops, or study groups—to become more able to be genuinely supportive to others who may be struggling with and stressed or distressed by sexual feelings.) Through self-isolation, they may be seeking to protect themselves from inquiry that might lead to discovery (by the therapist as well as by others) of the therapist's unacknowledged sexual feelings.

In other instances, therapists may be expressing through their isolative behavior a guilt that they may be but dimly, if at all, aware of. It is as if they feel that they have done something unethical by experiencing sexual feelings in therapy. In fact, in one national study, about 10% of the participants indicated their belief that simply to *feel* sexually attracted to a patient (regardless of whether the attraction is acted on by the therapist) per se was *always* unethical (Pope et al., 1987). This phenomenon— feeling that sexual attraction to a patient is per se unethical— may reflect the profession's historic tendency falsely to view sexual attraction to a patient as equivalent to or somehow inextricably bound up with therapist–patient sexual intimacy (see chapter 2). In this context, the therapists' self-isolation may express a sense of shame and guilt about supposedly unethical feelings of attraction to a patient. It is as if the therapist were punishing him- or herself through banishment or ostracism. Interestingly, even when the shame and guilt push the therapist toward isolation, he or she may still be unaware of the sexual impulses that are evoking the shame and guilt.

At the other extreme, the therapist may on some level be setting the stage for sexual intimacies with the patient. Moving away from contact with others may seem to protect the therapist against discovery that he or she is engaging in strange or questionable patterns of conduct with a patient or is somehow acting differently. (As with many efforts to escape detection, isolation seems to call attention to the therapist and to make colleagues curious about the therapist's withdrawal. Paradoxically, it may make detection of questionable behavior more—rather than less—likely.)

Whenever a therapist begins a process of isolation, withdrawing from customary patterns of supervision, consultation, and therapy, it may be a clue that unacknowledged sexual feelings are occurring.

Creating a Secret

One of the most salient clues that there may be unacknowledged sexual feelings is the therapist's efforts to impose secrecy on the patient. Typically, of course, therapy involves privacy and confidentiality. The therapist is required—with some carefully delineated legal exceptions—to keep private what the patient reveals as part of the therapeutic process. In some instances, however, the therapist will urge or direct the patient to keep secret the contents of therapy. The therapist may rationalize this secrecy through a variety of concepts: that the therapy will not "work" unless the patient keeps it in the session; that the patient must speak of certain "special" topics only to the therapist because only the therapist is capable of handling these issues safely; that other people—including other therapists—are too conventional, narrow-minded, inhibited, sexually repressed, or just downright stupid to understand the unique, advanced, revolutionary methods of the therapist; that no one else has the empathy and kindness that the therapist possesses, and therefore no one else will be capable of accepting the patient and giving him or her the necessary understanding and support; that therapist and patient share a very special relationship that no one else would. . .uh. . .appreciate and understand; that the patient must "save up" feelings about particular topics and "discharge" them only in therapy; and so on. Whatever the rationale, the shared sense of secrecy may enhance the feelings of intimacy between therapist and patient, may encourage them to feel "set apart" from the rest of society, and, not incidentally, may make it less likely that the patient would tell anyone else that the therapist were saying or doing something that, at best, would be highly questionable.

Whenever a therapist feels tempted to impose some sort of secrecy on the relationship with a patient, it is worthwhile to explore whether the impulse to secrecy is a clue that there may exist inadequately acknowledged sexual feelings that need to be identified, accepted, and examined. Particularly if the therapist feels that this is *not* a good case to obtain consultation for, this clue may be a valuable indicant that consultation could be very useful.

Seeking Repeated Reassurance From Colleagues

Consultation—particularly when the consultant is someone chosen to question, explore, advise, or guide rather than merely to validate—is one of the therapist's most valuable resources. Consultation can always play an important role, but there are times when therapists are likely to rely more heavily on it: early in the career, when the newness of being a therapist can magnify feelings of insecurity; when the therapist is returning to work after a serious illness, loss, or trauma, and wants additional support; and when the therapist is working with a patient who has many severe problems, some of which the therapist may be relatively unfamiliar with. Our view is that consultation is always a good idea. If a therapist is considering whether to obtain consultation, it is probably the better course to go ahead and consult. Like the judgment that one's own salary is much too high, getting too much consultation is an exceedingly rare occurrence.

There are some instances, however, in which increased consultation—particularly consultation of a particular type—may be a clue to unacknowledged sexual feelings. The therapist seeks repeated consultation about a patient, but the consultation sessions do not seem to move much beyond their starting point. The therapist seems to seek reassurance more than an opportunity for exploration and guidance. Each consultation session seems to take the same general form as the previous one: The same questions are asked, the same issues raised, and the same observations and reassurances given. The therapist does not have a particular question to ask as the focus for consultation but continues to struggle with a vague sense that "something isn't right."

Instances in which unacknowledged sexual feelings prompt repeated quests for reassurance from a consultant provide one of the most fascinating clues to the unacknowledged feelings. Although the therapist may be unaware of the reason for seeking consultation, he or she is taking active steps that make it more likely that the sexual feelings will come to awareness (with the help of the consultant). Like the interesting slips and meaningful mistakes noted in a previous section, repetitive consultation seeking about a particular patient can be potentially embarrassing because someone else (i.e., the consultant) may become aware of the therapist's sexual reactions to a patient before the therapist gains this awareness. A sensitive, informed, and respectful consultant, however, can minimize this potential embarrassment and can help the therapist to identify, accept, and understand the sexual feelings and accompanying reactions.

Boredom or Drowsiness as Protective Reactions

The final example of a possible clue to unacknowledged sexual feelings is boredom or drowsiness with a patient. The therapist may find it hard, if not impossible, to pay attention to what a patient is saying. The patient's words seem to deflect the therapist's awareness to the physical aspects of the consulting room, to memories of the days' events, to anticipation of patients scheduled for later in the day or week, or to daydreams and fantasies that seem completely unrelated to the patient. Sometimes a patient may seem to induce a drowsiness that falls over the therapist session after session after session. Each session seems interminable. The clock face seems frozen. No matter how alert and engaged the therapist was during the previous patient's session or will be during the subsequent patient's session, the therapist feels drugged, comatose, and daunted by the seemingly impossible task of keeping his or her eyes open and mind concentrated.

The emotional numbness associated with sustained boredom or drowsiness that recurs from session to session with a particular patient may be a clue that the therapist on some level is fighting against awareness of acutely uncomfortable feelings or impulses, and these feelings or impulses may be sexual. (They may also, of course, be hostile, depressed, frightened, and so on.) Picking up the clue for careful examination, of course, may be difficult in light of the dulled nature of the therapist's customary alertness and by the prospect that examination will lead to direct awareness of uncomfortable feelings or impulses.

The clues listed in this chapter are only a few examples of those that often occur when sexual feelings in therapy remain unacknowledged. As with the reactions discussed in the previous chapter, study groups can probably make best use of this chapter not only by using it as a basis for discussion but also by extending the list through drawing on the personal experiences and observations of the participants.

Having considered the purpose and plan of the learning experience for which this book was created (chapter 1), reviewed the profession's historic tendency to deny and avoid the topic of sexual feelings in therapy (chapter 2), established the conditions under which such feelings can be safely explored (chapter 3), conducted a self-assessment (chapter 4), reflected on some of the contextual influences that shape and color the way we experience and understand sexual feelings (chapter 5), and discussed and added to lists of frequent reactions to sexual feelings in therapy (chapter 6) and frequent clues to unacknowledged sexual feelings (chapter 7), readers are now ready to explore their reactions to the passages and scenarios in Part II. Before beginning that exploration, it might be useful and important for study groups to take a brief period to discuss the process of preparation they have completed through these first seven chapters. If there are lingering apprehensions, doubts, or confusions about task and process—or if new apprehensions, doubts, or confusions have arisen during the course of preparation—participants must take responsibility for giving them voice and attention. Spending a short period of time touching on each of the conditions for learning set forth in chapter 3 from this vantage point (i.e., the group having worked together through the first seven chapters and pausing before beginning Part II) may be particularly meaningful. The journey of exploration and discovery represented by Part II deserves a safe and supportive learning environment, one that fulfills the criteria set forth in chapter 3 and meets the individual needs of each participant. Open and honest discussion of these criteria and needs (some of which may have emerged or become apparent during the process of working through the first seven chapters) helps form the necessary foundation not only of the process of exploration and discovery of the feelings that are the topic of this book but also of the career-long process of continuing exploration and discovery, of creating and maintaining professional communities in which such exploration and discovery are a shared venture, and of developing the trust and helpfulness we need to work with each other as we encounter some of the most private aspects of our experience with patients.

II

Passages and Scenarios

Chapter

8

Passages

The following 23 passages are meant to provide an opportunity to explore feelings and reactions. The passages have been culled from almost a century of psychotherapy literature and will illustrate that the issues arising with sexual or erotic feelings in therapy are complex and evocative, and have long been with us. (The scenarios in chapter 9 illustrate additional situations that may lead to the discovery and discussion of feelings not elicited by the passages.)

We recommend that the first question that readers address after reading a passage or scenario be, "What am I feeling?" In some cases, the immediate personal response may be vague or elusive. There may be a temptation to rely on "stock" responses (that may seem more socially acceptable or easier to understand) or to substitute a more intellectual observation (perhaps based on some of the theory, research, or didactic material presented elsewhere in the book) as a hedge against the immediacy of an idiosyncratic emotional response. An awareness of these temptations and the texture of feelings from which they arise can be an important resource for exploration and discovery.

As emphasized previously, it is especially important to avoid an intellectual, punitive, and unfair passing of judgment on the participants in these descriptions (see chapter 1). The passages have been taken out of context and do not allow an adequately informed, fair judgment by those unacquainted with the full context and specifics and the evolving situation. Any such judgment not only does a disservice to the participants but also is an avoidance of the task: exploring and learning about personal feelings.

In some cases, the client may be the focus of a reader's attention. In others, the reader may identify empathically with the therapist. And in still others, seemingly inconsequential details of a passage may evoke the reader's memories (e.g., of his or her work as a therapist, of his or her own experience as a client, or of other personal experiences), fantasies, or concerns.

After addressing the primary questions (e.g., "What am I feeling?" or "What feelings does this passage evoke in me?"), readers may want to address some of the other suggested questions that follow each description. However, readers may also find it more useful to pursue their own questions.

The Therapist's Fear of Showing Feeling: A Passage From Clara Thompson

Clara Thompson, one of the "neo-Freudians," earned her M.D. at Johns Hopkins Medical School in 1920 and received additional training working as a staff psychiatrist at Johns Hopkins Hospital. At the hospital, her supervisor was Adolf Meyer, whom she credits with providing excellent training. In the early 1920s, she encountered Edward Kempf and Lucille Dooley, who were using psychoanalytic principles to treat individuals diagnosed as psychotic at St. Elizabeth's Hospital. Soon after, she met Harry Stack Sullivan and was impressed with interpersonal therapy. She became an analysand of Sandor Ferenczi and, later, of Erich Fromm. Maintaining a private practice since 1925, she taught at Johns Hopkins, the Washington School of Psychiatry, and the William Alanson White Institute, where she served as executive director. (For a more detailed presentation of this biographical material, see Roazen, 1971; Thompson, 1950.)

Thompson's book *Psychoanalysis: Its Evolution and Development* (1950) traced the intricate patterns of influence and change in analytic theory and practice. She described the period of the 1920s when the original Freudian notion of the analyst as a "blank screen" was sharply challenged. Sullivan was beginning to elaborate his theory of therapy as an interpersonal process. Rank set forth the idea that the analyst must become an active participant during therapy sessions. Perhaps the most influential at the time, Ferenczi emphasized that a necessary component of therapy was the therapist's feelings of friendliness toward the patient. He observed that patients would often comment on the analyst's behaviors and—as intuited or construed by the patient—the analyst's feelings or reactions. Ferenczi argued that the analyst must not ignore or merely interpret such comments. If the therapist could acknowledge instances in which the patient was correctly perceiving or understanding the therapist's feelings and reactions (i.e., instances in which the comments were not solely determined by transference distortions or mistaken inferences) then he or she could help the patient's reality testing.

Thompson also credited some of the movement toward analysts showing their feelings toward patients to problems in therapy that could occur when analysts attempted to be a "blank screen." Rank and Ferenczi characterized the analytic situation as sterile and artificial when the analyst acted as if he or she had no feelings. Patients sometimes seemed to lose their own ability to express feelings in such a barren atmosphere.

Yet such efforts to encourage analysts to acknowledge— when clinically warranted—their feelings to patients often met with firm resistance from many therapists. Thompson (1950) described a form of "countertransference anxiety" that seemed to freeze many analysts:

> Freud always knew that it was sometimes not possible for the analyst to remain entirely out of the picture, that sometimes, in spite of everything, he would react personally to the patient and what he said or did. This he saw as countertransference, by which he meant that analysts sometimes transfer elements from their past (or present) problems to the analytic situation. Thus one might be susceptible to the flattery of a patient's erotic interest or one might be hurt by

a hostile attack on a vulnerable spot. Because of the stress on the unfortunate aspects of the analyst's involvement, the feeling grew that even a genuine objective feeling of friendliness on his part was to be suspected. As a result, many of Freud's pupils became afraid to be simply human and show the ordinary friendliness and interest a therapist customarily feels for a patient. In many cases, out of fear of showing counter-transference, the attitude of the analyst became stilted and unnatural. (p. 107)

Questions

Does being a "professional" seem somehow at odds with "being human" or showing "friendliness" toward a patient?

Have you ever regretted your spontaneity with a patient? What do you think may have occurred?

Do you think that any of your patients perceive you as stilted and unnatural? Is there any truth to their perception? Is there any aspect of your professional appearance or style that seems awkward or artificial?

If they were interviewed and gave completely candid responses, what words do you think your patients might use to describe you and your manner?

What words do you think your patients might use to describe how they feel about you and your manner?

How do you go about recognizing your own countertransference?

Therapist Self-Disclosure of Attraction to a Patient: A Passage From Leslie Schover

Schover (1981) conducted an analogue study of therapist responses to sexual material presented by female and male therapy clients. Her participants included 12 men and 12 women who were psychiatrists, psychologists, and social workers. The therapists reviewed the case history of a female or male client, looked at a picture of the client, and listened to a recording of the client, who either talked about a problem involving sexual dysfunction or told the therapist that she or he was attracted to the therapist.

Before listening to the recording, the therapists filled out standardized self-report scales that assessed, among other variables, the degree to which they held liberal or conservative attitudes about sex. While therapists listened to the recording, it was interrupted seven times to allow the therapist an opportunity to say something to the client. After they had listened to the complete recording and given their responses to the client, the therapists were asked to fill out some self-report rating scales to indicate the degree to which they had experienced such feelings as anxiety and sexual arousal.

The female therapists tended to be more comfortable (i.e., less anxious) when the client discussed sexual dysfunction. Conservative male therapists tended to become aroused by descriptions of a female client's sexual dysfunction, but they also became anxious and tended to avoid addressing the issue or problem that the client was raising. Liberal male therapists tended to become sexually aroused when a female client said that she was attracted to the therapist, and encouraged her to say more.

One of the prominent trends was for male therapists to respond with self-disclosure about their own sexual attraction to the client when a female client expressed her attraction to the therapist. As one male social worker said to the client,

> Well I am turned on to you. I find you very attractive. . . . And again I feel a lot of pressure in this respect; that you want something from me, and, uh, I find it difficult because it seems as if I keep wanting to set limits, and you're keeping wanting to go beyond the limits. Uh . . . is that true that you do want more? (p. 489)

Questions

If you were the client, and your therapist had just said the words in the preceding passage to you, how would you react?

Would your reaction change according to the age, gender, race, or sexual orientation of the therapist?

What could a client say that you, as the therapist, might find sexually arousing? How would you respond?

What factors might lead you to avoid addressing a sexual issue that a client has just raised?

Do you have any "rules" or guidelines that you follow regarding self-disclosure to patients about your own sexual feelings?

When a client expresses sexual attraction to you, what do you consider in terms of what limits to set and how to talk about those limits with the client?

The Therapist's Attraction Causing Misdiagnosis and Mistreatment: A Passage From David Reiser and Hanna Levenson

In a provocative article, "Abuses of the Borderline Diagnosis: A Clinical Problem With Teaching Opportunities," Reiser and Levenson (1984) explore six ways in which the diagnosis of borderline personality disorder is often misapplied. These abuses include using a borderline diagnosis to avoid working with a client's sexual issues, to cover the therapist's sloppy diagnostic procedures, to rationalize a lack of success in the treatment, to prevent the use of psychopharmacological or other medical interventions that might be of help to the patient, to express the therapist's countertransference hate, and to rationalize the therapist's acting out.

In the following case history, Reiser and Levenson suggested that the therapist's sexual attraction to the patient led to the therapist's acting out and to his misuse of the borderline diagnosis. His difficulty accepting his attraction caused him to "freeze up." The authors described how the "therapist held back from an unusually attractive patient and refused to be human when she requested empathy and advice" (p. 1530). A brief summary of the treatment sessions follows.

A psychiatry resident began work with a college senior, described by clinicians on the unit as "strikingly beautiful" (p. 1530). She had sought therapy because she had suffered a variety of traumatic events. An automobile crash had killed one of her close friends. Marijuana possession had led to the arrest of her brother, who had entered mandated drug treatment. Her parents' marriage was troubled and divorce seemed imminent.

The young woman cried as she described these situations. She told the therapist that she felt guilty, that her mother looked to her for answers. She asked the therapist to help her decide what she should say to her mother.

Throughout the woman's account, the therapist maintained a blank silence. When asked a question, he did not reply but remained silent. Finally, he spoke: He asked the woman to describe her current feelings about her brother and then to describe her feelings about her brother at the time of his birth.

The patient attempted to comply with the resident's request but repeatedly returned to her question: How could she respond to her mother, who seemed to put the entire burden for solving the family's problems on the patient's shoulders? The therapist neither addressed the woman's question nor acknowledged that she was clearly distressed by the traumatic events and by her feelings that she must "make things right" for her mother.

The patient arrived on time for her second appointment, but the therapist did not appear. He had marked down the wrong date in his appointment book.

> The patient came back for one more session, during which the resident was again distant and aloof. Subsequently the patient cancelled all further appointments. The resident stated, "I think she was probably borderline." (p. 1530)

Questions

Have you ever experienced an incident with a client in which you felt "frozen?" What caused you to "freeze up?"

What aspects of a client's attractiveness or sexuality do you find most threatening, anxiety-provoking, or difficult to acknowledge?

What aspects of your own sexuality do you find most threatening, anxiety provoking, or difficult to acknowledge?

Has someone's attractiveness or sexuality ever evoked an angry response from you? Has it ever caused you to be inhibited and to lack spontaneity?

What aspect of your response to an attractive client would you find most difficult to discuss with your clinical supervisor or a colleague consultant?

Have you ever declined to treat a patient because he or she was too sexually attractive to you?

Working With a Client's Sense of His Physical Attractiveness: A Passage From Ellen Toby Klass and Joann Paley Galst

In her fascinating book *Women as Therapists, A Multitheoretical Casebook*, Cantor (1990) asked a therapist to present a case study and then invited therapists from different theoretical orientations to describe how they might have handled the treatment. The case study in the following passage was presented by Zager (1990). It concerned a young man who felt "depressed, ugly, and bad" (p. 145).

Klass and Galst (1990) described a cognitive behavioral approach to treating the young man. (For stylistic convenience, Klass and Galst used the first person singular, i.e., "I".) In addressing how they would work with the patient around his feelings of ugliness, they drew on cognitive behavioral techniques developed to foster greater self-acceptance among women of their bodies and images of their bodies. They described an approach that provides a sympathetic invitation for the client to put words to his deep feelings about himself and his appearance:

> This experience would provide exposure to avoided content (on the rationale of allowing extinction of conditioned emotional reactions), and the emotionality might also facilitate

needed change. I would then ask [the patient] how he learned to feel so ugly and would trace the feelings associated with specific incidents. Since [the patient] was so unquestioning about his unattractiveness, I would hope that this emotional and historical framework could help him truly entertain the idea that these self-evaluations were learned rather than necessarily factually correct. I would suggest that as a child and teenager, [the patient] had little choice but to think his peers were right. "As an adult, you may be able to learn other ways to feel about your attractiveness, hard as it is to believe that right now. . . ."

I would suggest that doing body mirror exercise at home might be very interesting, and I would help him devise tolerable hierarchical steps to do so. I would also try to broaden [the patient's] view of the basis for attractiveness . . . (pp. 215–216)

Questions

When a client discusses body image, what feelings does it evoke in you? To what extent do such factors as the client's age, gender, race, sexual orientation, cultural background, and socioeconomic status influence your feelings?

When a client talks about feeling ugly and unattractive, what feelings are evoked in you?

Have you ever found yourself comparing your client's attractiveness to your own attractiveness?

Have you ever envied a client's attractiveness?

Have you ever resented a client's attractiveness?

Have you ever been repelled because you experienced a client as extremely unattractive?

Have you ever felt pity for a client because you perceived him or her to be extremely unattractive?

What events or factors have been most influential in shaping your sense of your own attractiveness?

What role do our society's predominant standards of physical attractiveness play in your assessment and treatment of clients?

How do you feel when working with clients who are hyper-obese or extremely emaciated?

Imagine that you are working with two clients who are reasonably matched for all factors except an aspect of attractiveness. Both clients are extremely distressed because they think that they are extremely ugly, that no one would find them attractive. The only difference between the two is this: You believe that one of them is one of the most beautiful people you have ever encountered; you believe that the other is one of the most unattractive people you have encountered. Do you use the same therapeutic approach with both clients? Or does your personal appraisal of their attractiveness influence you to use different therapeutic interventions? What if each client were to ask you if you found him or her attractive? How would you feel? How would you respond?

When writing notes about clients regarding an intake screening, a mental status examination, a psychological assessment, or a course of therapy, to what extent do you mention client attractiveness? If you reviewed all of your charts, would attractiveness be mentioned in equal proportions in your male clients' charts and your female clients' charts?

Nonerotic Touch as Therapeutic: A Passage From Judd Marmor

A former president of the American Psychiatric Association, Judd Marmor (1972) examined the question of nonerotic touch as reassuring and healing. He believed that such touching could be therapeutic, depending on the situation and the motives of the therapist:

> In an anaclitic therapeutic approach to seriously ill psycho-somatic patients, such as those with ulcerative colitis, or status asthmaticus, a "maternal" holding or stroking of

hands may be both helpful and justified. Similar behavior may be indicated and useful with regressed psychotic patients. Non-erotic holding or hugging of pre-adolescent children, especially autistic and withdrawn ones, may even be essential to their therapy.

With most patients with neurotic and personality disorders, however . . . the psychotherapist should be extremely wary with regard to physical contacts if there is the slightest possibility that they might be interpreted or responded to as erotic. Once therapist and patient have gotten to know each other well, and a complete sense of mutual trust and security has been established between them, a friendly or reassuring pat on the shoulder may be a useful bit of non-verbal communication. But the therapist who does this must be quite sure of his own motives and feelings in so doing. If there is any hidden erotic element in such a gesture, the patient's unconscious will usually pick it up—to the detriment of the therapeutic process. (p. 8)

Questions

If you were a client in therapy, under what circumstances would you want your therapist to touch you?

If your own therapist touched you in a way that was uncomfortable for you or that you found inappropriate, frightening, or seductive, would you have any trouble telling the therapist?

In working as a therapist, have you ever made a gesture with a "hidden erotic element" (whether or not it involved touching the patient)? When and how did you become aware of the erotic nature or meaning of the gesture? Do you believe that the patient was aware—at the time or later—of the erotic quality of your gesture?

Imagine that you have just brought an intense intake interview to a close and are walking the client to the door. The client suddenly turns and stands with arms open wide about one foot from you. The client says, "I need a hug. I'm a hugging-type person." How do you feel and what thoughts occur to you?

Imagine several possible responses and speculate on their potential effects on the subsequent therapy process.

✤ ✤ ✤

The Patient's Sexual Images of the Therapist: A Passage From Jesse Geller, Rebecca Cooley, and Dianna Hartley

Geller, Cooley, and Hartley (1981–1982; see also Orlinsky & Geller, in press) conducted research about how patients internalize or represent their therapist. One aspect of their findings was that the degree to which patients could create internal images of their therapists and carry these beyond termination was a significant factor in a positive outcome.

A second aspect was that how they represented their therapist tended to fall into three general categories: imagistic (e.g., "I imagine my therapist sitting in his or her office"), haptic (e.g., "I am aware of a particular emotional atmosphere that gives me the sense that my therapist is 'with me' "), and conceptual (e.g., "I think of my therapist as making specific statements to me").

A third aspect was that their representation of their imagined involvement with the therapist fell into six categories: sexual and aggressive involvement, the wish for reciprocity, continuing the therapeutic dialogue, failures of benign internalization, the effort to create a therapist introject, and mourning. The six major components of the first factor (imagined sexual and aggressive involvement) are as follows:

I imagine having my therapist's child.
I imagine having sex with my therapist.
I imagine our kissing each other.
I imagine hurting my therapist in some way.
I imagine being held by my therapist.
I imagine being my therapist's child. (p. 140)

Questions

To what extent has your work as a therapist included considering how your clients "represent" you in their imagination?

To what extent was this topic addressed in your graduate training and supervision?

Do you believe that some of your patients have imagined, either during therapy or after termination, conceiving a child with you? Did they reveal this image to you? What feelings does it evoke in you?

Do you believe that some of your patients have imagined, either during therapy or after termination, having sex with you? Did they disclose this image to you? What feelings does it evoke in you?

Do you believe that some of your patients have imagined, either during therapy or after termination, kissing you? Did they mention this image to you? What feelings does it evoke in you?

Do you believe that some of your patients have imagined, either during therapy or after termination, hurting you? Did they reveal this image to you? What feelings does it evoke in you?

Do you believe that some of your patients have imagined, either during therapy or after termination, being held by you? Did they disclose this image to you? What feelings does it evoke in you?

Do you believe that some of your patients have imagined, either during therapy or after termination, being your child? Did they mention this image to you? What feelings does it evoke in you?

A Client Describes Sexual Images: A Passage From Joseph Reyher

In Reyher's (1978) approach to "emergent uncovering," the therapist (for whom Reyher uses the Sullivanian term *participant observer*) invites the patient (who is designated as the *collaborator*) to recline on a couch, close his or her eyes, and describe the images that occur. Experiencing such images and translating them into words in the presence of a participant observer can cause intense anxiety and other uncomfortable feelings. In the following passage, a young patient who had been experiencing problems with impotence described the images that occurred to him when he attempted to visualize a scene he had seen on television. The previous week, he had seen a commercial in which a woman advertised rugs. For some reason, he had become obsessed with the commercial. When he lay down on the couch, closed his eyes, and called up the visual image of the commercial in his mind's eye, the result was a sequence of sexual images:

> He described an older, attractive woman who selected a rug and reclined upon it, pulling a lower corner over her pelvic area. Then he saw a disembodied erect penis move toward her and stop about eight feet away. A drop of liquid formed on the tip of the penis and turned into a fish that swam over to her. As the fish drew near, the woman, now nude, pulled back the rug and the fish swam up her vagina partway and got stuck, with just its tail showing. The woman then laughed manically as the fish struggled vainly to extricate itself by violently swishing its tail. It finally succeeded, but it was reduced to a skeleton, and the woman was now his mother. The client's anxiety was so acute that he opened his eyes and did not want to resume free imagery for several sessions. (p. 66)

Questions

If you were the therapist, what feelings might this description evoke in you? At what point in the passage did the feelings begin? Did your feelings change during the course of the passage? In what ways, if any, do you think that whether you are a man or a woman may influence those feelings?

When the client opened his eyes, if he said that the image made him very anxious, what might you say to him? Would you remain silent?

Do you feel comfortable using therapy techniques (e.g., guided imagery and hypnosis) that readily lead to bizarre sexual imagery? Can you imagine a patient describing sexual images or fantasies that you would find it difficult to respond to or work with?

✢ ✢ ✢

A Client Becomes Aroused When Her Therapist Comes to Her Home: A Passage From Helen Block Lewis

In the following passage, Lewis (1971) described a pivotal event in her treatment of a young woman she called "Z." Z had sought treatment for a drinking problem that was causing her to miss work. She shared an apartment with her lover, but from time to time she would become drunk and pick up a male or female stranger for a "one night stand."

During the course of therapy, Z separated from her roommate and moved into her own apartment. According to Lewis, her shame and guilt caused her to feel angry at her therapist for encouraging her to live by herself. During a session, she expressed this anger, which Lewis attempted to recognize and interpret. Nevertheless, Lewis noticed that she herself seemed impatient and even somewhat scornful during this session, from which the patient left offended. Lewis further revealed that her own impatience led her to feel guilty. Then, in response to her own guilt as a therapist for the way she had handled the session, she felt anxious:

> This hour was the last session of the week, to be followed by a three-day weekend. On Saturday evening I had a desperate call from Z. who was drunk and weeping hysterically. I arrived at her apartment and found her half naked and disheveled, trying to sober up. She had begun to drink on awakening in the morning and had "perversely" and "defiantly" (her phrasing) continued all day. Pathetically, she wanted to "free-associate," now that I had come, in order to find out immediately why all this had happened. When I said I thought she needed at the moment to rest and recover herself, she was, typically, rebuffed. She then told me that she was sexually excited and wanted to make love to me. I reminded her that sexual excitement often followed her hu-

miliation at feeling neglected. Again she was rebuffed, but appeared calmer. It was apparent that my presence was somewhat irksome to her, that it embarrassed her. I suggested that she tell me when she was ready for me to leave. She demurred, but shook hands a few minutes later and saw me to the door. (p. 452)

Questions

Reread the passage, but substitute a male for a female therapist. Does this make any difference in your understanding of the events, in the feelings the passage evokes in you, and so forth?

Reread the passage, but substitute a male for a female patient. Does this make any difference in your understanding of the events, in the feelings the passage evokes in you, and so forth?

Imagine that you are the therapist in this passage. What thoughts occur to you about the patient being half naked? Do you mention or address this in any way? Do you feel any impulse or make any effort to ask her to put on some more clothes?

If you were the therapist in this passage, could you imagine any possibility that you might feel angry with this patient? If so, why? How would you respond to your feelings of anger?

If you were the therapist in this passage, could you imagine any possibility that you might become sexually aroused? If so, why? How would you respond to your feelings of arousal?

If you were the therapist in this passage, what would you consider in deciding what to include and what to exclude as you made your notes in the patient's chart?

If you were the therapist in this passage, what thoughts would you have about the next session with Z?

If you were the therapist in this passage, what thoughts would you have about how to respond to Z's phone call? Would it make any difference if Z had called and told you that she had taken an overdose of a drug?

✤ ✤ ✤

Seeing a Patient Removing Her Nightgown in Her Bedroom: A Passage From Robert Lindner

Robert Lindner (1914–1956) earned his doctorate in psychology at Cornell University, began advanced training in psychoanalysis, and was analyzed by Theodor Reik. His 1954 book *The Fifty-Minute Hour* was a best-seller; in it, he skillfully told the stories of six of his analytic patients. At age 40, he became aware of a serious heart problem that caused his death a year later.

One story in *The Fifty-Minute Hour* described Laura, a young woman who tended to go on binges of eating. She would literally stuff herself until she fell into unconsciousness. During the first year of analysis, Laura explored a childhood in which she had suffered serious forms of abuse. She seemed to receive no relief from talking about her experiences, nor did the therapy seem to improve her current life. In the 11th month, she recounted a dream that, when analyzed, revealed her intense fears of sexuality. This session seemed a turning point: For the first time, she seemed to understand the irrational nature of her thoughts about sex. That weekend, she enjoyed sex with a lover. During subsequent sessions, however, she was angry with her therapist, and the analysis once again became exceptionally difficult.

One weekend, the therapist was scheduled to leave town to give a talk. He looked forward to this as a semi-vacation. He was shocked to receive word that Laura had slashed her wrists and had been hospitalized.

The analysis continued while Laura was in the hospital and after her discharge. The next pivotal event occurred much later. Uncharacteristically, she failed to come in for her session. As Dr. Lindner was leaving the office, his secretary reported that she had just received a phone call; when she picked up the receiver, she heard a strange noise and then the caller hung up.

The therapist went home for a dinner party. Shortly before the party, his wife received a call. She could not understand what the caller was saying. She believed that the caller was drunk.

During the dinner party, the phone rang. Dr. Lindner answered. He heard strange noises but could not make out the words. When he asked who was calling, the voice said, "Laura." She managed to say that she was at home and that she was eating. She asked for help, and then the line went dead.

Extremely concerned, the therapist excused himself from the party and drove to his patient's apartment. Laura told him to go away but finally unlocked the door. The room was cluttered with empty food cartons. Laura was in a sheer nightgown and had a distended stomach, looking as if she were pregnant. The therapist described how his hand reflexively touched the distended stomach.

Laura had difficulty speaking but was finally able to say the word "baby." When the therapist asked whose baby it was, she replied that it was hers, and asked him to look:

> She bent forward drunkenly and grasped her gown by the hem. Slowly she raised the garment, lifting it until her hands were high above her head. I stared at the exposed body. There, where my fingers had probed, a pillow was strapped to her skin with long bands of adhesive. (p. 123)

This event became the focus of the last phase of Laura's therapy. She linked the binge eating to her unconscious wish to become pregnant. This understanding was vital to her, but there still seemed to be a piece of the puzzle missing. During a session, as she was talking about her wish to make babies, she said,

> "I guess I have to mike a new baby. . . . " Her hand went over her mouth. "My God!" she exclaimed. "Did you hear what I just said?"
> Mike was her father's name; and of course it was his baby she wanted. It was for this impossible fulfillment that Laura hungered—and now was starved no more. (p. 124)

Questions

Reread the passage, but substitute a female for a male therapist. Does this make any difference in your understanding of the events, in the feelings the passage evokes in you, and so forth? Would it be possible for the client to imagine having her female therapist's baby?

Imagine that you are the therapist in this passage as you enter the client's apartment. Do you have any concerns about the client being dressed in a nightgown? About the client raising the nightgown over her head?

If you were the therapist in this passage, what feelings would your reflexively touching the patient's stomach evoke in you? How might the patient respond to your touch? How would you assess her reaction? What would you consider when deciding how to proceed?

If you were the therapist in this passage, could you imagine any possibility that you might feel angry with this patient? If so, why? How would you respond to your feelings of anger?

If you were the therapist in this passage, could you imagine any possibility that you might feel angry with this patient? If so, why? How would you respond to your feelings of anger?

If you were the therapist in this passage, could you imagine any possibility that you might feel disgusted? If so, why? How would you respond to your feelings of disgust?

If you were the therapist in this passage, what would you consider in deciding what to include and what to exclude as you made your notes in the patient's chart?

If you, as the therapist, were being supervised, what thoughts and feelings would occur to you as you approached the next supervision session? What factors would influence what you choose to mention and not to mention to the supervisor? How do you imagine your supervisor responding to your account?

If you were the therapist in this passage, would you go to the patient's home? What factors influence your decision?

Imagine that one of your patients places a phone call to you and says, "I'm drunk and in my nighty and I want you to come and help me." What feelings do you experience as she says this? What would you say to her?

Telling a Client to Undress During a Therapy Session: A Passage From Milton Erickson

Milton Erickson, who died in 1980, was an extremely active hypnotist, hypnotizing over 30,000 people during his lifetime (J. Williams, 1980). Training at the University of Wisconsin and Colorado General Hospital, he received a doctorate in medicine and a master's degree in psychology. Founding president of the American Society for Clinical Hypnosis, he was a fellow of both the American Psychological Association and the American Psychiatric Association.

Erickson's hypnotic techniques have been described by Haley (1973) as a form of strategic therapy: "Therapy can be called strategic if the clinician initiates what happens during therapy and designs a particular approach for each problem" (p. 1). To accomplish profound change in one or only a few sessions, Erickson used a variety of techniques, such as fostering resistance, pointing out negative options, and creatively using metaphors (Haley, 1973).

The following intervention was described by Erickson in 1959 during a conversation with Jay Haley and John Weakland (Haley, 1985).

A young woman had become engaged, but kept putting off the engagement. She was afraid of marriage and began to develop phobias. Erickson's first intervention was to direct the woman to move out of her mother's house: "I made her move. A Spanish family. The grandmother . . . laid down the law . . ., but I had laid down the law first" (Haley, 1985, p. 127).

After working with her about her travel phobias, Erickson turned to the issue of sex. Every time the topic came up, the woman acted as if she could not communicate in any way. To address this issue, Erickson told her that she must bring to the next session the most abbreviated pair of shorts she could find. At the next session, he told her to show him the shorts. As they looked at the shorts, he posed a dilemma for her: Either she must come to the next session dressed in those shorts or, during the next session, he would make her put them on in the consulting room.

The woman arrived at the next session wearing the shorts. Then Erickson posed another dilemma: Either she must pay attention as he addressed the sexual issues that were troubling her or he would direct her to remove the shorts and put them back on while she was with him. She began to pay attention as he began to talk about the sexual issues that had been plaguing her.

During a subsequent session, he directed her to confront her sexual fears in a way that was both direct and symbolic:

> I said, "Now you need to know how to undress and go to bed in the presence of a man. So start undressing." Slowly, in an almost automatic fashion, she undressed. I had her show me her right breast, her left breast, her right nipple, her left nipple. Her belly button. Her genital area. Her knees. Her gluteal regions. I asked her to point where she would like to have her husband kiss her. I had her turn around slowly. She dressed. I dismissed her. (Haley, 1985, p. 128)

Erickson reported that she was then able to travel freely (i.e., without the debilitating phobias), to make the wedding arrangements, and to have a happy marriage including children. He also reported that she wrote him later to express her gratitude for the help he had given her.

In addressing the question of why the client followed his directions, Erickson explained that the key is the therapist's expectations that the patient will follow the instructions. The patient comes to understand that the therapist knows that the therapeutic behavior is absolutely essential. Erickson drew a connection to an influential lesson he had learned as an intern from a professor at the Colorado School of Medicine. The professor stressed that in some cases

> the only way you can get a woman to consent to have an amputation of the breast for cancer . . . is by stripping her

to the nude and doing a very careful medical examination
. . . with your eyes . . . and then you tell her, "I'm very,
very positive you need the amputation . . . I'm awfully
sorry." . . . You can get some women, who would otherwise
go to the grave, to enter the operating room gladly, hopefully. (Haley, 1985, pp. 128–129)

Questions

Erickson mentions that the woman comes from a Spanish family. What influence, if any, does this have on your understanding of and reaction to the events described in this passage?

What difference would it make (in your understanding of and
reaction to the events) if the therapist were female? Why?

What difference would it make if the patient were male? Why?

Would it make any difference if the therapist were a medical
doctor?

Would the age of the therapist or patient (e.g., very young,
middle-aged, or very old) make any difference in the way you
react to or understand the events described in this passage?

Would the race or ethnicity of the therapist or patient make any
difference in the way you react to or understand the events
described in this passage?

Imagine that you seek therapy for difficulties similar to those
experienced by the woman in this passage and that your therapist uses a similar approach. How would you react?

Do you believe that such interventions might increase the likelihood of a positive outcome or might shorten the course of
therapy? To what extent does your belief about efficacy or ef-
ficiency influence your decisions about learning and using such
interventions?

Under what circumstances would you "lay down the law" to
a patient? How do you feel about giving commands to a patient?

Have you had any experiences with professors or supervisors
in which their treatment philosophy profoundly influenced

your own approach? How did you evaluate the validity of their views? In the most memorable instance of such influence, how did the professor or supervisor "teach" you (e.g., lecture, dialogue, demonstration, modeling, or giving you directions about what to do)?

Instructing a Client to Imagine Her Breasts Tingling: A Passage From Theodore Barber

Theodore Barber has conducted extensive research and written prolifically on the phenomenon of hypnosis. In a review chapter (Barber, 1984), he described studies conducted by several other specialists in hypnosis to help women develop larger breasts through hypnosis. The women were given a version of the following instructions:

> Imagine that the sun (or a heat lamp) is shining on the breasts or that wet, warm towels are on the breasts and feel the heat as it flows through the breasts; imagine the breasts growing, as they did during puberty, and experience the feelings of tenderness, swelling, and tightness of the skin over the breasts; and imagine that the breasts are becoming warm, tingling, pulsating, sensitive, and that they are growing. (p. 85)

In considering the nature of such techniques, Barber suggested that it would be useful to examine the extent to which the techniques involved sexual arousal.

> When women are given suggestions by men to relax, let go, and imagine the breasts tingling, pulsating, and growing, they might recall or imagine sexual situations which could produce sexual arousal. . . . (p. 86)

Questions

As you imagine yourself giving hypnotic suggestions for a woman's breasts to feel warm, tingly, and so forth, do you feel sexually aroused? Do you think that the patient might be aware of your feelings? If so, how might she feel?

Do you feel more comfortable giving suggestions that might cause sexual arousal to men or to women? Why?

Do you ever feel concerned that when giving hypnotic (or other therapeutic) suggestions that might have an erotic element you might become tongue-tied or embarrassed? Has this ever happened to you?

To what extent do you consider your patients' values, morals, or mores when you speak of their breasts or genitals?

How do you choose what words to use when speaking of a patient's genitals or erotic behaviors? Do you ever use words that are different from those that the patient tends to use?

Do the words you use in the presence of the patient about the patient's genitals or erotic behaviors tend to be the same or to differ from the words you use for these sexual organs and activities when discussing the treatment with your supervisor?

A Client's Anger at a Therapist's Voyeurism: A Passage From Laura Brown

In an article discussing the negative consequences of posttermination sexual relationships involving lesbians, Brown (1988) emphasized an interesting point: When a client learns that her (or his) therapist has been sexually intimate with another client, either before or after termination, the client may begin to wonder about the therapist's reactions to sexual issues in therapy:

> To quote one former client of such a therapist, "The thought that she's been sitting around getting her jollies by listening to *my* sexual experiences and concerns enrages me!" These clients consistently espouse the view that the relationship, although genitally sexual only in posttermination, must have begun its sexual and romantic component in therapy; this

overt revelation of the countertransferential aspect of the psychotherapy process is distinctly unsettling even to so-phisticated clients and former clients who are themselves therapists. The fear that a therapist will not protect them from their own regressed or transferential feelings can be overwhelming, and may serve as a barrier to seeking out therapy for fear of encountering it in another therapist. (p. 253)

Questions

Do you enjoy hearing about the sexual activities of some patients more than others? What influences your reactions?

Have you ever found yourself asking for more details about a sexual encounter than was probably necessary for your work?

Do you ever feel like asking a patient not to talk about his or her body or sexuality? Why?

Have you ever sensed that a client was trying (consciously or unconsciously) to arouse you sexually? What feelings did the client's behavior evoke in you? Did you become aroused either at the time or later when recollecting the experience? What influenced you to disclose or not to disclose to the client your interpretation of the purpose of the behavior?

Does a Patient's Clothing Cause Sexual Involvement With a Therapist? A Passage From Shirley Feldman-Summers and Gwendolyn Jones

Conducting landmark research into the consequences of therapist–patient sexual involvement, Feldman-Summers and Jones (1984) posed an interesting question to patients: Was it their belief that "sexual contact between client and therapist occurs because the client dresses or behaves in a seductive manner?" (p. 1057).

Questions

What kind of clothing do you consider clearly reflects patient seductiveness? What kinds of patient behaviors seem to you to be clearly seductive in the context of therapy? To what extent do you think there is agreement or variation among you and your colleagues concerning clothing and behaviors that clearly indicate patient seductiveness?

How do you feel when a patient dresses in a way that seems to you subtly seductive? Extremely seductive? How does it affect your behavior?

Under what conditions would you comment on the seeming seductiveness of a patient's clothing, words, or behavior? To what extent would you feel comfortable making a statement to a patient about apparently seductive clothing, words, or behavior?

Is a patient being seductive when attending therapy sessions in clothes that reflect the fashions of the day (e.g., miniskirt or tight or torn blue jeans)?

Have you ever found yourself lost in contemplation of what your patient is wearing? Do you believe that the patient was aware of your attention to clothing? How might your attention to and contemplation of clothing affect your relationship with the patient and the process of therapy?

Have you ever found yourself wishing that one of your patients would wear revealing or sexy clothing or would act seductively? How did you react to and understand this wish?

Do you ever have fantasies about your patients dressing or acting more seductively? If so, why? If not, why?

Do you sometimes decide not to wear some favorite article of clothing because it might appear seductive to your patients? To your colleagues? To your supervisor?

✤ ✤ ✤

*Are Beliefs About Race and Sex Related? A Passage From
Leon Williams*

Leon Williams (1972) began his analysis of the issues by quoting Herndon's conclusion "that all race relations [in the United States] tend to be, however subtle, sex relations" (Herndon, 1965, p. 7):

> Racism like sexuality is learned behavior, and on a given plane, such as America's peculiar history of slavery, "Jim Crowism" and Victorian morality, that initial, fleeting insight into the sexuality of racism, strikes us with greater clarity.
>
> Herndon conceptualized this relationship best by calling the tangled myths of sexuality and racism the "sexualization of racism," a uniquely American phenomenon. He saw racism and sex in tandem, concluding that the two were inextricably connected.
>
> If this, then, is the case, we must explore racism and its sexual dimension as an additional factor which may serve as a powerful constraint on the [therapist's] judgment and skill as [the therapist] attempts to practice across racial lines. . . .
>
> Treating the two notions [race and sex] together is virtually unheard of, suggesting that powerful emotions and deeply unconscious factors have come into play to "cool out" our efforts to look critically and objectively at a subject which appears to lie at the root of social reality in America. (L. F. Williams, 1972, pp. 76, 80)

Questions

Are you more or less likely to become sexually aroused by a patient whose race is different from your own?

Are you more or less likely to touch a patient whose race is different from your own?

If a patient of a different race said that he or she were in love with you (or were having sexual fantasies about you), how would you feel? What would you say or do?

When you think about a patient of a different race, what is the first race that comes to mind? Why?

Is there any race for which you cannot imagine yourself making love with, or being a life partner with, a person of that race? If so, what influence might your propensities have on your therapy with people of that race?

How would you respond if a patient commented that you were racist? How would you respond if a supervisor commented that some of your views, assessments, or interventions were racist?

Do you believe that race is generally an important factor or generally not an important factor in therapy?

Imagine that you begin work with a patient who expresses views and engages in behaviors that you consider to reflect racism. How do you feel? How, if at all, does this perceived racism affect your relationship with the patient and your interventions?

How comfortable are you discussing racial issues in supervision and case conferences? Do you discuss racial issues in supervision and case conferences?

✤ ✤ ✤

Beatings, Grief, Love, and Sex: A Passage From Fritz Perls

Fritz Perls (1893–1970) was one of the founders of gestalt therapy. As accounts of his life and work have described (e.g., Perls, 1969, 1973, 1988; Shepard, 1976), he practiced psychoanalysis in Berlin until the Nazi movement forced his emigration. He was analyzed by Wilhelm Reich, was supervised by Helene Deutsch, Otto Fenichel, and Karen Horney, and worked for a brief period as an assistant to Kurt Goldstein. In the 1930s, Perls moved to South Africa, where he founded the South African Institute of Psychoanalysis.

Later moving to Miami, he found that his marriage was no longer fulfilling, and he began engaging, according to his own account, in affairs that were unaccompanied by any deep emotional attachment (Perls, 1969). Soon, however, he met a woman to whom he wrote an open letter in his autobiography, addressing her as "the most important person in my life" (1969,

p. 196). According to Shepard (1976), she had been attending individual therapy sessions with him for 3 to 5 days each week. Shepard quotes her description of the turning point in therapy. Perls had been giving her friendly, supportive kisses at the end of each session. At the end of one session, the kiss became erotic. According to Shepard (1976), she told him, "I need a therapist, not a lover" (p. 81). She then had a dream, which she described during a subsequent session. It was after she reviewed the dream that she, according to Shepard's account, decided to become Perls's lover.

Once he had arrived in the United States, Perls began to devote more time and energy to the development of gestalt therapy. In the early 1950s, he founded the New York Institute for Gestalt Therapy and the Cleveland Institute for Gestalt Therapy. In the 1960s, he found a community that felt like "home" to him: the Esalen Institute in Big Sur, California.

Perls viewed gestalt therapy as an existential approach that dealt with the whole person: "The difference between Gestalt Therapy and most other types of psychotherapy is essentially that we do *not* analyze. We *integrate*" (Perls, 1988, pp. 65–66). The integration took place in and focused on the present: "Psychotherapy then becomes not an excavation of the past, in terms of repressions, Oedipal conflicts, and primal scenes, but an experience in living in the present" (Perls, 1973, p. 15).

In the following passage, Perls recounts his intervention with a woman in a group at Esalen. The woman had begun physically fighting with members of the group. Unable to restrain her, the group called on Perls to help bring peace.

> When I came in she charged with her head down into my belly and nearly knocked me over. Then I let her have it until I had her down on the floor. Up she came again. And then a third time. I got her down again and said, gasping: "I've beaten up more than one bitch in my life." Then she got up, threw her arms around me: "Fritz, I love you." Apparently she finally got what, all her life, she was asking for.
>
> And there are thousands of women like her in the States. Provoking and tantalizing, bitching, irritating their husbands and never getting their spanking. You don't have to be a

Parisian prostitute to need that so to respect your man. A Polish saying is: "My husband lost interest in me, he never beats me any more." (Perls, 1969, p. 98)

One of the many fascinating aspects of this account is the sudden shift in the woman's feelings toward Perls. In his gestalt approach, he was exceptionally aware of such quick emotional transformations as they occurred not only for others but also for him, as the following passage illustrates: "And if I comfort a girl in grief or distress and the sobbing subsides and she presses closer and the stroking gets out of rhythm and slides over the hips and over the breasts . . . where does the grief end and a perfume begin to turn your nostrils from dripping to smelling?" (1969, p. 100).

Questions

Can you imagine yourself doing the following to a patient as an attempt to teach the person how to "be open" and "stay tuned" to the present moment?

- pinning the person down on the floor
- holding the person in your lap
- tying the person's hands together
- muffling the person's face with a pillow
- "fighting" using big, heavy, cloth bats

As you imagine these scenes, how do you feel?

Are the feelings any different when you change the gender, race, sexual orientation, social status, or age of the imaginary patient?

How might such interventions affect someone suffering from each of the following diagnostic groups?

- depression
- problems being assertive
- posttraumatic stress syndrome
- schizophrenia
- multiple personality
- panic disorder

How do you decide what limits to set for your own behavior during therapy? How do you decide whether to use "street language?"

❖ ❖ ❖

A View of the Patient's Attraction as Transference: A Passage From Freud

Freud (1915/1963) viewed sexual attraction toward the therapist as a form of transference. The patient took feelings and conflicts toward other important (usually earlier) people, such as the patient's mother or father, and "transferred" them to the therapist. According to Freud, the therapist must avoid taking the patient's attraction personally:

> He must recognize that the patient's falling in love is induced by the analytic situation and is not to be ascribed to the charms of his person, that he has no reason whatever therefore to be proud of such a "conquest," as it would be called outside analysis. And it is always well to be reminded of this. (p. 169)

In the passage below, Freud outlined the ways in which he believed that the erotic transference differed from attractions that occurred in other settings and situations:

> The transference-love is characterized . . . by certain features which ensure it a special position. In the first place, it is provoked by the analytic situation; secondly, it is greatly intensified by the resistance which dominates this situation; and thirdly, it is to a high degree lacking in regard for reality, is less sensible, less concerned about consequences, more blind in its estimation of the person loved, than we are willing to admit of normal love. (p. 173)

Questions

Has a patient ever expressed sexual attraction to you? How did you feel?

Do you believe that a patient's sexual attraction to you might represent something other than "transference" as Freud described it?

If a patient seems attracted to you but does not mention it, under what circumstances, if any, might you raise the topic?

If you have been in therapy as a patient or client, were you ever attracted to your therapist? If so, did you discuss it with your therapist? How sensitive, respectful, and skilled did your therapist seem in addressing your feelings?

When the Therapist Doesn't Know That the Client Is Attracted to Her: A Passage From Marny Hall

Hall (1985) described vividly the ways in which clients may fear and be uncomfortable with sexual attraction to their therapists. She described, for example, one man who took elaborate steps to ensure that he would not be attracted to his therapist. He went out of his way to select a therapist who did not have the physical characteristics that he found attractive. By the second therapy session, however, he was experiencing an elaborate sexual fantasy about the therapist. In the following passage, Hall described a different situation, in which the therapist remained unaware that her female client was intensely attracted to her:

> Sky was so attracted to Cecile, her therapist, that she drove by her house frequently, hoping to catch a glimpse. She called Cecile late at night and hung up when she answered. After three months of this (all of which remained unknown to Cecile), Sky decided that her feelings were hopeless and she stopped therapy. (p. 152)

Questions

To what degree to you think that a therapist's physical attributes are important in eliciting a patient's sexual attraction?

Have you ever felt that you were unusually slow in discovering that a patient was sexually attracted to you? In thinking about it later, were there subtle (or not so subtle) signs of the patient's attraction that you failed to notice or make sense of? Were there any personal factors that made it difficult for you to recognize these signs?

What behaviors have patients used to express their attraction to you? Have any of these ever frightened you?

As a therapist, have you ever had a patient stop therapy without explanation? Why do you think he or she withdrew? What did you do? What other approaches might you have used?

Have you ever experienced "hang-up" phone calls that you thought might be made by a particular patient? How did you feel? How did you decide whether to raise the issue with the patient?

A Patient's Distorted View of the Therapist: A Passage From Linnda Durre

Durre bases her approach to therapy on a unique blend of such diverse approaches as gestalt therapy and psychodynamic therapy. She has emphasized that "the importance of 'falling in love' with one's therapist can be interpreted as positive transference, and its successful resolution in a nonsexual manner is crucial to the process of the therapeutic relationship and the progress that the client will make in therapy" (Durre, 1980, p. 228).

As part of her study of women who had become sexually involved with their therapists, she asked them about how they viewed their therapists and how that view had evolved. Her study suggests that some, and perhaps many, patients idealize their therapist to the extent that the therapist appears to possess almost superhuman attractiveness and perfection:

> "I just thought that he was the handsomest man I ever saw," one woman told me in an interview for this study. "Then

about one year after my therapy was completed, I saw him again, and realized that he was bald, grossly overweight, had bad skin, bad breath, and was a sloppy dresser. A caring, sensitive man, but nothing like what I had imagined. How could I have not seen that?" she asked herself. Many other women shared the same perceptions of their therapists at first: that he was good-looking, kind, understanding , supportive, had no problems of his own, or, as one woman stated, "certainly none that he couldn't solve easily and by himself." They later found out that many of their perceptions were not grounded in reality and some were far from the truth. (Durre, 1980, pp. 236–237)

Questions

Do you recall a patient idealizing you? In what ways? What feelings did the idealization evoke in you? Did the patient's idealization ever give you a "lift," make you feel better about yourself and your life? Did idealization ever make you feel inadequate (i.e., that you couldn't live up to the patient's view of you)?

Imagine that a patient says to you, "Well, of course you wouldn't know the kind of problems I face. You're so smart, talented, kind, and good-looking. You and I are so different!" How would you feel? What would you say to the patient?

Have you ever said or done something that, upon later reflection, seemed to encourage a patient to idealize you?

Have you ever idealized a patient? What aspects did you idealize (e.g., skills, looks, integrity, courage, or life-style)? What prompted you to idealize the patient? How do you understand the relationship between your idealization of the patient and your feelings about yourself and your life?

Have you ever worked with a patient whom you believed was actually (i.e., without idealization) happier and better adjusted than you were? What feelings did this evoke in you? How did it influence your relationship with the patient and your interventions?

Imagine that one of the women described in the passage has just started therapy with you. She has previously been involved in a sexual relationship with her therapist. What do you imagine her feelings might be toward you as her new therapist?

✤ ✤ ✤

Fantasizing Love and Marriage With a Patient: A Passage From Harold Searles

Describing his own experiences with love in the countertransference, Searles (1959) contrasted his reactions to two of his patients at the Chestnut Lodge Research Institute in Rockville, Maryland. During his first few years at Chestnut Lodge, Searles treated a man in his mid-thirties who was diagnosed as suffering from paranoid schizophrenia. During the second year of treatment, he became aware that he was experiencing romantic and sexual feelings about his patient. These feelings made him quite anxious. He almost panicked when, during one of the sessions, he and the patient were sitting silently, listening to a sweetly romantic song playing on a distant radio, "when I suddenly felt that this man was dearer to me than anyone else in the world, including my wife" (p. 185). His reaction to his patient (or to his feelings about his patient) made him so uncomfortable that, on a variety of pretexts, he was soon no longer working with the man.

Years later, once he had worked through his discomfort through his own analysis, Searles began working with another patient whom he described as extremely unattractive in dress and physical appearance (at least according to conventional standards) and suffering from a severe disorder. The first 2 years of therapy were marked by substantial negative transference and countertransference. But gradually Searles found himself attracted to the patient. "One morning, as I was putting on a carefully-selected necktie, I realized that I was putting it on for him . . . " (p. 185).

During the next 2 years of treatment, the patient described the relationship as "being married" and told of his fantasies of marrying his therapist. Searles described how one day, as he and the patient were riding in a car, he experienced a fantasy that he and the patient were engaged to be married. He imagined what the future might be like if he and the patient were to go on shopping trips together and to share experiences common to loving couples.

> When I drove home from work at the end of the day I was filled with a poignant realization of how utterly and tragically unrealizable were the desires of this man who had been hospitalized continually, now, for fourteen years. But I felt that, despite the tragic aspect of this, what we were going through was an essential, constructive part of what his recovery required; these needs of his would have to be experienced, I felt, in however unrecognizable a form at first, so that they could become reformulated, in the course of our work, into channels which would lead to greater possibilities for gratification. (p. 185)

Questions

Does your ability to recognize, acknowledge, accept, and understand your attraction to a client depend at all on the gender of the client?

Does your ability to discuss your feelings of attraction in supervision or case conferences depend at all on the gender of the client?

Have you ever fantasized marriage with a same-sex client? With an opposite-sex client? What feelings did these fantasies evoke in you? Do you believe that the client in such fantasies was aware of your feelings about him or her?

Have you ever been aware of wanting to refer or terminate a client because your reactions to the client made you anxious? What did you do?

Have you ever been repulsed by a client's physical appearance? How did your reaction affect the therapy and your relationship with the client? Do you think that the client was aware of your reaction?

Have you ever been surprised as your feelings about a client changed over the course of therapy? Have you ever found it difficult to acknowledge these changes?

Self-Disclosure as an Expression of Jealousy: A Passage From Myron Weiner

In his book *Therapist Disclosure: The Use of Self in Psychotherapy*, Weiner (1978) illustrated the way in which a patient's obviously transferential and "distorted" perception of the therapist may actually intuit correctly a therapist's countertransference:

> Mrs. A.E. told her therapist that a friend had described one of his medical colleagues as unusually good-looking. The therapist responded, "He's gorgeous." In their next session, the patient returned to a concern she had expressed early in therapy—that the therapist might be homosexual. This temporarily blocked dealing with dream material she had reported in which there were homosexual overtones. The block was resolved by helping her see that she was projecting the feared part of herself onto the therapist and by the therapist's pointing out that they were only talking about homosexual thoughts and feelings and not defining her as a heterosexual or homosexual person. The therapist then took on the task within himself of dealing with his gratuitous comment, which was an acting out of his envy of the colleague's good looks and success and his wish to disparage him as "too pretty." (p. 191)

Questions

Imagine that you are the patient in this passage. What feelings did you experience when your therapist commented that his colleague was "gorgeous?" How does that reaction affect your feelings toward the therapist? Would your feelings change if the colleague were female?

Have you, as a therapist, ever been aware of jealousy, anger, love, sexual attraction, or other feelings toward someone whom a patient discussed? Do you believe that those feelings influenced your relationship or behavior with the patient? Do you believe that the patient was aware of your feelings? How could you tell? Under what conditions, if ever, would you discuss these feelings with your client?

✛ ✛ ✛

A Voyeuristic Response to an Incest Survivor: A Passage From Christine Courtois

Now in independent practice as a counseling psychologist, Courtois has specialized in understanding the process of sexual victimization and providing help to survivors of sexual assault for over two decades. In 1972, she cofounded (and served as codirector with Ruth Anne Koenick) the University of Maryland's University Women's Crisis Center. Originally a rape crisis center, the facility soon began providing services to women who had experienced (and in some instances continued to experience) incest. Six years later, Courtois conducted a study of female incest survivors, patterning her research on the studies of battered women conducted by Lenore Walker.

In her book *Healing the Incest Wound: Adult Survivors in Therapy* (1988), Courtois described two types of voyeuristic responses to patients who have endured incest. In the first type, the clinician treats the incest survivor almost as if he or she were a laboratory animal or a visitor from another planet whose primary purpose was to teach the therapist about the exotic, fascinating, and sometimes horrifying topic of forbidden sexual intimacies with a relative. The therapist–client relationship focuses on the client's potential use to the therapist as a teaching vehicle, a means by which the therapist can learn about incest. Courtois observed that some therapists may even thank their clients for being such good educators and sources of information.

> This perspective is dangerous because it encourages the "survivor as heroine" aspect of the incest, minimizes its harmfulness, and recreates the dynamic of the survivor taking

care of others, this time the therapist. As one survivor put it: "I parented my parents and thought that was enough. I didn't want to have to teach or take care of my therapist. Her job was to take care of me."

In the second type of privileged voyeurism, the therapist focuses on the sexual aspects and details of the abuse to the exclusion of other issues. Survivors who have experienced this therapist reaction tell of feeling pressured to describe in detail the most intimate and often the most humiliating sexual aspects of the abuse early in treatment to satisfy the therapist's prurient interests. They also describe being made to feel like they are on the witness stand and are constantly redirected from the other issues back to the sexual details. The therapist often appears spellbound or tantalized by the survivor's incest history. Clearly, such behavior is another experience of victimization. (pp. 237–238)

Questions

In what ways, if at all, have you used patients as a source of information about forms of victimization, dysfunctional processes, or clinical phenomena? How has this process of learning affected the therapy and your relationship with the patient?

Have you ever been sexually aroused by a client's description of sexual abuse? How did you respond to the arousal? Do you believe that the client was aware of your arousal?

If you have been a patient in therapy, have you ever felt that your therapist was behaving voyeuristically toward you?

During clinical supervision, have you ever felt that you were "on the witness stand" and were "constantly redirected from the other issues back to the sexual details" in a way that was at odds with your supervisory needs?

A Sex Therapy Patient Responding Erotically to the Therapist: A Passage From Helen Singer Kaplan

Helen Singer Kaplan holds doctorates in medicine and philosophy, is on the faculty of Cornell University, and directs the

Sex Therapy and Education Program of the Payne Whitney Clinic of New York Hospital. Her approach differs from that of the original Masters and Johnson program in that she does not believe it necessary for the treatment to involve a couple or to be conducted by a team of cotherapists.

Kaplan emphasizes that the therapist must be alert to the occurrence of erotic transference: "Clearly, in sex therapy, which entails open discussion of the intimate details of the patient's sexual behavior, feelings, and fantasies, there is a greater danger that the patient will develop an erotic transference toward the therapist" (1976, p. 243). However, Kaplan has found that, in sex therapy, such erotic transferences are rare unless the therapist is either openly or subtly seductive. Thus, when such responses occur more than rarely, it is a clue that the therapist may be unaware of countertransference: "If one of our trainees reports more than once a year an erotic response on the part of the patient, we assume that he is doing something seductive, something countertransferential that is outside of his awareness" (1977, p. 186).

According to Kaplan, sexual feelings about patients in sex therapy are common and, if they do not represent unrecognized countertransference, may be harmless and perhaps even beneficial if they are reactions to the patient's or couple's dynamics, and may help the therapist to understand the treatment needs and process: "A therapeutic situation is an emotional one in the best sense of the word. Rather than stamp it out as undesirable, the therapist should sensitize himself to his feelings and keep closely in touch with his emotional responses . . ." (1976, p. 245).

What is crucial is the recognition that unexamined countertransference may prompt the therapist to act in a countertherapeutic manner and may elicit a wide range of feelings and actions from a patient.

> When a therapist has an unconscious and neurotic need to demonstrate his sexual superiority over the husband, he may elicit erotic feelings in the wife. It is easy under such circumstances for the male sex therapist to unconsciously transmit a message to the sexually distressed wife along the following

lines—"Of course you can't function with him. You're won-
derful, and he's clumsy and stupid. But I'm sensitive and
know all about sexuality. If I were your lover, you would
function." (1976, p. 244)

Questions

Do you agree that erotic reactions are rare in sex therapy unless
the therapist is "either openly or subtly seductive?"

What different kinds of openly seductive behaviors can you
imagine?

What different kinds of subtly seductive behaviors can you
imagine?

As a therapist, have you ever engaged in openly or subtly
seductive behavior of which you were unaware? How did you
become aware of the meaning or intent of your behavior? Was
the client aware of the seductive nature of your behavior?

Imagine that you have been engaging in subtly seductive behavior with a patient but have been unaware of it. You begin
to notice that the patient is sexually aroused. Trying to understand why the patient is aroused, you discover your own seductive intent and behavior. After the session, you prepare to
tell your supervisor about what has happened. How do imagine
that your supervisor will respond?

To what extent has your supervision addressed the issue of
your own seductive behavior as a potential cause of a patient's
erotic reaction?

*A Patient's Difficulties in Talking About Sexual Fantasies: A
Passage From Mardi Horowitz*

Serving as director of the Center for the Study of Neuroses (a
National Institute of Mental Health Clinical Research Center)
at the Langley Porter Institute in San Francisco, Horowitz has
conducted extensive research into how people encode their

experience in three modes of representation: (a) bodily or kin-
esthetic, (b) imagistic, and (c) linguistic. One focus of his research is the way in which therapy can help a patient to translate
material from one mode to another. In the following passage,
he described a patient's difficulties talking in therapy about the
visual images she experiences during intercourse with her husband:

> A young married woman was sometimes sexually frigid. At
> other times she was able to achieve an orgasm during inter-
> course with her husband. Her only route to sufficient erotic
> excitation for orgasm was to have a specific visual fantasy
> during love making. In this fantasy she pictured herself as
> a prostitute permitting humiliating acts to be performed
> upon her for money. She felt guilty and tried to avoid recall
> of these fantasies or acknowledgment of their implications.
> She also feared revealing the images to the therapist because
> she was ashamed of them and feared that they might be
> regarded as abnormal. Also, translation of the images into
> words would destroy the compartmentalization of her men-
> tal life: she would have to recognize the images and their
> implications, and that meant that she might have to give up
> her only current route to sexual pleasure. (Horowitz, 1978,
> pp. 120–121)

Questions

Are there any aspects of your own sexuality about which you
feel guilty or ashamed? Have you experienced any visual sexual
images that you would be reluctant to translate into words?
How does your own sexuality influence your reactions to this
woman?

If you were the therapist, how would you conceptualize the
patient's difficulty revealing her sexual images to you? What
other possibilities are there besides the explanation set forth in
the passage?

If you were the therapist, would you attempt to help the woman
translate her sexual images into words? If so, how would you
proceed? If not, how would you approach the issue?

Can you imagine yourself, as therapist, becoming excited or aroused as a patient describes the sexual images in the passage or any other sexual images he or she might experience? Do you believe your excitement or arousal would increase or decrease if, instead of translating the images into words, the patient were to bring in or draw pictures of them?

Chapter

9

Scenarios

The passages of the previous section offered readers opportunities to explore their reactions to situations selected from
the psychotherapy literature and to participate in a shared
learning experience with other psychotherapists and counselors. The scenarios that follow present similar opportunities;
however, because each scene addresses the reader directly (and
is phrased in the second person), these scenarios may invite a
more immediate and intense identification. The most useful
scenes may be those that catch the reader off guard or off
balance, that evoke from the reader an unexpected and perhaps
puzzling response. However much they may temporarily
threaten our sense of ourselves as self-aware and centered in
our knowledge of ourselves, these surprising personal reactions
can help illuminate inner territory that has previously remained
out of awareness, or at least unexamined. To return to chapter
3's ocean metaphor, the reader should be ready to take a swim
and feel competent in the water, whatever the currents and
conditions may be. There is, of course, not necessarily one best
way to stay afloat and make headway when the ocean gets
rough.

   We recommend that, as with the passages in chapter 8, readers first address their emotional reaction to each scenario (e.g.,
"What am I feeling?" or "What feelings does this scenario evoke

in me?"). And again, as with the passages, we have suggested other questions that readers may consider and discuss.

Scenario 1: The Movie

It has been an extremely demanding week, and you're looking forward to going to the new movie with your life partner. The theater is packed but you find two seats on the aisle not too close to the screen. You feel great to have left work behind you at the office and to be with your lover for an evening on the town. As the lights go down, you lean over to give your partner a passionate kiss. For some reason, while kissing, you open your eyes and notice that, sitting in the seat on the other side of your partner and watching you, is a therapy patient who has, just that afternoon, revealed an intense sexual attraction to you.

Questions

If you were the therapist, what, if anything, would you say to the patient at the time of this event? What would you say during the next therapy session?

How would the patient's presence affect your subsequent behavior at the theater?

How might this event affect the therapy and your relationship with the patient?

What, if anything, would you say to your partner—either at the theater or later—about what had happened? Are there any circumstances under which you would phone the patient before the next scheduled appointment to discuss the matter?

Imagine that during a subsequent therapy session the patient begins asking about whom you were with at the theater. How would you feel? What would you say?

What if the patient were a business client of your partner (or knew your partner in another context) and they begin talking before the movie begins. What feelings would this discovery evoke in you? What would you consider in deciding how to handle this matter?

To what extent do you believe that therapists should be free to "be themselves?" To what extent should they behave in public as if a patient might be observing them?

Scenario 2: Marriage Counseling

You have just completed your third marriage counseling session with a couple who have been together for 4 years. As you walk back to your desk, you find that one of them has left a note for you. Opening the note, you find the client's declaration of overwhelming feelings of love for you, the desire for an affair, and a promise to commit suicide if you tell the other member of the couple about this note.

Questions

Would you initially address this matter privately with the client who left the note or with the two clients as a couple? What do you consider as you make this decision?

How would your understanding of and response to this client's "love" for you differ, if at all, if you were conducting individual rather than couple counseling?

What feelings does the client's threat of suicide evoke in you? How do you address this issue?

As you imagine this scenario, do you tend to believe that the other client is aware of his or her partner's loving feelings toward you?

When you see a couple in therapy, what ground rules, agreements, or formal contracts do you create regarding confidentiality, "secrets," and the scheduling of sessions with only one member of the couple? Do you provide any of this information in written form?

When providing couple counseling, do you keep one chart for the couple or individual charts for the two clients? How do you decide what information should be included in (or excluded from) the charts? Would you include the note described in the scenario in the chart?

✤ ✤ ✤

Scenario 3: Sounds

You are working in a busy mental health center in which the doors to the consulting rooms, while offering some privacy, are not completely soundproofed. As long as therapist and client are talking at a normal level, nothing can be heard from outside the door. But words spoken loudly can be heard and understood in the reception area.

A patient, Sal, sits in silence during the first 5 minutes of the session, finally saying, "It's been hard to concentrate today. I keep hearing these sounds, like they're ringing in my ear, and they're frightening to me. I want to tell you what they're like, but I'm afraid to."

After offering considerable reassurance that describing the sounds would be OK and that you and Sal can work together to try to understand what is causing the sounds, what they mean, and what you might do about them, you notice that Sal seems to be gathering the courage to reveal them to you.

Finally, Sal leans back in the chair and imitates the sounds. They build quickly to a very high pitch and loud volume. They sound exactly like someone becoming more and more sexually aroused and then experiencing an intense orgasm.

You are reasonably certain that these sounds have been heard by the receptionist, some of your colleagues, the patients sitting in the waiting room, and a site visitor from the Joint Commission on Accreditation of Healthcare Organizations who is deciding whether the hospital in which your clinic is based should have its accreditation renewed.

Questions

As you imagined the scene, was the client male (e.g., Salvador) or female (e.g., Sally)? Does the client's gender make any difference in the way you feel?

If Sal began to make the sounds again, would you make any effort to interrupt or to ask the client to be a little quieter? Why?

If none of the people who might have heard the sounds mentioned this event to you, would you make any effort to explain what had happened?

Imagine that just as Sal finishes making these sounds, someone knocks loudly on the door and asks, "What's going on in there?" What do you say or do?

Would your feelings or behavior be any different if the sounds were of a person being beaten rather than having an orgasm?

How would you describe this session in your chart notes?

If you were being supervised, would you feel at all apprehensive about discussing this session with your supervisor?

What approach do you usually take toward your clients making loud noises that might be heard outside the consulting room?

Scenario 4: Initial Appointment

In independent practice, you've been working in your new office for about a year. In the last few months, several of your patients have completed therapy and new referrals haven't been coming in. It has become difficult to cover your expenses. Finally, a prospective patient schedules an initial appointment. During the first session, the patient says that the problem is sexual in nature and asks if you are comfortable and experienced in working with that sort of problem. You answer truthfully that you are. You are told that the patient would only be able to work with a therapist of a particular sexual orientation, without specifying what that orientation is. Then the patient asks, "What is your sexual orientation?"

Questions

Imagine that the question takes you by surprise. What might you say to the patient if the question took you off guard?

Reflect on the various ways you might respond to this question. If you had adequate time to consider the question, how do you think you would respond? Is this response different from the one you might tend to make if the question caught you off guard?

Imagine that the patient has been in therapy with you for 6 months and then asks this question. Would you give a different answer than if he or she were a new patient?

If you were choosing a therapist, would the therapist's sexual orientation make any difference in your decision?

Do you believe that there are any false stereotypes about therapists based on their sexual orientation? If so, what are they? How, if at all, do they affect therapy research, theory, and training? How, if at all, do they affect hiring practices, promotions, and formal or informal policies within mental health facilities? How, if at all, have they affected your training and practice? What feelings do these false stereotypes that you believe exist evoke in you?

Do you believe that there are any actual group differences between therapists based on their sexual orientation? If so, what are they? How, if at all, do they affect therapy research, theory, and training? How, if at all, do they affect hiring practices, promotions, and formal or informal policies within mental health facilities? How, if at all, have they affected your training and practice? What feelings do these group differences that you believe exist evoke in you?

How do you decide what kinds of personal information to reveal to a patient?

Scenario 5: Size

During your first session with a new patient, he tells you that he has always been concerned that his penis was too small. Suddenly, he pulls down his pants and asks you if you think it is too small. (Consider the same scenario with a new patient who is concerned about the size of her breasts.)

Questions

What would you, as therapist, *want* to do first? Why? What do you think you *would* do first? Why?

What difference would it make if this were a patient whom you had been treating for a year rather than a new patient?

How, if at all, would your feelings and actions be different according to whether treatment were conducted on an inpatient or an outpatient basis?

How, if at all, would your feelings and actions differ according to the gender of the patient?

Imagine that the male and female patients in the scenario are 15 years old. What feelings does the scenario evoke in you? What do you do? What fantasies occur to you about what might happen after the event described in the scenario?

Scenario 6: Open Discussion

You are working with a patient who is terrified of sex. Even thinking about sexual behaviors tends to make him or her feel guilty, anxious, and uncomfortable.

You discuss this patient with your supervisor, and note the progress that the patient is making in discussing more openly the very few sexual activities that he or she enjoys. Your supervisor asks you what kind of sexual activities you enjoy.

Questions

How would you *like* to respond? Why?

How do you believe you *would* respond? Why?

How would your feelings and behaviors vary, if at all, according to such factors as the supervisor's age, gender, race, or professional status and influence?

How would your feelings and behaviors vary, if at all, according to whether you were sexually attracted to your supervisor?

Scenario 7: The Pet

A patient tells about a ritual that takes place once a week or so involving a pet dog. The patient's dog is stroked in such a way that the dog becomes sexually excited. Then the patient plays with the dog until the patient and then the dog experience an orgasm. The patient asks you if this is normal and if you think it is OK.

Questions

When you first imagined the scenario, what were the patient's gender, age, cultural background, race, sexual orientation, and socioeconomic status? Is the patient you imagined attractive to you? How is the patient dressed? What other attributions would you make about this patient based only on the information provided in the scenario?

If the patient had a different gender, age, race, sexual orientation, socioeconomic status, and cultural background than you first imagined, would your feelings change? How?

Are you likely to reveal your feelings about the ritual to the patient? Would you give a prompt and direct answer to the patient's question? If so, what would you consider saying? If not, why not? Would you state your intention not to answer or would you simply not answer (e.g., remain silent, provide information that is not responsive to the question, or respond to the patient's question with a question of your own)?

Over the course of your life, have your beliefs about what is sexually "normal" and "OK" or your understanding of those two concepts remained relatively stable or changed considerably? How do your own beliefs about what is "normal" and

"OK" affect the work you do and your relationships with patients?

Scenario 8: Reaction

A client begins describing sexual fantasies in great detail. You find that you become sexually aroused and are blushing. The patient notices that you seem different somehow and asks you, "What's wrong?"

Questions

Is it likely that you will respond to the client's question directly? Why or why not?

What do you consider as you decide what to do next?

As you imagine yourself becoming sexually aroused in front of a patient, what feelings do you experience? Would you mention these feelings to the client? To a supervisor? To a colleague? To a supervisee?

As you imagine yourself blushing in front of a client, what feelings do you experience? Would you reveal these feelings to the client? To a supervisor? To a colleague? To a supervisee?

What effects do you imagine your arousal and blushing might have had on the client?

As you first imagined this scenario, was the client sexually aroused while describing the fantasies?

Are you aware of any desire for the client to continue describing the fantasies? Any desire to move closer to the client? Any desire to extend the length of the session? Any desire that the session were already over? Any desire that the client had not described the fantasies in such detail? Any wish that you had met this client outside of the therapeutic relationship so that you could enjoy a sexually intimate relationship? Any desire to terminate or transfer this client?

The session is now over and you are preparing to meet with your supervisor. Are you any more eager or reluctant to meet with your supervisor than you customarily would be? Do you believe that you would describe the client's fantasies in great detail to your supervisor? Would you mention your own sexual arousal to your supervisor?

You describe this session to a colleague. The colleague says, "I think you must have been acting seductively. In some subtle ways, you must have been giving signals encouraging the client to talk in a way that would stimulate you sexually." What do you feel when your colleague says this? What do you think?

You describe this session to a colleague. The colleague says, "I think this client was trying to seduce you." What do you feel when your colleague says this? What do you think?

You describe this session to a colleague. The colleague says, "Aren't you concerned that this client might file a complaint against you for sexual misconduct?" What do you feel when your colleague says this? What do you think?

You describe this session to a colleague. The colleague says, "Some people have all the luck. I wish one of my clients would do that!" What do you feel when your colleague says this? What do you think?

When a client describes sexual fantasies in great detail, under what circumstances might you fail to include any mention of the topic in the client's chart? Under what circumstances might you include detailed descriptions of the fantasies in the chart? What are your feelings and thoughts as you anticipate the possible consequences of including or omitting sexual material while charting?

You are now sitting in your office 5 minutes before the next session with this client. Do you find yourself either more or less eager to meet with this client than you usually are?

In future sessions, would you make any effort to encourage or discourage the client from describing sexual fantasies in great detail?

Scenario 9: The Goal

Your patient describes to you her troubled marriage. Her husband used to get mad and hit her ("not too hard," she says) but he's pretty much gotten over that. Their sex life is not good. Her husband enjoys anal intercourse, but she finds it frightening and painful. She tells you that she'd like to explore her resistance to this form of sexual behavior in her therapy. Her goal is to become comfortable engaging in the behavior so that she can please her husband, enjoy sex with him, and have a happy marriage.

Questions

What are you feeling when the patient says that her husband used to get mad and hit her? What are you thinking?

What are you feeling when she says that she finds anal intercourse frightening and painful? What are you thinking?

What do you feel when she describes her goals in therapy? What are you thinking?

In what ways do you believe that your feelings may influence how you proceed with this patient?

Scenario 10: Lunch Break

Just as you are about to head out for your 2-hour lunch break, your life partner surprises you by showing up, taking you to a fancy hotel, ordering room service, and sharing with you an unexpected but delightful romantic interlude, finally dropping you off at your office just in time for your next patient, who is waiting for you in the reception area. You and your patient enter your office and sit down. Your face is still flushed from your sexual encounter. Your patient says, "You look like you're blushing. What's going on?"

Questions

If the client's question caught you off guard and you answered immediately, what do you imagine that you would say?

Would you answer the client's question directly? Why or why not?

Under what conditions might you invent a reason for your blushing in order to answer the client's question? How do you believe that telling the client something that is not strictly true might influence the therapy and your relationship with the client? Have you ever told a client something that you knew was false or misleading? Why? Have you ever told a supervisor something that you knew was false or misleading? Why?

If, on your way back into the office, a colleague rather than a client would have asked the same question, would your response have been different? If so, why?

To what extent do you believe that each of the clients you work with acknowledges that you have a private life away from work and your sessions with him or her? To what extent is each client curious about your life? What fantasies do you think your clients have about your life? Do their fantasies include your sexual behavior? To what extent do your clients' concerns and fantasies about your life become a topic of therapy?

III

Deciding What To Do

Chapter

10

Confronting an Impasse

A repeated theme of this book is that there are no clear, one-size-fits-all answers to what sexual feelings about patients mean or their implications for the therapy. Various theoretical orientations provide different, sometimes opposing ways of approaching such questions. Each person and situation is unique. Each therapist must explore and achieve a working understanding of his or her own unfolding, evolving feelings and the ways in which they may provide a source of guidance about what to say or do next. A cookbook approach may hinder rather than help this process.

The tenets of this book place fundamental trust in the individual therapist, adequately trained and consulting with others, to draw his or her own conclusions. Virtually all therapists have learned primary resources for helping themselves explore problematic situations. They may, for example, (a) introspect, (b) study the available research and clinical literature, (c) consult, (d) seek supervision, and (e) begin or resume personal therapy. But there are times when, even after the most sustained exploration, the course is not clear. The therapist's best understanding of the situation suggests a course of action that seems productive yet questionable and perhaps potentially harmful. To refrain from a contemplated action may shut the door to the therapist's spontaneity, creativity, intuition, and ability to help; to refrain may stunt the patient's progress or impede recovery.

However, to engage in the contemplated action may lead to disaster. It may be helpful for therapists, having reached an impasse, to examine the potential intervention in light of the following 10 considerations.

The Fundamental Prohibition

No consideration is more fundamental than this: Is the contemplated action consistent with the prohibition against therapist–patient sexual intimacy? Under no circumstances should a therapist ever engage in sexual intimacies with a patient. No matter what the situation. No matter who the patient. No matter what the patient has said or done. No matter how the therapist or the patient feels. Therapist-patient sexual intimacies are in all instances wrong and must be avoided.

In all situations, it is solely the therapist's responsibility to ensure that he or she never engages in sexual intimacies with a patient. The locus of responsibility for the therapist's behavior in this regard can never be shifted; it remains always and completely with the therapist.

Consequently, when considering how to respond to sexual feelings, what course of action might be appropriate, the therapist must frankly ask, Does this possible course of action in any way involve sexual intimacy with the patient? If the answer to that question is anything but a clear "no," the contemplated action must be rejected.

The Slippery Slope

The second consideration may require much more self-exploration and a deeper knowledge of oneself. Is the contemplated course of action likely to lead to or create a risk for sexual intimacies with the patient? The contemplated action may not, in and of itself, constitute or even connote sexual intimacies with the patient. Yet it may represent, depending on the personality, strengths, and weaknesses of the therapist, a subtle first step on a slippery slope. In most cases, only the therapist can honestly address this consideration.

Consider the following scenario. You find yourself feeling *something*—you are not quite sure what—for a patient. You are aware that you feel a closeness to her, a kind of connectedness and rapport that is unusual for you. Each session, she comes in and sits on the couch. You sit in your chair. However, at the next session, she begins sitting in the chair, leaving the couch for you to sit on. After several sessions of this pattern—she coming in and sitting on the chair, you then taking a seat on the couch—she announces, in the middle of a session, that she doesn't like being so far away from you, so she comes over and sits on the other end of the couch.

What do you do?

Obviously, therapist and patient sitting at far ends of a long couch does not constitute sexual intimacy. Nor does she give any indication that she wants to be any closer to you.

Depending on their theoretical orientation, their personal style, the specific therapeutic relationship, the needs of the patient in the scenario, and other factors, many therapists would probably make some comment about this new seating pattern.

But what would you do during the rest of the session and during future sessions?

It is our belief that there is no one-size-fits-all answer that uniformly applies across all theoretical orientations, situations, and so on. But if such factors would allow this "closer" seating arrangement, the therapist needs to consider what it means and where it may lead. In *some* cases, it might reflect a tacit agreement between therapist and patient to move physically closer. *Some* therapists in some versions of this scenario might recognize that incremental movements toward increased physical closeness, if continued, might set the stage for sexual intimacies. No specific movement, in and of itself, would seem particularly remarkable, risky, or inappropriate. Each would have ample justification (or rationalization). The lack of a drastic or sudden action could allow physical closeness to increase gradually until therapist and patient achieved a physical intimacy that was subtly or clearly sexual.

Each therapist must carefully consider actions that may lead, by small, seemingly insignificant-in-themselves increments, toward sexual intimacy. Those who wonder if they are progressing down this slippery slope may find it useful to complete the self-evaluation checklist presented by Pope and Bouhoutsos (1986).

Consistency of Communication

The third consideration invites the therapist to review the course of therapy from the start to the present: Has the therapist clearly and consistently communicated to the patient that sexual intimacies cannot and will not occur, and is the contemplated action consistent with that communication? The question of sexual intimacy may not arise with all patients. If the question does arise, it may not surface until therapy is well under way. Although approaches to therapy seem to have an almost infinite variety, there is probably no therapist who begins with the words, "Hello, I'm Dr. _____ . I want you to know that under no circumstances will we ever engage in sex." Nevertheless, therapists must and do communicate the ground rules of therapy to their patients. The communications differ in each therapy relationship, according to theoretical orientation, personal style, the unique situation, and so on. Under no circumstances should a therapist ever communicate, either explicitly or implicitly, that sexual intimacy with the patient is a possibility. No communication should be inconsistent with the fundamental prohibition against sexual intimacies between therapist and patient.

It is important to be alert to subtle or unintentional communications contrary to the prohibition against therapist–patient sex. Some therapists may enjoy and tacitly seek to encourage a patient's sexual feelings, attraction, or desire. They may be reluctant to clarify the prohibition because to do so might result in the patient examining the feelings therapeutically (rather than expressing them in a way that the therapist finds personally arousing or gratifying) or turning his or her attention to other issues. Through words or deeds, these therapists may act in a creatively seductive manner, inviting, reinforcing, and trying to maintain the patient's sexual interest.

Clarification

The fourth consideration requires the therapist to assess whether taking the contemplated action should be deferred until sexual and related issues have been clarified. Imagine, for example, that the patient has told the therapist that he or she would like each session to end with a reassuring hug. Assume that the therapist's theoretical approach *per se* does not preclude this form of physical contact. Assume also that the hugging might be construed as addressing one or more of the patient's important clinical needs. Finally, assume that the therapist is not sexually attracted to the patient, does not anticipate becoming sexually aroused if such brief hugs were to end each session, and that hugging does not seem to stir up any conflicts or confusions on the part of the therapist.

What issues would adding this ritualized hug to the process of therapy raise? For some patients, abusive childhood experiences may have prevented their learning that hugs can be nonsexual; for them, this sort of physical contact involves deeper levels of sexual expression. For others, the hugs may represent an attempt to please the therapist, another pattern that may have been learned in childhood. Still others may be challenging or testing a boundary. In such cases, the therapist may need to discuss these issues with the patient before making a decision about whether to end each session with a hug.

The Patient's Welfare

The fifth consideration is one of the primary touchstones of all therapy: Is the contemplated action consistent with the welfare of the patient? The therapist's feelings—especially when they are sexual—can be so powerful, complex, and personally immediate that they can create a context of their own. In this context, the therapist can respond to vivid personal feelings, impulses, desires, fears, and fantasies while the patient's clinical needs lose their salience.

Complex legal issues may make this consideration more difficult. In some instances, a therapist may take an action that may not be construed by all concerned as clearly consistent with the welfare of the patient. For example, a therapist may be legally required to report that the patient has engaged in child abuse or has threatened to kill a third party, even though some therapists may believe that such reports are not consistent with the welfare of the patient.

Despite the legal and related complexities, it is important to consider the degree to which any contemplated action promotes, is consistent with, is irrelevant to, or is contrary to the patient's welfare. Both therapist and patient, for example, may enjoy talking at length about the patient's sexual fantasies. But the therapist must frankly address the questions: Does such discussion serve a legitimate therapeutic purpose? Is it consistent with the patient's welfare? Does it help address the needs or questions that prompted the patient to seek therapy or that emerged during the course of therapy? Regarding the previous example (i.e., discussing at length the patient's sexual fantasies), there is no predetermined or universal answer that spans all therapeutic situations. In some instances, such discussion may be vital to the patient's progress. In others, it may be extremely destructive. Nothing can spare therapists from struggling with such questions each time they arise.

Consent

The sixth consideration is another primary touchstone of therapy: Is the contemplated action consistent with the basic informed consent of the patient? Consent is one of the most difficult issues with which therapists must contend (see, e.g., Pope & Vasquez, 1991). Legal requirements for informed consent to treatment and informed refusal of treatment vary according to jurisdiction. There are often instances in which patients are subjected to interventions that are contrary to their voluntary consent. For example, a person who is actively suicidal, homicidal, or gravely disabled may, again depending on applicable law for the jurisdiction, be involuntarily hospitalized. However, patients are generally accorded rights to informed consent or informed refusal. Each act or set of actions by a therapist must be carefully considered in light of its consistency with the person's autonomy and his or her right to choose what forms of treatment to try or to avoid.

It is worth emphasizing a special proviso, even though it is redundant with the first consideration that was previously discussed: Under *no* circumstances can a patient be construed to have legitimized therapist–patient sexual intimacies because he or she "consented" to them (see Pope & Bouhoutsos, 1986). Again, the prohibition against therapist–patient sexual intimacies is absolute and without exception, and it is the therapist who bears *sole* responsibility for his or her own behavior and for never participating in sexually intimate behavior with a patient. Nothing can justify a therapist's choice to violate this fundamental ethical responsibility and to place a patient at risk for deep and lasting harm.

Adopting the Patient's View

The seventh consideration is one that invites the therapist to empathize imaginatively with the patient: How is the patient likely to understand and respond to the contemplated action? Therapy is one of many endeavors in which *exclusive* attention to theory, intention, and technique may distract from other sources of information, ideas, and guidance. Therapists-in-training may cling to theory, intention, and technique as a way of coping with the anxieties and overwhelming responsibilities of the therapeutic venture. Seasoned therapists may rely almost exclusively on theory, intention, and technique out of learned reflex, habit, and the sheer weariness that approaches burnout. There is always risk that the therapist will fall back on repetitive and reflexive responses that verge on stereotype. Without much thought or feeling, the anxious or tired therapist may, if analytically minded, answer a patient's question by asking why the patient asked the question; if holding a client-centered orientation, may simply reflect or restate what the client has just said; if gestalt trained, may ask the client to say something to an empty chair; and so on.

One way to help avoid responses that are driven more by anxiety, fatigue, or similar factors is to consider carefully how the therapist would think, feel, and react if he or she were the patient. Regardless of the theoretical soundness, intended outcome, or technical sophistication of a contemplated intervention, how will it likely be experienced and understood by the patient? Can the therapist anticipate at all what the patient might feel and think? The therapist's attempts to try out, in his or her imagination, the contemplated action and to view it from the perspective of the patient may help prevent, correct, or at least identify possible sources of misunderstanding, miscommunication, and failures of empathy.[7]

Competence

The eighth consideration is one of competence: Is the therapist competent to carry out the contemplated intervention? Ensuring that a therapist's education, training, and supervised experience is adequate and appropriate for his or her work is an important clinical and ethical responsibility. "The Ethical Principles of Psychologists and Code of Conduct" of the American Psychological Association (1992), for example, emphasizes that

> Psychologists. . .recognize the boundaries of their particular competencies and the limitations of their expertise. They provide only those services and use only those techniques for which they are qualified by education, training, or experience. . . . They maintain knowledge of relevant scientific and professional information related to the services they ren-

---

[7]Therapists may also find it useful to attempt to understand the phenomenon of therapist–patient sexual intimacy from the point of view of the patient. Several books presenting excellent first-person accounts have been published (e.g., Bates & Brodsky, 1989; Noel & Watterson, 1992). Though not a first-person account, Hare-Mustin's (1992) discussion of poet Anne Sexton's psychotherapy is particularly useful in clarifying how limited perspectives can obscure the harm that tends to be associated with therapist–patient sex.

der, and they recognize the need for ongoing education.
(p. 3)

As an extreme example, consider a hypothetical male therapist who discovers, in the second month of work with a patient, that the patient is the victim of child sex abuse. The patient says that he or she fears the therapist and finds it difficult to talk because sexual memories keep intruding. The therapist has listened to colleagues discuss "reenactment therapy" and decides that this might be an appropriate intervention to try on a trial basis with this patient. He asks the patient to describe the memory, which involved anal intercourse. The therapist then suggests that he and the patient get down on the floor, fully clothed, to pantomime the action. Although the therapist has no real knowledge of "reenactment therapy," the approach seems to make sense to him in light of his knowledge of learning theory and behavior therapy. He believes that reenacting the traumatic memory through pantomime, in the safety and security of the therapy office, will enable the patient to become systematically desensitized to the traumatic associations. He anticipates that after one or two slow, careful reenactments, the patient will no longer generalize the learned fear (as well as other negative feelings) to the therapist.

Especially if they are knowledgeable about interventions for people who were sexually abused as children, readers will probably be able to envision some likely disastrous consequences of the therapist's contemplated actions in this scenario. Whenever therapists consider possible interventions or courses of action (e.g., emotional flooding, systematic desensitization, using touch to help induce a hypnotic trance, "emergent uncovering" of sexual feelings, or psychodrama), it is crucial that they candidly assess the degree to which they have adequate knowledge and training.

Uncharacteristic Behaviors

The ninth consideration involves alertness to unusual actions: Does the contemplated action fall substantially outside the range of the therapist's usual behaviors? That the contemplated action is unusual does not suggest *per se* that something is wrong with it. The creative therapist will likely try creative interventions. The typical therapist—if there is such a person—will likely engage in atypical behaviors from time to time. But possible actions that seem considerably outside the therapist's general approaches probably warrant special consideration.

For most therapists, therapy is conducted in the consulting room. Some theoretical orientations, however, may not preclude the therapist from seeing a patient outside the office if there is clear clinical need and justification. For example, Stone (1982) described a woman suffering from schizophrenia who was hospitalized during a psychotic break. The woman heaped verbal abuse on her therapist, claiming that the therapist did not really care about her. Suddenly, the patient disappeared from the unit.

> The therapist, upon hearing the news, got into her car and canvassed all the bars and social clubs in Greenwich Village which her patient was known to frequent. At about midnight, she found her patient and drove her back to the hospital. From that day forward, the patient grew calmer, less impulsive, and made great progress in treatment. Later, after making substantial recovery, she told her therapist that all the interpretations during the first few weeks in the hospital meant very little to her. But after the "midnight rescue mission" it was clear, even to her, how concerned and sincere her therapist had been from the beginning. (p. 171)

Searching for a patient outside the hospital or office is an extremely atypical event for most, if not all, therapists. When the therapist undertakes such an atypical action, is it clear that such out-of-the-office contact is warranted by the patient's clinical needs and situation? Contemplated actions that are out of the ordinary invite extremely careful evaluation.

On a much more complex level, it is useful to consider the factors that define, reflect, or influence what is "usual" behavior for the therapist. For example, does the therapist typically use nonerotic touch (e.g., handshakes, reassuring pats on the back, or briefly holding the patient's hand to express sympathy) with patients? Careful examination of the patterns of touch may reveal bias or other factors that may hold important meaning or implications. For example, there is evidence that differential use of nonsexual touch with male and female patients is statistically associated with therapist–patient sexual intimacy (Holroyd & Brodsky, 1980).

Consultation

The tenth consideration concerns secrecy: Is there a compelling reason for not discussing the contemplated action with a colleague, consultant, or supervisor? One red flag to the possibility that a course of action is inappropriate is the therapist's reluctance to disclose it to others. One question a therapist may ask about any proposed action is this: If I took this action, would I have any reluctance for all of my professional colleagues to know that I had taken it? If the answer is "yes," the reasons for the reluctance are worth examining. If the answer is "no," it is worth considering if one has adequately taken advantage of the opportunities to discuss the matter with a trusted colleague. If discussion with a colleague has not helped to clarify the issues, consultation with additional professionals, each of whom may provide different perspectives and suggestions, may be useful.

Reflecting on one's motivation for seeking consultation and one's methods of selecting potential consultants can be an important part of the consultation process. In times of temptation, often there is ample motive to seek superficial, phony, or pro forma consultation as a way to obtain approval or "permission" for a questionable behavior. The apparent consultation is an attempt to quash or override doubts rather than to explore them. Methods for selecting potential consultants can help undermine or ensure the integrity of the consultation process. Only the least persistent therapist would be unable to find, in a moderate or large community, a consultant who would say "yes" to virtually any proposed intervention. Survey research, for example, suggests that there is a tiny, atypical minority of therapists who even believe that sexual intimacies with clients may sometimes be therapeutic (see appendix C).

Making use of consultation as a regular component of clinical activities rather than as a resource used only on atypical occasions is one way to extend the learning process beyond the time span of the specific study group in which this book has served as a focus of exploration and discovery. Consultation with a variety of colleagues on a frequent basis can strengthen the sense of community in which therapists work. It can provide a safety net, helping therapists to ensure that their work does not fall into needless errors, unintentional malpractice, or harmful actions that are due to lack of knowledge, guidance, perspective, challenge, or support. It can create a sense of cooperative venture in which the process of professional development, exploration, and discovery continue.

References

Abramowitz, S. I., Roback, H. B., Schwartz, J. M., Yasuna, A., Abramowitz, C. V., & Gomes, B. (1976). Sex bias in psychotherapy: A failure to confirm. *American Journal of Psychiatry, 133,* 706–709.

American Psychological Association. (1992). Ethical principles of psychologists and code of conduct. *American Psychologist, 47,* 1597–1611.

Baer, R. (1981). *Homosexuality and American psychiatry.* New York: Basic Books.

Baldwin, L. C. (1986). The therapeutic use of touch with the elderly. *Physical and Occupational Therapy in Geriatrics, 4,* 45–50.

Ballou, M. B. (1990). Approaching a feminist-principled paradigm in the construction of personality theory. In L. S. Brown & M. P. P. Root (Eds.), *Diversity and complexity in feminist theory* (pp. 23–40). New York: Haworth.

Barber, T. X. (1984). Changing "unchangeable" bodily processes by (hypnotic) suggestions: A new look at hypnosis, cognitions, imaging, and the mind-body problem. In A. A. Sheikh (Ed.), *Imagination and healing* (pp. 69–127). Farmingdale, NY: Baywood.

Bass, A. (1989, April 3). Sexual abuse of patients—Why? High incidence may be due to therapists sense of impunity, inaction by professional groups. *Boston Globe,* pp. 27–28.

Bates, C. M., & Brodsky, A. M. (1989). *Sex in the therapy hour: A case of professional incest.* New York: Guilford Press.

Bergin, A. E. (1983). Religiosity and mental health: A critical reevaluation and meta-analysis. *Professional Psychology: Research and Practice, 14,* 170–184.

Bergin, A. E. (1988). Three contributions of a spiritual perspective to counseling, psychotherapy, and behavior change. *Counseling and Values, 33,* 21–31.

Bergin, A. E. (1991). Values and religious issues in psychotherapy and mental health. *American Psychologist, 46,* 394–403.

Bergin, A. E., & Jensen, J. P. (1990). Religiosity of psychotherapist: A national survey. *Psychotherapy, 27,* 3–7.

Bergin, A. E., & Payne, I. R. (1991). Proposed agenda for a spiritual strategy in personality and psychotherapy. *Journal of Psychology and Christianity, 10,* 197–210.

Beutler, L. E., & Crago, M. (Eds.). (1991). *Psychotherapy research: An international review of programmatic studies.* Washington, DC: American Psychological Association.

Note. Readers seeking a wider range of published resources are referred to the reference sections of appendixes A, B, and C.

Beutler, L. E., Crago, M., & Arizmendi, T. G. (1986). Research on therapist variables in psychotherapy. In S. Garfield & A. E. Bergin (Eds.), *Handbook of psychotherapy and behavior change* (pp. 257–310). New York: Wiley.

Borenzweig, H. (1983). Touching in clinical social work. *Social Casework, 64,* 238–242.

Borys, D. S., & Pope, K. S. (1989). Dual relationships between therapist and client: A national study of psychologists, psychiatrists, and social workers. *Professional Psychology: Research and Practice, 20,* 283–293.

Bosanquet, C. (1970). Getting in touch. *Journal of Analytical Psychology, 15,* 42–55.

Bouhoutsos, J. C., Holroyd, J., Lerman, H., Forer, B., & Greenberg, M. (1983). Sexual intimacy between psychotherapists and patients. *Professional Psychology: Research and Practice, 14,* 185–196.

Bowers, P. F., Banquer, M., & Bloomfield, H. H. (1974). Utilization of non-verbal exercises in the group therapy of outpatient chronic schizophrenics. *International Journal of Group Psychotherapy, 24,* 13–24.

Braude, M. (1984, May). *Sexual feelings between psychiatrists and patients.* Symposium presented at the annual meeting of the American Psychiatric Association, Los Angeles, CA.

Breuer, J., & Freud, S. (1957). In J. Strachey & A. Freud (Eds. & Trans.), *Studies on hysteria.* New York: Basic Books. (Original work published 1895)

Briere, J. (1989). *Therapy for adults molested as children.* New York: Springer.

Brodsky, A. M. (1977). Countertransference issues in the woman therapist: Sex and the student therapist. *Clinical Psychologist, 30,* 12–14.

Brodsky, A. M. (1989). Sex between patient and therapist: Psychology's data and response. In G. O. Gabbard (Ed.), *Sexual exploitation in professional relationships* (pp. 15–25). Washington, DC: American Psychiatric Press.

Brown, L. S. (1985). Power, responsibility, boundaries: Ethical concerns for the lesbian feminist therapist. *Lesbian Ethics, 1,* 30–45.

Brown, L. S. (1988). Harmful effects of posttermination sexual and romantic relationships with former clients. *Psychotherapy, 25,* 249–255.

Brown, L. S. (1989). Beyond thou shalt not: Theory about ethics in the lesbian community. *Women and Therapy, 8,* 13–26.

Brownfain, J. J. (1971). The APA professional liability insurance program. *American Psychologist, 26,* 648–652.

Buckley, P., Karasu, T. B., Charles, E., & Stein, S. P. (1979). Theory and practice in psychotherapy: Some contradictions in expressed belief and reported practice. *Journal of Nervous and Mental Disease, 167,* 218–223.

Bullis, R. K., & Harrigan, M. P. (1992). Religious denominational policies on sexuality. *Families in Society, 73,* 304–312.

Burton, A., & Heller, L. G. (1964). The touching of the body. *Psychoanalytic Review, 51,* 122–134.

California Department of Consumer Affairs. (1990). *Professional therapy never includes sex.* (Available from Board of Psychology, 1430 Howe Avenue, Sacramento, CA 95825)

Cantor, D. W. (1990). *Women as therapists: A multitheoretical casebook.* Northvale, NJ: Jason Aronson.

Carkhuff, R., & Pierce, R. (1967). Differential effects of therapist race and social class upon patient depth of self-exploration in the initial clinical interview. *Journal of Consulting Psychology, 31,* 632–634.

Cochran, S. D., Hacker, N. F., Wellisch, D. K., & Berek, J. S. (1987). Sexual functioning after treatment for endometrial cancer. *Journal of Psychosocial Oncology, 5,* 47–61.

Courtois, C. A. (1988). *Healing the incest wound: Adult survivors in therapy.* New York: Norton.

Dahlberg, C. C. (1970). Sexual contact between client and therapist. *Contemporary Psychoanalysis, 5,* 107–124.

Davidson, V. (1977). Psychiatry's problem with no name. *American Journal of Psychoanalysis, 37,* 43–50.

Dollard, J., Doob, L. W., Miller, N. E., Mowrer, O. H., & Sears, R. R. (1939). *Frustration and aggression.* New Haven: Yale University Press.

Durre, L. (1980). Comparing romantic and therapeutic relationships. In K. S. Pope (Ed.), *On love and loving: Psychological perspectives on the nature and experience of romantic love* (pp. 228–243). San Francisco: Jossey-Bass.

Ellenberger, H. F. (1972). The story of "Anna O": A critical review with new data. *Journal of the History of the Behavioral Sciences, 8,* 267–279.

Espin, O. M., & Gawelek, M. A. (1992). Women's diversity: Ethnicity, race, class, and gender in theories of feminist psychology. In L. S. Brown & M. Ballou (Eds.), *Personality and psychopathology* (pp. 88–107). New York: Guilford Press.

Etnyre, W. S. (1990). Body image and gay American men. In R. J. Kus (Ed.), *Keys to caring: Assisting your gay and lesbian clients* (pp. 45–58). Boston: Alyson.

Eyman, J. R., & Gabbard, G. O. (1991). Will therapist–patient sex prevent suicide? *Psychiatric Annals, 21,* 669–674.

Feldman-Summers, S., & Jones, G. (1984). Psychological impacts of sexual contact between therapists or other health care practitioners and their clients. *Journal of Consulting and Clinical Psychology, 52,* 1054–1061.

Feldman-Summers, S., & Kiesler, S. B. (1974). Those who are number two try harder: The effect of sex on attributions of causality. *Journal of Personality and Social Psychology, 30,* 846–855.

Fidell, L. S. (1970). Empirical verification of sex discrimination in hiring practices in psychology. *American Psychologist, 25,* 1094–1098.

Forer, B. (1980, February). *The psychotherapeutic relationship: 1968.* Paper presented at the annual meeting of the California State Psychological Association, Pasadena.

Freud, S. (1950). *The interpretation of dreams* (A. Brill, Trans.). New York: Modern Library. (Original work published 1900)

Freud, S. (1961a). Joseph Breuer (1925). In J. Strachey (Ed. & Trans.), *The standard edition of the complete psychological works of Sigmund Freud* (Vol. 19; pp. 279–282). London: Hogarth. (Original work published 1925)

Freud, S. (1961b). The psychopathology of everyday life. In J. Strachey (Ed. and Trans.), *The standard edition of the complete psychological works of Sigmund Freud* (Vol. 6) London: Hogarth. (Original work published 1901)

Freud, S. (1963). Observations on transference-love. In P. Rieff (Ed.) & J. Strachey (Trans.), *Sigmund Freud: Therapy and technique* (pp. 167–179). New York: Collier Books. (Original work published 1915)

Fuchs, L. L. (1975). Reflections on touching and transference in psychotherapy. *Clinical Social Work Journal, 3,* 167–176.

Galanter, M., Larson, D., & Rubenstone, E. (1991). Christian psychiatry: The impact of evangelical belief on clinical practice. *American Journal of Psychiatry, 148,* 90–95.

Ganzarain, R., & Buchele, B. (1986). Countertransference when incest is the problem. *International Journal of Group Psychotherapy, 36,* 549–566.

Ganzarain, R., & Buchele, B. (1988). *Fugitives of incest: A perspective from psychoanalysis and groups.* Madison, CT: International Universities Press.

Garfield, S., & Bergin, A. (1978). *Handbook of psychotherapy and behavior change: An empirical analysis.* New York: Wiley.

Garfield, S., & Bergin, A. (1986). *Handbook of psychotherapy and behavior change.* New York: Wiley.

Garnets, L., Hancock, K. A., Cochran, S. D., Goodchilds, J., & Peplau, L. A. (1991). Issues in psychotherapy with lesbians and gay men: A survey of psychologists. *American Psychologist, 46,* 964–972.

Garnets, L., Herek, G. M., & Levy, B. (1990). Violence and victimization of lesbians and gay men: Mental health consequences. *Journal of Interpersonal Violence, 5,* 366–383.

Gartrell, N. (1981a). The lesbian as a "single" woman. *American Journal of Psychotherapy, 35,* 502–509.

Gartrell, N. (1981b). Reply. *American Journal of Psychotherapy, 35,* 515–516.

Gechtman, L. (1989). Sexual contact between social workers and their clients. In G. O. Gabbard (Ed.), *Sexual exploitation in professional relationships* (pp. 27–38). Washington, DC: American Psychiatric Press.

Geller, J. D. (1978). The body, expressive movement, and physical contact in psychotherapy. In J. L. Singer & K. S. Pope (Eds.), *The power of human imagination: New methods in psychotherapy* (pp. 347–378). New York: Plenum Press.

Geller, J. D. (1988). Racial bias in the evaluation of patients for psychotherapy. In L. Comas-Diaz & E. Griffith (Eds.), *Clinical guidelines in cross-cultural mental health* (pp. 112–134). New York: Wiley.

Geller, J. D., Cooley, R. S., & Hartley, D. (1981–1982). Images of the psychotherapist. *Imagination, Cognition, and Personality, 1,* 123–146.

Genevay, B. (1990). Being old, sexual, and intimate: A threat or a gift? In B. Genevay & R. S. Katz (Eds.), *Countertransference and older clients* (pp. 148–168). Newbury Park, CA: Sage.

Gill, C. J. (1985). The family/professional alliance in rehabilitation viewed from a minority perspective. *American Behavioral Scientist, 28,* 424–428.

Glover, E. (1955). *The technique of psychoanalysis*. Madison, CT: International Universities Press.

Gonsiorek, J.C. (1988). Mental health issues of gay and lesbian adolescents. *Journal of Adolescent Health Care, 9*, 114–122.

Goodstein, R. K. (1982). Individual psychotherapy and the elderly. *Psychotherapy: Theory, Research and Practice, 19*, 412–418.

Gurman, A. S., & Razin, A. M. (1977). *Effective psychotherapy: A handbook of research*.

Guttman, H. (1984). Sexual issues in the transference and countertransference between female therapists and male patients. *Journal of the American Academy of Psychoanalysis, 12*, 187–197.

Haley, J. (1973). *Uncommon therapy: The psychiatric techniques of Milton H. Erickson, M.D.* New York: Ballantine Books.

Haley, J. (Ed.). (1985). *Conversations with Milton H. Erickson, M.D., Vol. 2: Changing couples*. New York: Norton.

Hall, M. (1985). *The lavender couch: A consumer's guide to psychotherapy for lesbians and gay men*. Boston: Alyson.

Hare-Mustin, R. T. (1992). Cries and whispers: The psychotherapy of Anne Sexton. *Psychotherapy, 29*, 406–409.

Henley, N. M. (1973). Status and touch: Some touching observations. *Bulletin of the Psychonomic Society, 2*, 91–93.

Henley, N. M. (1977). *Body politics: Power, sex, and nonverbal communication*. Englewood Cliffs, NJ: Prentice-Hall.

Herek, G. M. (1990). The context of anti-gay violence: Notes on cultural and psychological heterosexism. *Journal of Interpersonal Violence, 5*, 316–333.

Herman, J. L. (1981). *Father–daughter incest*. Cambridge, MA: Harvard University Press.

Herman, J. L. (1992). *Trauma and recovery*. New York: Basic Books.

Herndon, C. C. (1965). *Sex and racism in America*. New York: Grove Press.

Hollingshead, A. B., & Redlich, F. C. (1958). *Social class and mental illness: A community study*. New York: Wiley.

Holroyd, J. C. (1983). Erotic contact as an instance of sex-biased therapy. In J. Murray & P. R. Abramson (Eds.), *Handbook of bias in psychotherapy* (pp. 285–308). New York: Praeger.

Holroyd, J. C., & Brodsky, A. M. (1977). Psychologists' attitudes and practices regarding erotic and nonerotic physical contact with patients. *American Psychologist, 32*, 843–849.

Holroyd, J. C., & Brodsky, A. M. (1980). Does touching patients lead to sexual intercourse? *Professional Psychology, 11*, 807–811.

Hopkins, J. (1987). Failure of the holding relationship: Some effects of physical rejection on the child's attachment and on his inner experience. *Journal of Child Psychotherapy, 13*, 5–17.

Horowitz, M. J. (1978). *Image formation and cognition* (2nd ed.). New York: Appleton-Century-Crofts.

Howard, K., Orlinsky, D., & Hill, J. (1969). The therapist's feelings in the therapeutic process. *Journal of Clinical Psychology, 25*, 83–93.

Jacobson, E. (1938). *Progressive relaxation*. Chicago: University of Chicago Press.

Jensen, J. P., & Bergin, A. E. (1988). Mental health values of professional therapists: A national interdisciplinary survey. *Professional Psychology: Research and Practice, 19,* 290–297.

Johnson, C. B., Stockdale, M. S., & Saal, F. E. (1991). Persistence of men's misperceptions of friendly cues across a variety of interpersonal encounters. *Psychology of Women Quarterly, 15,* 463–475.

Jones, E. (1961). *The life and work of Sigmund Freud.* (Edited and abridged by L. Trilling & S. Marcus). New York: Basic Books.

Kaplan, H. S. (1976). *The new sex therapy: Active treatment of sexual dysfunctions.* New York: Bruner/Mazel.

Kaplan, H. S. (1977). Training of sex therapists. In W. H. Masters, V. E. Johnson, & R. D. Kolodny (Eds.)., *Ethical issues in sex therapy and research* (pp. 182–189). Boston: Little, Brown.

Kardener, S. H., Fuller, M., & Mensch, I. N. (1973). A survey of physicians' attitudes and practices regarding erotic and nonerotic contact with patients. *American Journal of Psychiatry, 133,* 1324–1325.

Kavaler-Adler, S. (1991). Some more speculations on Anna O. *American Journal of Psychoanalysis, 51,* 161–171.

Kimmel, D. G. (1988). Ageism, psychology, and public policy. *American Psychologist, 43,* 175–178.

Klass, E. T., & Galst, J. P. (1990). A cognitive–behaviorist views the case. In D. W. Cantor (Ed.), *Women as therapists: A multitheoretical casebook* (pp. 198–274). Northvale, NJ: Jason Aronson.

Knesper, D. J., Pagnucco, D. J., & Wheeler, J. R. C. (1985). Similarities and differences across mental health services providers and practice settings in the United States. *American Psychologist, 40,* 1352–1369.

Kohrman, R., Fineberg, H., Gelman, R., & Weiss, S. (1971). Technique of child analysis: Problems of countertransference. *International Journal of Psychoanalysis, 52,* 487–497.

Korchin, S. (1976). *Modern clinical psychology: Principles of intervention in the clinic and community.* New York: Basic Books.

Kus, R. J. (1990). Introduction. In R. J. Kus (Ed.), *Keys to caring: Assisting your gay and lesbian clients* (pp. 7–10). Boston: Alyson.

Leland, J. (1976). Invasion of the body. *Psychotherapy: Theory, Research and Practice, 13,* 214–218.

Lester, E. (1985). The female analyst and the eroticized transference. *International Journal of Psychoanalysis, 66,* 283–293.

Lewis, H. B. (1971). *Shame and guilt in neurosis.* Madison, CT: International Universities Press.

Lindner, R. (1954). *The fifty-minute hour.* New York: Dell.

Macdougall, J. C., & Morin, S. F. (1979). Sexual attitudes and self-reported behavior of congenitally disabled adults. *Canadian Journal of Behavioral Science, 11,* 189–204.

Malyon, A. K. (1981–1982). Psychotherapeutic implications of internalized homophobia in gay men. *Journal of Homosexuality, 7,* 59–69.

Malyon, A. K. (1982). Biphasic aspects of homosexual identity formation. *Psychotherapy: Theory, Research & Practice, 19,* 335–340.

Malyon, A. K. (1986a). *Brief follow-up to June 24, 1986, meeting with the American Psychiatric Association work group to revise DSM-III.* Unpublished manuscript.

Malyon, A.K. (1986b). *Presentation to the American Psychiatric Association work group to revise DSM-III.* Unpublished manuscript.

Mann, D. (1989). Incest: The father and the male therapist. *British Journal of Psychotherapy, 42,* 143–153.

Marmor, J. (1972). Sexual acting out in psychotherapy. *American Journal of Psychoanalysis, 22,* 3–8.

Martin, H. (1991). The coming-out process for homosexuals. *Hospital and Community Psychiatry, 42,* 158–162.

Masson, J. M. (1988). *Against therapy.* New York: Atheneum.

McKneely, D. (1987). *Touching: Body therapy and depth psychology.* Toronto, Ontario, Canada: Inner City Books.

McMinn, M. R. (1991). Religious values, sexist language, and perceptions of a therapist. *Journal of Psychology and Christianity, 10,* 132–136.

Mednick, M. T. (1989). On the politics of psychological constructs: Stop the bandwagon, I want to get off. *American Psychologist, 44,* 1118–1123.

Mintz, E. (1969). Touch and the psychoanalytic tradition. *Psychoanalytic Review, 56,* 365–376.

Mitchum, N. T. (1987). Developmental play therapy: A treatment approach for child victims of sexual molestation. *Journal of Counseling and Development, 65,* 320–321.

Morin, S. F., & Rothblum E. D. (1991). Removing the stigma: Fifteen years of progress. *American Psychologist, 46,* 947–949.

Munoz, R. F. (1985). Commentary. *Business and Professional Ethics Journal, 4,* 177–182.

Nash, E. A., Hoehn-Saric, R., Battle, C. C., Stone, A. R., Imber, S. B., & Frank, J. D. (1965). Systematic preparation of patients for short term psychotherapy: II. Relations to characteristics of patient, therapist, and the psychotherapeutic process. *Journal of Nervous and Mental Disease, 140,* 374–383.

Noel, B., & Watterson, K. (1992). *You must be dreaming.* New York: Poseidon Press.

Okun, B. (1989). Therapists' blind spots related to gender socialization. In D. Kantor & B. Okun (Eds.), *Intimate environments: Sex, intimacy, and gender in families* (pp. 129–162). New York: Guilford Press.

Orlinsky, D. E., & Geller, J. D. (in press). Psychotherapy's internal theater of operation: Patients' representations of their therapists and therapy as a new focus of research. In N. E. Miller, J. Docherty, L. Luborsky, & J. Barber (Eds.), *Psychodynamic treatment research.* New York: Basic Books.

Palombo, J. (1985). Self-psychology and countertransference in the treatment of children. *Child and Adolescent Social Work Journal, 2*, 36–48.

Pedersen, P. D., Draguns, J. G., Lonner, W. J., & Trimble, E. J. (1989). Introduction and overview. In P. D. Pedersen, J. G. Draguns, W. J. Lonner, & E. J. Trimble (Eds.), *Counseling across cultures* (3rd ed.; pp. 1–2). Honolulu: University of Hawaii Press.

Perls, F. S. (1969). *In and out of the garbage pail.* New York: Bantam.

Perls, F. S. (1973). *The gestalt approach & Eye witness to therapy.* New York: Science and Behavior Books.

Perls, F. S. (1988). *Gestalt therapy verbatim.* Highland, NY: Center for Gestalt Development. (Original work published 1969)

Person, E. (1985). The erotic transference in women and in men: Differences in consequences. *Journal of the American Academy of Psychoanalysis, 13*, 159–180.

Poggi, R., & Berland, D. (1985). The therapist's reactions to the elderly. *The Gerontologist, 25*, 508–513.

Pollock, G. (1973). Bertha Pappenheim: Addenda to her case history. *Journal of the American Psychoanalytic Association, 21*, 328–332.

Pope, K. S. (1990). Therapist–patient sex as sex abuse: Six scientific, professional, and practical dilemmas in addressing victimization and rehabilitation. *Professional Psychology: Research and Practice, 21*, 227–39.

Pope, K. S. (in press). Licensing disciplinary actions for psychologists who have been sexually involved with a client: Some information about offenders. *Professional Psychology: Research and Practice.*

Pope, K. S., & Bouhoutsos, J. C. (1986). *Sexual intimacies between therapists and patients.* New York: Praeger.

Pope, K. S., Butcher, J. N., & Seelen, J. (1993). *The MMPI, MMPI-2, and MMPI-A in court: Assessment, testimony, and cross-examination for expert witnesses and attorneys.* Washington, DC: American Psychological Association.

Pope, K. S., & Garcia-Peltoniemi, R. E. (1991). Responding to victims of torture: Clinical issues, professional responsibilities, and useful resources. *Professional Psychology: Research and Practice, 22*, 269–276.

Pope, K. S., Keith-Spiegel, P., & Tabachnick, B. G. (1986). Sexual attraction to patients: The human therapist and the (sometimes) inhuman training system. *American Psychologist, 41*, 147–158.

Pope, K. S., Levenson, H., & Schover, L. R. (1979). Sexual intimacy in psychology training: Results and implications of a national survey. *American Psychologist, 34*, 682–689.

Pope, K. S., & Tabachnick, B. G. (1993). Therapists' anger, hate, fear, and sexual feelings: National survey of therapist responses, client characteristics, critical events, formal complaints, and training. *Professional Psychology: Research and Practice, 24*, 142–152.

Pope, K. S., Tabachnick, B. G., & Keith-Spiegel, P. (1987). Ethics of practice: The beliefs and behaviors of psychologists as therapists. *American Psychologist, 42*, 993–1006.

Pope, K. S., & Vasquez, M. J. T. (1991). *Ethics in psychotherapy and counseling: A practical guide for psychologists.* San Francisco: Jossey-Bass.

Pope, K. S., & Vetter, V. A. (1991). Prior therapist–patient sexual involvement among patients seen by psychologists. *Psychotherapy, 28,* 429–438.

Rappaport, B. (1975). Carnal knowledge: What the wisdom of the body has to offer psychotherapy. *Journal of Humanistic Psychology, 15,* 49–70.

Redlich, F. C., & Kellert, S. R. (1978). Trends in American mental health. *American Journal of Psychiatry, 135,* 22–28.

Redlich, F. C., & Pope, K. S. (1980). Ethics of mental health training. *Journal of Nervous and Mental Disease, 168,* 709–714.

Reich, W. (1942). *The discovery of the orgone: The function of the orgasm* (T. Wolfe, Trans.). New York: Farrar, Straus & Giroux.

Reiser, D. E., & Levenson, H. (1984). Abuses of the borderline diagnosis: A clinical problem with teaching opportunities. *American Journal of Psychiatry, 141,* 1528–1532.

Religion in America (Report No. 236). (1985). Princeton, NJ: The Gallup Report.

Reyher, J. (1978). Emergent uncovering psychotherapy: The uses of imagoic and linguistic vehicles in objectifying psychodynamic processes. In J. L. Singer & K. S. Pope (Eds.), *The power of human imagination: New methods in psychotherapy* (pp. 51–93). New York: Plenum Press.

Roazen, P. (1971). *Freud and his followers.* New York: Da Capo Press.

Robinson, W. L., & Calhoun, K. S. (1982–1983). Sexual fantasies, attitudes and behavior as a function of race, gender and religiosity. *Imagination, Cognition and Personality, 2,* 281–290.

Russell, D. (1988). Language and psychotherapy: The influence of nonstandard English in clinical practice. In L. Comas-Diaz & E. Griffith (Eds.), *Clinical guidelines in cross-cultural mental health* (pp. 33–68). New York: Wiley.

Sarason, S. B. (1985). *Caring and compassion in clinical practice.* San Francisco: Jossey-Bass.

Schlachet, B. C. (1984). Female role socialization: The analyst and the analysis. In C. M. Bordy (Ed.), *Women therapists working with women: Theory and process of feminist therapy* (pp. 56–65). New York: Springer.

Schonbar, R., & Beatus, H. R. (1990). The mysterious metamorphoses of Bertha Pappenheim: Anna O. revisited. *Psychoanalytic Psychology, 7,* 59–78.

Schover, L. R. (1981). Male and female therapists' responses to male and female client sexual material: An analogue study. *Archives of Sexual Behavior, 10,* 477–492.

Schover, L. R. (1989). Sexual exploitation by sex therapists. In G. O. Gabbard (Ed.), *Sexual exploitation in professional relationships* (pp. 139–149). Washington, DC: American Psychiatric Press.

Schwartz, J. M., & Abramowitz, S. I. (1978). Effects of female client physical attractiveness on clinical judgment. *Psychotherapy, 15,* 251–257.

Searles, H. F. (1959). Oedipal love in the countertransference. *International Journal of Psychoanalysis, 40,* 180–190.

Sechehaye, M. A. (1951). *Symbolic realization*. Madison, CT: International Universities Press.

Shapiro, D. (1965). *Neurotic styles*. New York: Basic Books.

Shepard, M. (1971). *The love treatment: Sexual intimacy between patients and psychotherapists*. New York: Wyden.

Shepard, M. (1976). *Fritz*. New York: Bantam Books.

Shor, J., & Sanville, J. (1974). Erotic provocations and dalliances in psychotherapeutic practice: Some clinical cues for preventing and repairing therapist–patient collusion. *Clinical Social Work Journal, 2*, 83–95.

Spotnitz, H. (1972). Touch countertransference in group psychotherapy. *International Journal of Group Psychotherapy, 22*, 455–463.

Sprecher, S., & Hatfield, E. (1985). Interpersonal attraction. In G. Stricker & R. H. Keisner (Eds.), *From research to clinical practice: The implications of social and developmental research for psychotherapy* (pp. 179–216). San Francisco: Jossey-Bass.

Srole, L., Langner, T. S., Michael, S. T., Kirkpatric, P., Opler, M. K., & Rennie, T. A. C. (1977). *Mental health in the metropolis: The Midtown Manhattan Study, Book II*. New York: Harper Torchbooks.

Stein, T. (1988). Theoretical considerations in psychotherapy with gay men and lesbians. *Journal of Homosexuality, 15*, 75–95.

Stephan, W., Berscheid, E., & Walster, E. (1971). Sexual arousal and heterosexual perception. *Journal of Personality and Social Psychology, 20*, 93–101.

Stone, A. (1990, March). No good deed goes unpunished. *Psychiatric Times*, pp. 24–27.

Stone, M. T. (1982). Turning points in therapy. In S. Slipp (Ed.), *Curative factors in dynamic psychotherapy* (pp. 259–279). New York: McGraw-Hill.

Stricker, G. (1991). How people change: A brief commentary. In R. C. Curtis & G. Stricker (Eds.), *How people change: Inside and outside therapy* (pp. 211–214). New York: Plenum Press.

Strupp, H. S. (1980). Humanism and psychotherapy: A personal statement of the therapist's essential values. *Psychotherapy: Theory, Research and Practice, 17*, 396–400.

Sue, D. W. (1981). *Counseling the culturally different: Theory and practice*. New York: Wiley.

Tavris, C. (1992). *The mismeasure of woman*. New York: Simon & Schuster.

Thompson, C. (1950). *Psychoanalysis: Its evolution and development*. New York: Hermitage House.

Unger, R. K. (1979). *Female and male*. New York: Harper & Row.

Unger, R. K., & Crawford, M. (1992). *Women and gender*. New York: McGraw-Hill.

Walster, E., Aronson, V., Abrahams, D., & Rottman, L. (1966). The importance of physical attractiveness in dating behavior. *Journal of Personality and Social Psychology, 4*, 508–516.

Walster, E., & Walster, G. W. (1978). *A new look at love*. Reading, MA: Addison-Wesley.

Weiner, M. F. (1978). *Therapist disclosure: The use of self in psychotherapy*. Woburn, MA: Butterworths Press.

Weisberg, J., & Haberman, M. (1989). A therapeutic hugging week in a geriatric facility. *Journal of Gerontological Social Work, 13*, 181–186.

Williams, J. (1980, March 29). Milton H. Erickson, hypnosis authority. *New York Times*, p. 28.

Williams, L. F. (1972). Sex, racism, and social work. In H. L. Gochros & L. G. Schultz (Eds.), *Human sexuality and social work* (pp. 75–81). New York: Association Press.

Word, C., Zanna, M. P., & Cooper, J. (1974). The nonverbal mediation of self-fulfilling prophesies in interracial interaction. *Journal of Experimental Social Psychology, 10*, 109–120.

Wright, R. H. (1985). The Wright way: Who needs enemies? *Psychotherapy in Private Practice, 3*, 111–118.

Zager, K. (1990). The case. In D. W. Cantor (Ed.), *Women as therapists: A multitheoretical casebook* (pp. 145–152). Northvale, NJ: Jason Aronson.

Zicherman, V. (1984). Sociocultural considerations and the emergence of sexual feelings in male patients seeing female therapists. *Journal of the American Academy of Psychoanalysis, 12*, 545–551.

Zwerner, J. (1982). Yes, we have troubles but nobody's listening: Sexual issues of women with spinal cord injury. *Sexuality and Disability, 5*, 158–171.

Appendixes

Appendix A
Sexual Attraction to Clients: The Human Therapist and the (Sometimes) Inhuman Training System

Kenneth S. Pope, Patricia Keith-Spiegel, and Barbara G. Tabachnick

Abstract: Although we currently possess considerable information about the incidence and consequences of sexually intimate relationships between psychotherapists and clients, there is virtually no documentation of the extent to which psychotherapists are sexually attracted to clients, how they react to and handle such feelings, and the degree to which their training is adequate in this regard. "Feelings" toward clients are generally relegated to vague and conflicting discussions of countertransference, without benefit of systematic research. Survey data from 575 psychotherapists reveal that 87% (95% of men, 76% of women) have been sexually attracted to their clients, at least on occasion, and that, although only a minority (9.4% of men and 2.5% of women) have acted out such feelings, many (63%) feel guilty, anxious, or confused about the attraction. About half of the respondents did not receive any guidance or training concerning this issue, and only 9% reported that their training or supervision was adequate. Implications for the development of educational resources to address this subject are discussed.

Although the primary focus of this article is the presentation of data concerning therapists' sexual attraction to their clients

Reprinted from the *American Psychologist* (1986), *41*, 147–158. Citations that were in press in the original article have been updated.

and the implications for education and training, the context within which this research was conducted should be noted. Sexually intimate behavior between therapists and their clients has emerged as an increasingly serious problem within the profession, as revealed by an examination of the records in three arenas—ethics cases, malpractice suits, and licensing board hearings.

Ethics cases concerning therapist–client sex have only recently begun to proliferate, but ethical standards prohibiting this activity date back at least as far as the Hippocratic Oath: "In every house where I come, I will enter only for the good of my patients, keeping myself far from all intentional ill-doing and all seduction, and especially from the pleasures of love with women and men" (*Dorland's Medical Dictionary*, 1974, p. 715). The American Psychological Association (APA), however, did not explicitly prohibit sexual intimacies with clients until the late 1970s (APA, 1977). Despite the recency of this explicit prohibition, the most frequently filed ethics complaints are related to Principle 6a ("Sexual intimacies with clients are unethical") of the *Ethical Principles for Psychologists* (APA, 1981). The APA Ethics Committee has been investigating about 30 cases during the past year, a substantial increase over the 14 such cases in 1981 and the 21 such cases in 1982 (D. Mills, personal communication, February 6, 1984).

Similarly, during the last 15 years, malpractice cases have shown a sharp increase. About 1 out of every 10 malpractice suits handled through the APA insurance trust involves allegations of sexual misconduct (Wright, 1981). Asher (1976) reported that the previous insurance carrier had declined to provide further coverage to psychologists because sexual intimacy cases had accounted for 5 of the approximately 45 claims since the start of coverage in 1974. Yet as late as 1970, the courts had neither examined nor ruled upon the liability of a psychologist who engaged in therapist–client sexual intimacy (O'Byrne, 1970).

In a third arena, licensing, complaints concerning therapist–client sexual intimacy have recently become a focus both of the activity of the state psychology boards and of the consequent civil litigation reviewing the boards' authority. States differ in the degree to which they regulate the practice of psychology, as well as in the ways in which they monitor violations of those regulations. In California, however, therapist–client sexual intimacy is currently the basis for 56% of disciplinary actions taken by the Psychology Examining Committee (Vinson, 1984). The psychology licensing boards' authority to take actions regarding therapist–client sexual relations involving psychologists (and, with few exceptions, other therapists) was not upheld by the courts until the 1970s. For instance, as late as 1965, the Colorado Supreme Court, in *Colorado State Board of Medical Examiners v. Weiler* (1965), thwarted the board's attempt to revoke a therapist's license for his allegedly creating a treatment plan involving intercourse for his female patient with himself as her partner. In *Morra v. State Board of Examiners of Psychologists* (1973), however, the Kansas Supreme Court affirmed the right of the board to revoke the license of a psychologist who had tried to persuade two of his patients to engage in sexual intimacies with him. Likewise, in *Cooper v. Board of Medical Examiners* (1975), a California Appellate Court upheld the right of the board to revoke a psychology license primarily on the basis of sexual intimacies between the psychologist and three patients.

There was only one attempt prior to the 1970s to conduct systematic empirical studies of the actual behavior of therapists in this regard. In 1938, Glover (1955) surveyed members of the British Psycho-analytical Society. The form was extraordinarily long, complex, and detailed (yet yielded an 83% return rate), inquiring into virtually all aspects of the members' work and relationships with their patients. There was no report of analyst–patient sexual intimacy. In fact, virtually all respondents reported "avoidance of social ('fringe') contact during analytical sessions" and "limitation of small talk" (p. 345). Over two thirds of the sample reported that they took special measures to avoid extra-analytical contact during analysis.

Forer, in an unpublished 1968 survey (B. Forer, personal communication, November 8, 1984) of the members of the Los Angeles County Psychological Association, found that 17% of the men in private practice indicated that they had engaged in therapist–client sexual intimacies, whereas no such sexual experiences were reported by women in private practice or by men working in institutional settings. Kardener, Fuller, and Mensh (1973) surveyed the male members of the Los Angeles County Medical Society. Ten percent of the subsample of psychiatrists reported engaging in erotic contact with clients, with 5% reporting sexual intercourse.

There have been two recent national studies of therapist–client sex, both limiting their sample to psychologists. Holroyd and Brodsky (1977) found that 7.7% of their sample of psychologists conducting psychotherapy "answered positively any of the questions regarding erotic-contact behaviors or intercourse during treatment" (pp. 847–848). Pope, Levenson, and Schover (1979) found that 7% of their sample of psychologists conducting psychotherapy reported engaging in sexual intimacies with their clients. Overall, the initial evidence suggests a rate of about 5% to 10% of psychotherapists engaging in sexual intimacies with their clients.

Despite dated, isolated claims about the benefits—or at least lack of harm—associated with therapist–client sex (McCartney, 1966; Romeo, 1978; Shepard, 1971), research has shown the destructive consequences of such behavior. Basing her analysis on an original study and a review of previous research (such as Belote, 1974; Chesler, 1972; Dahlberg, 1971; Taylor & Wagner, 1976), Durre (1980) concluded that "amatory and sexual interaction between client and therapist dooms the potential for successful therapy and is detrimental if not devastating to the client" (p. 243). Durre's research cited

> many instance of suicide attempts, severe depressions (some lasting months), mental hospitalizations, shock treatment, and separations or divorces from husbands. . . . Women reported being fired from or having to leave their jobs because of pressure and ineffectual working habits caused by their depression, crying spells, anger, and anxiety. (p. 242)

In a more recent study, Bouhoutsos, Holroyd, Lerman, Forer, and Greenberg (1983) found that in 90% of the reported cases of therapist–client sexual intimacies, clients were damaged (according to their subsequent therapists). The harm ranged from inability to trust and hesitation about seeking further help from

health (or other) professionals, to severe depressions, hospi-
talizations, and suicide.

The sequelae of a patient's sexual relationship with a therapist
may form a distinct syndrome, with both acute and chronic
phases (Pope, 1985, 1986). Aspects of the Therapist–Patient Sex
Syndrome include cognitive dysfunction (especially in the areas
of attention and concentration, frequently involving flashbacks,
intrusive thoughts, and unbidden images), identity and boundary disturbance, ambivalence, lability of mood (frequently involving severe depression), inability to trust (often focused on
conflicts about dependence, control, and power), sexual confusion, suppressed rage, and feelings of guilt and emptiness.
For long periods of time, the patient may be at substantial
suicidal risk. The syndrome appears to bear similarities to various aspects of borderline (and histrionic) personality disorder,
posttraumatic stress disorder, rape response syndrome, reaction to incest, and reaction to child or spouse battering.

We have begun to explore instances in which a psychologist
"acts out" a sexual attraction to a client and thus violates the
prohibition. But, especially in terms of research, we know virtually nothing about the attraction itself. What seems to cause
this attraction? How frequently does it occur among all therapists, not just those who become sexually intimate with their
clients? Do therapists feel uncomfortable, guilty, or anxious
when they notice such attraction? Do they tell their clients? Do
they consult with their colleagues? Why do therapists refrain
from "acting out" this attraction (in cases when they do refrain)?
In what instances is it useful and beneficial to the therapy? In
what instances is it harmful or an impediment? Do therapists
believe that their graduate training provided adequate education regarding attraction to clients?

The primary purposes of this article are to raise such questions, to initiate serious discussion and research by providing
data, and to examine implications for psychology training.

Views on Therapists' Attractions to Clients

When the subject of therapist–client attraction has been addressed in the literature—unfortunately in the absence of sys-

tematic research—the discussion has been almost exclusively in terms of transference and countertransference.[1] In her review of this literature, Tower (1956) noted that virtually every writer on the subject of countertransference stated unequivocally that no form of erotic reaction to a patient is to be tolerated.

Within the psychoanalytic framework, a therapist's attraction to a client was originally seen as a reaction to the client's transference. In 1915, Freud stressed that the patient's transference must be understood as a specific therapeutic phenomenon not identical to the experience of "falling in love" as it occurs outside the context of therapy. The analyst

> must recognize that the patient's falling in love is induced by the analytic situation and is not to be ascribed to the charms of his person, that he has no reason whatsoever therefore to be proud of such a "conquest," as it would be called outside analysis. (Freud, 1915/1963, p. 169)

Freud wrote that he emphasized this phenomenon of "transference love" because it "occurs so often" (p. 167), because "it is so important in reality and . . . its theoretical interest" (p. 167), and because his writings on the subject could provide the analyst with "a useful warning against any tendency to countertransference which may be lurking in his own mind" (p. 169).

---

[1]Efforts were made to find theoretical literature, outside the psychodynamic framework, addressing this subject. For example, a large range of articles concerning behavioral and cognitive therapy had been recently collected for a review chapter (Levenson & Pope, 1984), but none addressed sexual attraction to clients. To strengthen our attempts to locate a nonpsychodynamic literature concerning therapists' sexual attraction to their clients, we contacted psychologists familiar with a range of approaches to psychotherapy or with particular knowledge of the cognitive–behavioral orientations, among them L. E. Beutler, A. E. Kazdin, D. H. Meichenbaum, J. L. Singer, and H. H. Strupp. We also contacted psychologists familiar with the theoretical and research literature on therapist-client sexual intimacy, among them J. C. Bouhoutsos, A. M. Brodsky, J. C. Holroyd, and J. L. Sonne. None was aware of a nonpsychodynamic theoretical literature concerning therapists' sexual attraction to clients (Personal communications, April 8 and 9, 1985).

This countertransference that Freud felt the analyst must be warned against was a reaction to the patient's transference rather than to the patient himself or herself. Kernberg (1975) stated the classical definition of countertransference as "the unconscious reaction of the psychoanalyst to the patient's transference" (p. 50). That is, in the same way that the analyst could not ascribe the patient's love to "the charms of his person," the analyst's response was not to the "charms of the patient" but rather a reaction to the transference.

Freud believed strongly that this countertransference must never be acted out.

> If her advances were returned, it would be a great triumph for the patient, but a complete overthrow for the cure. . . . The love-relationship actually destroys the influence of the analytic treatment on the patient; a combination of the two would be an inconceivable thing. (Freud, 1915/1963, p. 174)

The classical view of countertransference, as first set forth by Freud, became the predominant view. The defining characteristics were as follows: (a) The therapist's reaction is irrational or distorting—that is, a transference; and (b) the therapist is reacting to the client's transference.

Proponents of the classical view are numerous. Grossman (1965), for example, proposed that "the word countertransference be limited to mean only one thing: reaction to transference" (p. 252). Ruesch (1961) maintained:

> Countertransference is transference in reverse. The therapist's unresolved conflicts force him to invest the patient with certain properties which bear upon his own past experiences rather than to constitute reactions to the patient's actual behavior. All that was said about transference, therefore, also applies to countertransference, with the addition that it is the transference of the patient which triggers into existence the countertransference of the therapist. (p. 175)

In a similar vein, Greenson (1967) wrote,

> Errors due to countertransference arise when the analyst reacts to his patient as though the patient were a significant

person in the analyst's early history. Countertransference is
a transference reaction of an analyst to a patient, a parallel
to transference, a counterpart of transference. (p. 348)

The development of this conceptualization regarding countertransference had a number of implications for the conceptualization of a therapist's attraction to a client. First, the attraction was viewed as countertransference. Second, because
countertransference represented the therapist's own transference, the therapist was involved in a distortion (seeing the client
in terms of a figure or conflict from the therapist's past) of which
he or she was unaware. Third, because the countertransference
was an inappropriate or irrational response to the client's transference, the therapist was, in effect, "mishandling" the transference phenomenon. As a result, a therapist's attraction to a
client became, almost by definition, a therapeutic error, something to hide and to be ashamed of.

The work of Winnicott (1949), Heimann (1950), and Little
(1951) has formed the impetus, over the last 35 years, for a
substantial literature asserting that countertransference, correctly managed, is a valuable therapeutic resource (e.g., Singer,
1970; Tauber, 1979; Weiner, 1975). However, the idea that countertransference, despite its positive potential, also constitutes
a weakness or error antithetical to the goals of therapy remains
widespread. Typical writings assert that countertransference
reactions are "undesirable and the analysis would be better off
without them" (Baum, 1969–1970, p. 635); that "countertransference is by definition a distraction from an important goal of
psychotherapy" (Weiner, 1978, p. 185); and that the phenomenon comprises "not only the analyst's personal neurotic tendencies . . . but also . . . blind spots and limiting factors" (Cohen
& Farrell, 1984, p. 26). Langs (1973) developed the thesis that
virtually all mistakes committed by well-trained and experienced therapists are caused directly by countertransference.
"Unrecognized countertransference is the single most frequent
basis for therapeutic failure. It is countertransference, rather
than transference . . . , that is by far the hardest part of analysis—and therapy" (Langs, 1982, p. 132). Taken as a whole,
the literature indicates that the failure to acknowledge and ex-

amine countertransference blocks its therapeutic potential and unleashes its destructive effects. Consequently, to the degree that sexual attraction is considered countertransference, it is particularly regrettable when training systems fail to promote the acknowledgment and examination of this phenomenon.

Interestingly, this psychodynamic conceptualization of the client's attraction to the therapist as transference, the therapist's attraction to the client as countertransference, and the necessity of avoiding a therapist–client "love affair" so that the transference can be adequately handled and the treatment can continue, have found their way into our legal standards. In *Zipkin v. Freeman* (1968), a female plaintiff had been referred to a psychiatrist for treatment of headaches and diarrhea. According to court records, the symptoms were gone after a couple of months, but the woman agreed to continue treatment in order to get at the underlying causes of her difficulties. She came to feel more and more affectionate toward her therapist. She claimed that when she told him she was in love with him, he said that the feeling was mutual. According to her testimony, the therapist advised her to leave her husband and live in a room above the therapist's office. (She later moved to a farm in which the therapist had invested.) She recounted that they engaged in sex together, that they traveled outside the state together, and that she attended "group therapy" that involved nude swimming. On the basis of these and other allegations, the psychiatrist was successfully sued for malpractice.

In writing his opinion for the majority of the Missouri Supreme Court in this case, Judge Seiler stated,

> The gravamen of the petition is that the defendant did not treat Mrs. Zipkin properly and as a result she was injured. He mishandled the transference phenomenon, which is a reaction the psychiatrists anticipate and which must be handled properly. (*Zipkin v. Freeman*, 1968, p. 761)

The judge expanded this theme:

> Once Dr. Freeman started to mishandle the transference phenomenon, with which he was plainly charged in the petition

and which is overwhelmingly shown in the evidence, it was inevitable that trouble was ahead. It is pretty clear from the medical evidence that the damage would have been done to Mrs. Zipkin even if the trips outside the state were carefully chaperoned, the swimming done with suits on, and if there had been ballroom dancing instead of sexual relations. (*Zipkin v. Freeman*, 1968, p. 761)

The case of *Zipkin v. Freeman* has two important implications. First, it conceptualizes the therapist–client sexual intimacy in terms of transference and the therapist's handling of that transference. Thus, therapists—even those whose theoretical orientation does not include the transference concept—may be held accountable for the inappropriate handling of a phenomenon that they may view as an invalid concept or at least one with minimal importance for therapy. Second, in discussing therapist–client sexual intimacy in terms of the therapist's responsibility to handle appropriately the transference, the court indicated that even less extreme expressions of the therapist's attraction to the patient (e.g., swimming, dancing) may constitute malpractice.

The mental health professions, despite the citations mentioned above, seem to shy away from dealing in an honest, open way with the phenomenon of sexual attraction to clients. Yet, it should be, in our opinion, a central issue in the training of psychotherapists. In addition, the distinctly negative view regarding attraction to clients has led many therapists to develop what Tower (1956) termed "countertransference anxieties." These anxieties have affected the ways in which therapists relate to their patients and conduct therapy. For example, Thompson (1950) stated that

> because of the stress on the unfortunate aspects of the analyst's involvement, the feeling grew that even a genuine objective feeling of friendliness on his part was to be suspected. As a result many of Freud's pupils became afraid to be simply human and show the ordinary friendliness and interest a therapist customarily feels for a patient. In many

cases, out of a fear of showing counter-transference, the attitude of the analyst became stilted and unnatural. (p. 107)

A stilted, unnatural manner and the suppression of ordinary friendliness and interest are but a few of the detrimental effects of making attraction to clients taboo. In many cases, clients may be punished for their sexual feelings. Fine (1965) described how a therapist, reacting inappropriately to the strong sexual desire of the patient, may harmfully misdiagnose the patient. In other cases the therapist may be held to blame for the client's sexual feelings. Kaplan (1977) wrote, "If one of our trainees reports more than once a year an erotic response on the part of the patient, we assume that he is doing something seductive, something countertransferential that is outside of his awareness" (p. 186). In still other cases, the taboo on attraction may influence therapists' choice of clients. The data of Abramowitz, Abramowitz, Roback, Corney, and McKee (1976), for instance, suggested that female therapists actively avoid treating attractive male clients.

In such an antilibidinal atmosphere, it is little wonder that even such an experienced, well-respected, authoritative therapist as Searles described the courage it required for him to publish his work concerning genital excitement during analytic hours as well as erotic and romantic dreams about patients. "I reacted to such feelings with considerable anxiety, guilt, and embarassment" (Searles, 1959/1965, p. 290). An analogue study by Schover (1981) found male therapists reacting "with anxiety and verbal avoidance of the material" (p. 477) when a female "client" discussed sexual material.

If such feelings are intimidating for experienced therapists, they pose an even greater problem for therapists in training. Tower (1956) described the erotic feelings and impulses that she believed virtually all therapists feel toward their patients, and the fears and conflicts regarding these feelings that lead therapists to withhold discussing the attraction with their own therapists or supervisors. In discussing supervision in training institutions, Lehrman (1960) maintained that "such guilt-ridden erotic feelings are a major, if not the major, problem of young male psychotherapists treating attractive female patients" (p. 546).

Given the taboos against acknowledging attraction to a client, the lack of virtually any systematic research in the area is understandable. Yet it is dismaying. An understanding of this phenomenon, based upon empirical data, could form a crucial but long-neglected part of our training as psychologists.

Most graduate programs have not dealt with this issue (Holroyd, 1983; Kenworthy, Koufacos, & Sherman, 1976; Landis, Miller & Wettstone, 1975). Indeed, the sexual attraction experienced between those involved in the training programs themselves may be a troublesome and difficult-to-address part of the problem. Research by Pope, Levenson, and Schover (1979) revealed that, nationwide, 10% of the students within psychology graduate training programs engaged in sexual relationships with their teachers and clinical supervisors. One out of four recent female graduates had engaged in such sexual relationships. Thirteen percent of the educators engaged in relationships with their students and supervisees. Only 2%, however, believed that such relationships could be beneficial to trainees and educators. These practices present a variety of serious clinical, ethical, and legal dilemmas for psychology educators and students (Pope, Schover, & Levenson, 1980).

The extent to which such relationships exert a "modeling effect" for later professional behavior as a therapist awaits more systematic research. However, the initial research (Pope, Levenson, & Schover, 1979) produced preliminary evidence suggesting the possibility of just such a consequence. For women, sexual contact as students was related to later sexual contact as professionals. That is, 23% of the women who had had sexual contact with their educators also reported later sexual contact with their clients, whereas only 6% of those who had had no sexual contact with their educators had sexual contact as professionals with clients. The sample of men who had had sexual contact with their educators was too small to test the relationship to later sexual contact as professionals with clients.

The profession of psychology would benefit from a careful examination of the attraction therapists feel for their clients. Teaching, theory, and practice with regard to this issue are currently uninformed by research. The study reported in the following sections represents an attempt to gather some initial information.

Method Used

A cover letter, a brief 17-item questionnaire (15 structured questions and 2 open-ended questions), and a return envelope were sent to 1,000 psychologists (500 men and 500 women) randomly selected from the 4,356 members of Division 42 (Psychologists in Private Practice) as listed in the 1983 APA Membership Register. The anonymous questionnaires were numbered in the order received and transferred to a data file for statistical analysis.

The questionnaire requested respondents to provide information about their gender, age group, and years of experience in the field. Information was elicited about the respondents' incidence of sexual attraction to male and female clients; reactions to this experience of attraction; beliefs about the clients' awareness of and reciprocation of the attraction; the impact of the attraction on the therapy process; how such feelings were managed; the incidence of sexual fantasies about clients; why, if relevant, respondents chose to refrain from acting out their attraction through actual sexual intimacies with clients; what features determined which clients would be perceived as sexually attractive; incidence of actual sexual activity with clients; and the extent to which the respondents' graduate training and internship experiences had dealt with issues related to sexual attraction to clients.

Results of the Study

Demographic Characteristics

Questionnaires were returned by 585 respondents (58.5%). Of these, 339 (or 57.9% of the sample) were men, and 246 (or 42.1% of the sample) were women.

The return-rate difference between male and female respondents was significant, $\chi^2(1, N = 1,000) = 35.62, p < .001$. Sixty-eight percent of the male respondents returned their questionnaires as compared to 49% of the female respondents. The differential return rate resulted in a male-to-female therapist ratio of about 1.4:1. In an effort to shed light on the reason for this differential return rate, we sent a brief follow-up letter three months later to 100 female respondents randomly selected from the original survey sample, requesting information about their response to the questionnaire; if they had not returned the questionnaire, we asked why. The responses of the 40 female psychologists who responded only to the follow-up were not very helpful in illuminating the reasons for the discrepancy. The single most common response was "too busy."

Approximately half (48.9%) of the respondents were between the ages of 30 and 45; 39.0% were between 46 and 60; and 12.1% were over 60 years of age. For purposes of descriptive convenience, respondents 45 years of age and under are designated as the "younger therapists" and those 46 and over are designated as the "older therapists." Two hundred and eighty-six respondents (172 men and 114 women) were younger therapists; 299 respondents (167 men and 132 women) were older therapists. This age distribution can be compared with the VandenBos and Stapp (1983) survey of mental health service providers, in which the median age for various subgroups ranged from 39.1 to 46.3 years. Their sample's pooled median was approximately 40 years; our sample's median age was approximately 46 years.

Respondents averaged 16.99 ($SD = 8.43$) years of professional experience, with no significant differences between male and female psychologists. Younger therapists averaged 11.36 ($SD = 3.93$) years of experience, and older therapists averaged 21.79 ($SD = 8.13$) years of experience.

Rate of Therapists' Sexual Attraction to Male and Female Psychotherapy Clients

Only 77 of the 585 respondents reported never being attracted to any client. Significantly more therapists, then, were attracted

Table 1

Therapists' Attraction to Male and Female Clients

	\multicolumn{2}{c}{None}		\multicolumn{2}{c}{Male only}		\multicolumn{2}{c}{Female only}		Both male and female	

Type of client to whom therapist is attracted

Therapists	None N	None %	Male only N	Male only %	Female only N	Female only %	Both male and female N	Both male and female %
All men	17	5.0	2	0.6	275	81.1	45	13.3
Younger	7	4.1	1	0.6	140	81.4	24	13.9
Older	10	6.0	1	0.6	135	80.8	21	12.6
All women	60	24.4	123	50.0	6	2.4	57	23.2
Younger	14	12.3	61	53.5	1	0.9	38	33.3
Older	46	34.8	62	47.0	5	3.8	19	14.4

to at least one client than not, $\chi^2(1, N = 585) = 317.54$, $p <$ .003.[2] Among the 508 who were attracted, 125 reported attraction to male clients only, 281 to female clients only, and 102 to both male and female clients. Table 1 presents the frequencies and percentages of attractions for the sex and age groups of the therapists.

---

[2]Most of the analyses in this article utilized 3-way tests of association (logit) analyses. These were used to evaluate the response categories as a function of sex and age (under 45 and over 45 years of age) categories. Of interest were the 3-way associations among response, age, and sex; the 2-way associations between response and sex and between response and age; and the test for equal frequency of the use of response categories. In all planned analyses, we used the more conservative tests for each effect at $p < .003$ to compensate for the increased probability of Type-I error with multiple tests. Similarly, ANOVA results were evaluated at $p < .003$. For post hoc comparisons, the significance level was set at $p < .001$.

Table 2 describes in detail the frequencies and percentages of attraction to male and female clients by male and female therapists.

A 2 × 2 × 2 between-within-within unweighted means AN-OVA was performed on therapist rate of attraction to clients as a function of therapist age category (younger and older), sex of therapist, and sex of client. The rating scale was based on frequency of attraction. Respondents indicating that they were never attracted to a client received a 1, respondents who were rarely attracted (operationally defined as once or twice in the

Table 2

Therapists' Frequency of Attraction to Clients

| | Frequency of attraction | | | | | | | |
| | Never | | Rarely | | Occasionally | | Frequently | |
Clients	N	%	N	%	N	%	N	%
Female clients								
All men	19	5.6	94	27.8	172	50.9	53	15.7
Younger	8	4.7	44	25.7	92	53.8	27	15.8
Older	11	6.6	50	29.9	80	47.9	26	15.6
All women	181	74.2	51	20.9	11	4.5	1	0.4
Younger	73	65.2	29	25.9	9	8.0	1	0.9
Older	108	81.8	22	16.7	2	1.5	0	0.0
Male clients								
All men	288	86.0	35	10.4	9	2.7	3	0.9
Younger	146	85.4	19	11.1	4	2.3	2	1.2
Older	142	86.6	16	9.8	5	3.0	1	0.6
All women	66	26.8	101	41.1	76	30.9	3	1.2
Younger	15	13.2	51	44.7	46	40.3	2	1.8
Older	51	38.6	50	37.9	30	22.7	1	0.8

survey form) received a 2, those who were occasionally attracted (operationally defined as 3 to 10 times) received a 3, and frequently attracted therapists (operationally defined as more than 10 times) received a 4. Results indicated that male therapists were significantly more often attracted to clients (mean rating = 1.98) than were female therapists (M = 1.70), $F(1, 575)$ = 41.00, $p <$ .003, that younger therapists were significantly more often attracted to clients (M = 1.94) than were older therapists (M = 1.74), $F(1, 575)$ = 22.32, $p <$ .003, and that therapists generally were more attracted to female (M = 2.16) than to male (M = 1.55) clients, $F(1, 575)$ = 135.29, $p <$ .003. An expected significant interaction between therapists' sex and the sex of clients to whom the therapists were attracted indicated that male therapists were more often attracted to female (M = 2.77) than male (M = 1.18) clients and female therapists were more often attracted to male (M = 2.08) than female (M = 1.32) clients, $F(1, 575)$ = 1877.79, $p <$ .003. An additional interaction between the sex of the therapists and the age of the therapists indicated a larger sex difference in rate of attraction for older therapists, $F(1, 575)$ = 10.68, $p <$ .003. Younger therapists of both sexes differed little in their rate of attraction to clients (M = 2.01 for male therapists; M = 1.88 for female therapists). But among older therapists, the older women were less often attracted to clients (M = 1.53) than were the older men (M = 1.95).

Contemplation of Sexual Involvement With Clients, Fantasies, and Actual Involvement

The vast majority of respondents (82%) reported that they had never seriously considered actual sexual involvement with a client, $\chi^2(1, N = 581)$ = 259.44, $p <$ .003. Of the 104 therapists who had considered sexual involvement, 91 had considered it only once or twice. Male therapists had considered sexual involvement with clients more than had female therapists (27% vs. 5%), $\chi^2(1, N = 581)$ = 51.85, $p <$ .003. Therapists did not differ significantly according to age.

A content analysis was performed on responses to an open-ended question, "In instances when you were attracted [to a client] but did not become sexually involved, why did you refrain from the involvement?" Many respondents offered more than one reason, with the result that there were 1,091 separate content items. Table 3 lists the major reasons offered in order of frequency mentioned. Patterns were proportionately similar for male and female therapists except for two categories, fear of retaliation by clients and the illegality factor, which were offered only by male therapists as reasons for not acting out sexual feelings toward clients.

Respondents were asked, "While engaging in sexual activity with someone other than a client, have you ever had sexual fantasies about someone who is or was a client?" Most therapists (71.3%) reported that they never had such fantasies, $\chi^2(1, N = 513) = 183.1$, $p < .003$. Such fantasies were reported to have occurred rarely by 19.3%, occasionally by 8.6%, and frequently by 0.7%. Male therapists reported having more sexual

Table 3

Reasons Offered for Refraining From Sexual Intimacies With Clients

Content category	Frequency
Unethical	289
Countertherapeutic/exploitative	251
Unprofessional practice	134
Against therapists' personal values	133
Therapist already in a committed relationship	67
Fear of censure/loss of reputation	48
Damaging to therapist	43
Disrupts handling of transference/countertransference	28
Fear of retaliation by client	19
Attraction too weak/short-lived	18
Illegal	13
Self-control	8
Common sense	8
Miscellaneous	32

fantasies about clients than did female therapists (27% vs. 14%), $\chi^2(1, N = 513) = 12.55, p < .003$. Younger therapists were more likely to have had such fantasies about clients than were older therapists (28% vs. 14%), $\chi^2(1, N = 513) = 13.58, p < .003$.

The vast majority of respondents (93.5%) have never acted out sexually with their clients, $\chi^2(1, N = 569) = 515.02, p < .003$. Sexual intimacies with clients occurred rarely (once or twice) for 5.6% of the sample, occasionally (3 to 10 instances) for 0.7%, and frequently (more than 10 times) for 0.2% (one respondent). Male therapists engaged in sexual intimacies with clients more often than did female therapists (9.4% vs. 2.5%), $\chi^2(1, N = 569) = 11.94, p < .003$.

Characteristics of Clients to Whom Therapists Are Sexually Attracted

Client characteristics that elicited feelings of sexual attraction from therapists were assessed by an open-ended question: "How would you describe the clients to whom you've been attracted? Are there any particular salient qualities or similarities among them?" Fifty-nine respondents who did report being sexually attracted to clients indicated that they could not discern any particular similarities or stated that they were the same characteristics they found sexually attractive in people who were not clients, but they did not elaborate what these were.

Over 80% of the respondents who reported being attracted to clients did offer one or more characteristics. The 997 descriptive items were sorted into 19 content categories presented in order of frequency as Table 4. Male and female therapists' responses were fairly balanced proportionately for all of the categories except two. "Physical attractiveness" was mentioned far more often by men (209 times) than by women (87 times), and "successful" was mentioned more often by women (27 times) than by men (6 times).

Therapist Assessment of and Reactions to Client Attraction

Respondents who reported attraction to clients were asked if sexual attraction toward clients had ever been beneficial to the

Table 4

Characteristics of Clients to Whom Psychotherapists Are Attracted

Characteristic	Frequency
Physical attractiveness (beautiful, healthy looking, athletic, nicely dressed, etc.)	296
Positive mental/cognitive traits or abilities (intelligent, articulate, insightful, creative, well-educated, etc.)	124
Sexual (sexy, sexual ideal, sexually active, sexual material discussed in therapy, etc.)	88
Vulnerabilities (needy, childlike, sensitive, fragile, etc.)	85
Positive overall character/personality (pleasant, good character, well-mannered, stylish, interesting, without significant pathology, positive outlook, etc.)	84
Kind (nice, warm, open, loving attitude toward children, etc.)	66
Fills therapist's needs (accepting, supportive, boosts therapist's image, touches therapist's vulnerabilities, fills needs for power, alleviates therapist's depression, pressures at home, loneliness, needs for intimacy, etc.)	46
Successful (accomplished, wealthy, from a good background, etc.)	33
"Good patient" (works well in or responds well to therapy, responsible, gratifying to work with, good therapeutic relationship, etc.)	31
Client's attraction (awareness of client being attracted to therapist and/or client's attraction to men or women generally)	30
Independence (self-sufficient, nonconforming, strong, confident, assertive, etc.)	23
Specific personality characteristics not falling into other categories (pleasure-oriented, honest, workaholic, funny, introverted, etc.)	14
Resemblance to someone in therapist's life (like mother, father, spouse, lover, someone from past, etc.)	12
Availability (client unattached)	9
Pathological characteristics (hysterical, low self-esteem, paranoid, narcissistic, severely disturbed, etc.)	8
Long-term client (attraction as part of the nature of long-term psychotherapy)	7
Sociability (sociable, extraverted, etc.)	6
Miscellaneous (close to termination, intimate feelings, client is also a psychologist, age specification, etc.)	15

therapy process. More therapists (69%) than not said that their sexual attraction had been beneficial in at least some instances, $\chi^2(1, N = 464) = 66.87, p < .003$. There was a tendency for male therapists to report more beneficial effects than did female therapists (73% vs. 60%), $\chi^2(1, N = 464) = 8.17, p = .004$.

Regarding potential negative effects, respondents were asked if their sexual attraction had ever been harmful or an impediment to the therapy process. Half (49.3%) of the therapists indicated that their sexual attraction had, at least on occasion, exerted a negative influence. Female therapists were more likely than male therapists to report that their sexual attraction was never harmful (60% vs. 44%), $\chi^2(1, N = 485) = 12.98, p < .003$. Younger and older therapists did not differ significantly in this respect.

A post hoc comparison revealed that the significant sex-by-harm interaction was eliminated if those who believed that the clients were aware of the therapist's attraction were selected out and compared on the negative effect item. Thus, it appears that if the client is believed to be aware of the therapist's attraction, the therapy is more likely to be perceived as harmed or impeded (68%) than if the client is believed to be unaware (42%), $\chi^2(1, N = 472) = 26.42, p < .001$.

To assess therapists' concern about their attraction to clients, respondents were asked, "When you are attracted to a client, does it tend to make you feel uncomfortable, guilty, or anxious?" More therapists indicated experiencing such feelings (63%) than not, $\chi^2(1, N = 488) = 32.98, p < .003$. Younger therapists tended to feel more discomfort than did older therapists (69% vs. 57%), $\chi^2(1, N = 488) = 7.49, p = .006$. No significant differences emerged between male and female therapists in this regard.

Client Awareness and Mutuality of Attraction

Respondents who had been attracted to clients were asked, "In instances when you were attracted to a client, was the client aware of it?" More therapists (71%) believed that the client was probably not aware than believed that the client was aware, $\chi^2(1, N = 492) = 88.97, p < .003$. Female therapists were more likely than male therapists to believe that their clients were unaware of the attraction felt toward them (81% vs. 65%), $\chi^2(1, N = 492) = 14.53$, $p < .003$. For this item, a significant three-way association emerged. Older male therapists were more likely than younger ones to believe that clients were aware of their attraction (40% vs. 30%), whereas younger female therapists were more likely than older ones to believe that clients were aware of the attraction (26.5% vs. 11%), $\chi^2(1, N = 492) = 18.74$, $p < .003$.

Mutuality was assessed by the question, "In instances when you were attracted to a client, was the client also attracted to you?" Most therapists (83%) believed that the attraction had been mutual. Only 9% said that the attraction felt toward a client had never been reciprocated, and 8% indicated that they did not know or were not sure, $\chi^2(2, N = 452) = 483.1$, $p < .003$. There were no significant sex or age group differences.

Graduate Training and Consultation Seeking

We were interested in learning if the respondents' graduate training programs and internships had provided courses or other structured education about sexual attraction to clients. Over half (55%) indicated that they had received no education about such matters, 24% had received "very little," 12% had received "some," and only 9% believed that sexual attraction issues had been given adequate coverage. Thus, the more extensive the training, the fewer the respondents who had received it, $\chi^2(3, N = 583) = 274.21$, $p < .003$. No significant sex or age differences related to training experience emerged.

Fifty-seven percent of the respondents reported that they had sought supervision or consultation upon becoming aware of feeling sexually attracted to a client, $\chi^2(1, N = 483) = 10.47$, $p < .003$. Younger therapists were more likely than older therapists to seek consultation (64% vs. 50%), $\chi^2(1, N = 483) = 8.60$, $p < .003$. Male and female therapists did not differ significantly on the rate of seeking consultation. Post hoc tests revealed that those who reported feeling uncomfortable, anxious, or guilty about their sexual attraction (70%) were more likely to seek supervision or consultation than were those who had no associated discomfort (37%), $\chi^2(1, N = 474) = 49.43$, $p < .001$. Furthermore, those who had at least some graduate training about sexual attraction to clients were more likely to seek consultation (66%) than were those with no such training (49%), $\chi^2(1, N = 474) = 12.92$, $p < .001$.

Discussion

The long-standing absence of systematic research on this topic might give the impression that psychologists—unlike other human beings—are incapable of experiencing sexual attraction to those they serve, or that the phenomenon is at most a strange and regrettable aberration, limited mostly to those relative few who engage in sexual intimacies with their clients.

This study presents some initial data providing clear evidence that attraction to clients is a prevalent experience among both male and female psychologists. Our data suggest that this widespread phenomenon is one for which graduate training programs and clinical internships leave psychologists almost entirely unprepared. As discussed in the introduction, inattention to this topic in educational programs may be due partly to the taboo nature of the phenomenon and to the belief that such attraction is dangerous and antitherapeutic. It may also be the consequence, in part, of the fact that there is virtually no research-based information about the subject, that there is "nothing to teach."

If training programs, by their behavior and example, suggest that the issue of attraction is to be shunned and that feelings of attraction are to be treated as dangerous and antitherapeutic, it is not surprising that individual psychologists tend to experience feelings of attraction with wary suspicion and unsettling discomfort. In our survey, more younger psychologists than older psychologists reported such negative feelings, which suggests that whatever efforts training programs have made in the recent past to address these issues have not been fully successful.

An encouraging finding is that 57% of the psychologists sought consultation or supervision when attracted to a client.

This is especially true of younger psychologists and those who felt uncomfortable, guilty, or anxious about the attraction. Although seeking help from a colleague may in part reflect the view that attraction is a sign that something has gone wrong with the therapy, such consultation and supervision can give psychologists access to guidance, education, and support in handling their feelings.

Most psychologists (71%) who were sexually attracted to their clients believed that their clients were unaware of the attraction. Thus the phenomenon seems to be one that generally goes unmentioned in the psychotherapy relationship itself. Moreover, the findings suggest that for a substantial group (at least 20%) of the respondents, their attraction to clients not only received inadequate coverage (or no coverage at all) during their graduate training but also went unmentioned to their clients, consultants, or supervisors. Thus, these psychologists seemingly have refrained from talking about the attraction with anyone else, at least within the context of their professional work.

Even though sexual attraction for some psychologists remained unspoken to colleagues and clients, it nevertheless could find expression in the fantasy life and sexual behavior (not involving the client) of a minority of the profession. The age and gender differences are consistent with the research regarding sexual fantasizing in general, which shows higher rates for males and for younger adults (Pope, 1982). It is important to note, however, that the questionnaire item was limited to sexual fantasies occurring during sexual activity with someone else. Thus, the rates of more general sexual fantasizing about clients may be much higher.

Especially in light of the literature from a variety of theoretical orientations emphasizing the clinical usefulness of therapists' fantasies about their clients (see Singer & Pope, 1978), such sexual fantasizing deserves careful research as well as frank acknowledgment in psychology training programs. Geller, Cooley, and Hartley (1981–1982) have pioneered a research strategy for systematically exploring the ways in which therapy clients mentally represent their therapists (through fantasy, mental imagery, imagined conversations, etc.) Such a strategy could be adapted to study the ways in which therapists mentally represent the clients to whom they are sexually attracted.

Although 29% of the respondents experiencing sexual attraction to clients engaged in sexual fantasies regarding those clients, a much smaller number engaged in actual sexual intimacies with the clients. The percentages of all respondents (9.4% of men; 2.5% of women) engaging in such intimacies with clients are similar to findings of the two previous national surveys of psychologists (Holroyd & Brodsky, 1977; Pope, Levenson, & Schover, 1979).

Previous research—most of which was conducted in the late 1970s—has suggested that of therapists who act out sexually, 75% to 80% do so repeatedly; one therapist was reported to have been involved with over 100 clients (Pope & Bouhoutsos, 1986). However, in the current study, of those who engaged in sexual intimacies with their clients, 86% did so once or twice, 10% did so between 3 and 10 times, and only one psychologist (female) reported a frequency of over 10 times. Perhaps the courts and regulatory agencies have removed from practice or altered the practices of some psychologists who engaged in extreme and frequent violation of the prohibitions against therapist-client sex. The publicity accompanying such cases, as well as the increased attention to imposing explicit sanctions for such violations, may have deterred or restrained many others.

The current research provides some preliminary information about the clients to whom therapists are sexually attracted. When asked to describe the personal attributes of the clients who elicited the sexual attraction, male and female psychologists did not differ, for the most part, in their responses. However, males, far more than females, mentioned physical characteristics. On the other hand, females far more than males, mentioned that the "successfulness" of their clients was what attracted them sexually. This difference seems an obvious reflection of the sex role stereotypes characteristic of the general culture.

Most respondents believed that sexual attraction to clients had been, at least in some cases, useful or beneficial to the therapy. Men seemed to view sexual attraction to clients as not only more beneficial but also more harmful than did women. Respondents' reports concerning whether clients were aware of the therapists' attraction were significantly related to the belief that attraction was harmful. Although the association does not constitute causation, it is still tempting to speculate that the therapists' reponses reflected a belief that what clients do not know will not hurt them.

Why do therapists refrain from acting out their attraction to clients? It was gratifying to note that the major reasons seemed to express professional values, a regard for the client's welfare, or personal values compatible with professional standards. Fears of negative consequences and self-serving reasons were mentioned, though less frequently.

Therapist Gender and Sexual Attraction

That sexual attraction to clients is a common experience among female as well as male psychologists is a finding worth emphasizing in several respects. First, the relevant countertransference literature (as well as the therapist–client sexual intimacy literature) often uses the pronoun *he* when referring to the therapist and the pronoun *she* when referring to the client in instances in which there are no specific antecedents. Some of the material quoted in the introduction reveals this trend (for example, Freud, 1915/1963; Greenson, 1967; Kaplan, 1977; Ruesch, 1961). This usage is understandable (most therapists are men; most clients are women) but nonetheless is a violation of the guidelines for nonsexist writing and is misleading. It implies (incorrectly) that the only therapists who experience sexual attraction to clients are men and that the only clients to whom therapists are attracted are women. It may serve to place an even greater taboo upon the sexual attraction a female psychologist may experience toward her clients and may thus cause or amplify the anxiety, discomfort, or guilt that accompanies this attraction.

Second, the early widely publicized malpractice suits concerning therapist–client sexual intimacy involved male therapists and, as a consequence, the discussions of this issue focused almost exclusively on male therapists. More recently, however, factors that had served to inhibit the filing of such suits against female therapists have become less effective (Turkington, 1984, p. 15), and the group of therapists who sexually exploit their clients is now seen to include female as well as male psychologists.

Third, the findings of the current study suggest that therapist gender, as a variable, may be systematically associated with the various aspects of attraction to clients. For example, whereas the percentage of therapists attracted exclusively to their own sex was 0.6% for men and 2.4% for women, 23% of the female therapists as compared to 13% of the male therapists reported sexual attraction to both male and female clients. Further research is needed to examine the validity, meaning, and implications of such findings. For the research and associated literature to be truly illuminating and useful, it must be acknowledged that the sexual exploitation of clients and the distinctly different phenomenon of sexual attraction to clients are not limited to male therapists. Furthermore, it should be noted that attraction to clients, though a common experience, is apparently not universal: Five percent of the men and 24% of the women in this study reported no sexual attraction to their clients.

Training Implications

The data suggest that personal ethics and a regard for client welfare are more compelling than fear of negative consequences as reasons for refraining from sexual intimacies with clients. Therefore, efforts to rely predominantly on a system of imposing external sanctions for such behavior may be much less effective in preventing violations than an approach focused on formal training, both in graduate institutions and in continuing education programs.

To be successful, a training approach must first of all acknowledge the value of honest, serious discussions about therapists' attraction to clients. Therapists and therapists in training must be acknowledged as fully human, as capable of feeling sexual attraction to those to whom they provide professional services. The taboo must be lifted.

Second, addressing the issue must not be limited to a one-hour lecture, set apart from the "normal" curriculum. Education regarding this topic can be an appropriate part of almost all clinical and professional course-work and training. Similarly, the topic should be reflected in textbooks and other teaching materials and techniques, such as role playing and videotaped vignettes (see Schultz & McGrath, 1978). A review of the standard texts for teaching psychotherapy revealed that no mention is made of sexual arousal on the part of the neophyte therapist, nor therefore, are instructions given on how to deal with it should it occur (Bouhoutsos, 1984). More recent books (e.g., Keith-Spiegel & Koocher, 1985) have begun to provide basic information and guidelines in this area.

Third, the material presented should include information based on systematic research. The virtual absence of research on the topic of therapists' attraction to their clients lends more force and urgency to the standard and obligatory call for further research. Among the pressing issues to be addressed by systematic study is the basic validity and generalizability of these initial findings. The current study of therapists' attraction to clients, along with the initial research concerning therapist–client sexual intimacy and student–teacher sexual intimacy, represents an initial attempt to gather basic data in previously unexplored areas. The findings must be considered provisional pending more sophisticated replications and elaborations. It is worth noting, however, that the rate of reported therapist–client sexual intimacy in the current study corresponds well with estimates based on the two previous national surveys (Holroyd & Brodsky, 1977; Pope, Levenson, & Schover, 1979). Future research will be useful in exploring in more detail the meaning of "sexual attraction" and how, for example, it might be differentially defined or experienced depending on sex, age, and other factors.

Fourth, the phenomenon of therapist–client sexual intimacy must be clearly differentiated from the experience of sexual attraction to clients. The latter seems to suffer from guilt by association, and the general failure to discuss the experience openly does little to clarify the situation.

Fifth, educational programs must provide a safe environment in which therapists in training can acknowledge, explore, and discuss feelings of sexual attraction. If students find or suspect that their teachers are critical and rejecting of such feelings and that such feelings are treated as the sign of an impaired or erring therapist, then effective education is unlikely.

Even if sexual attraction to clients is not viewed as a therapeutic offense, the acknowledgement of the attraction—as in the case of Searles (1959/1965) mentioned in the introduction—is often associated with feelings of vulnerability and trepidation. Students may fear that their disclosures of sexual attraction will lead to their educators asking intrusive questions about their personal lives, making insensitively flip or humorous comments, failing to maintain appropriate confidentiality (i.e., gossiping), or trying to satisfy their voyeuristic tendencies through titillating conversation.

Students need to feel that discussion of their sexual feelings will not be taken as seductive or provocative or as inviting or legitimizing a sexualized relationship with their educators. As discussed in the introduction, sexual intimacies between teachers or supervisors and their students, most often in the context of a working relationship, are not uncommon. Educators must display the same frankness, honesty, and integrity regarding sexual attraction that they expect their students to emulate. Psychologists need to acknowledge that they may feel sexual attraction to their students as well as to their clients. They need to establish with clarity and maintain with consistency unambiguous ethical and professional standards regarding appropriate and inappropriate handling of these feelings.

References

Abramowitz, S. I., Abramowitz, C. V., Roback, H. B., Corney, R. T., & McKee, W. (1976). Sex-role related countertransference in psychotherapy. *Archives of General Psychiatry, 33*, 71–73.

American Psychological Association. (1977). *Ethical principles of psychologists* (rev. ed.). Washington, DC: Author.

American Psychological Association. (1981). *Ethical principles of psychologists* (rev. ed.). Washington, DC: Author.

American Psychological Association. (1983). *APA membership register.* Washington, DC: Author.

Asher, J. (1976, March). Confusion reigns in APA malpractice plan. *APA Monitor*, pp. 1, 11.

Baum, O. E. (1969–1970). Countertransference. *Psychoanalytic Review, 56*, 621–637.

Belote, B. (1974). *Sexual intimacy between female clients and male psychotherapists: Masochistic sabotage.* Unpublished doctoral dissertation, California School of Professional Psychology, San Francisco, CA.

Bouhoutsos, J. (1984). Sexual intimacy between psychotherapists and clients: Policy implications for the future. In L. Walker (Ed.), *Women and mental health policy* (pp. 207–227). Beverly Hills, CA: Sage.

Bouhoutsos, J., Holroyd, J., Lerman, H., Forer, B., & Greenberg, M. (1983). Sexual intimacy between psychotherapists and patients. *Professional Psychology, 14,* 185–196.

Chesler, P. (1972). *Women and madness.* New York: Avon Books.

Cohen, F., & Farrell, D. (1984). Models of the mind. In H. H. Goldman (Ed.), *Review of general psychiatry* (pp. 23–36). Los Altos, CA: Lange Medical Publications.

Colorado State Board of Medical Examiners v. Weiler, 402 P.2d 606 (Col. 1965).

Cooper v. Board of Medical Examiners, 49 Cal. App. 3d 931, 123 Cal. Rptr. 563 (1975).

Dahlberg, C. C. (1971). Sexual contact between patient and therapist. *Medical Aspects of Human Sexuality, 5,* 34–56.

Dorland's medical dictionary. (1974). (25th ed.) Philadelphia: Saunders.

Durre, L. (1980). Comparing romantic and therapeutic relationships. In K. S. Pope (Ed.), *On love and loving: Psychological perspectives on the nature and experience of romantic love* (pp. 228–243). San Francisco: Jossey-Bass.

Fine, R. (1965). Erotic feelings in the psychotherapeutic relationship. *Psychoanalytic Review, 52,* 30–37.

Freud, S. (1963). Further recommendations in the technique of psychoanalysis: Observations on transference-love. In P. Rieff (Ed.), *Freud: Therapy and technique* (pp. 167–180). New York: Collier Books. (Original work published 1915)

Geller, J. D., Cooley, R. S., & Hartley, D. (1981–1982). Images of the psychotherapist: A theoretical and methodological perspective. *Imagination, Cognition, and Personality: Consciousness in Theory, Research, Clinical Practice, 3,* 123–146.

Glover, E. (1955). *The technique of psycho-analysis.* New York: International Universities Press.

Greenson, R. R. (1967). *The technique and practice of psychoanalysis* (Vol. 1). New York: International Universities Press.

Grossman, C. M. (1965). Transference, countertransference, and being in love. *Psychoanalytic Quarterly, 34,* 249–256.

Heimann, P. (1950). On countertransference. *International Journal of Psychoanalysis, 31,* 81–84.

Holroyd, J. C. (1983). Erotic contact as an instance of sex-biased therapy. In J. Murray & P. R. Abramson (Eds.), *The handbook of bias in psychotherapy* (pp. 285–308). New York: Praeger.

Holroyd, J. C., & Brodsky, A. M. (1977). Psychologists' attitudes and practices regarding erotic and nonerotic physical contact with patients. *American Psychologist, 32,* 843–849.

Kaplan, H. S. (1977). Training of sex therapists. In W. H. Masters, V. E. Johnson, & R. D. Kolodny (Eds.), *Ethical issues in sex therapy and research* (pp. 182–189). Boston: Little, Brown.

Kardener, S. H., Fuller, M., & Mensh, I. N. (1973). A survey of physicians' attitudes and practices regarding erotic and nonerotic contact with patients. *American Journal of Psychiatry, 130,* 1077–1081.

Keith-Spiegel, P., & Koocher, G. (1985). *Ethics in psychology: Standards and cases.* New York: Random House.

Kenworthy, T. A., Koufacos, C., & Sherman, J. (1976). Women and therapy: A survey on internship programs. *Psychology of Women Quarterly, 1,* 125–137.

Kernberg, O. (1975). *Borderline conditions and pathological narcissism.* New York: Aronson.

Landis, C. E., Miller, H. R., & Wettstone, R. P. (1975). Sexual awareness training for counselors. *Teaching of Psychology, 2,* 33–36.

Langs, R. J. (1973). *The technique of psychoanalytic psychotherapy* (Vol. 1). New York: Aronson.

Langs, R. J. (1982). Countertransference and the process of cure. In S. Slipp (Ed.), *Curative factors in dynamic psychotherapy* (pp. 127–152). New York: McGraw-Hill.

Lehrman, N. S. (1960). The analyst's sexual feelings. *American Journal of Psychotherapy, 14,* 545–549.

Levenson, H., & Pope, K. S. (1984). Behavior therapy and cognitive therapy. In H. H. Gold (Ed.), *Review of general psychiatry* (pp. 538–548). Los Altos, CA: Lange Medical Publications.

Little, M. (1951). Countertransference and the patient's response to it. *International Journal of Psychoanalysis, 32,* 32–40.

McCartney, J. (1966). Overt transference. *Journal of Sex Research, 2,* 227–237.

Morra v. State Board of Examiners of Psychologists, 510 P.2d 614 (S.Ct. Kan. 1973).

O'Byrne, B. (1970). Civil liability of doctor or psychologist for having sexual relationship with patient. *American Law Reports, 33,* 1393–1396.

Pope, K. S. (1982). *Implications of fantasy and imagination for mental health: Theory, research, and interventions.* (Contract No. 449904865, Order No. 82M024784505D). Bethesda, MD: National Institute of Mental Health.

Pope, K. S. (1985, August). *Diagnosis and treatment of Therapist–Patient Sex Syndrome.* Paper presented at the meeting of the American Psychological Association, Los Angeles.

Pope, K. S. (1986, May). *Therapist–patient sex syndrome: Research findings.* Paper presented at the annual meeting of the American Psychiatric Association.

Pope, K. S., & Bouhoutsos, J. C. (1986). *Sexual intimacy between therapists and patients.* New York: Praeger.

Pope, K. S., Levenson, H., & Schover, L. (1979). Sexual intimacy in psychology training: Results and implications of a national survey. *American Psychologist, 34,* 682–689.

Pope, K. S., Schover, L. R., & Levenson, H. (1980). Sexual behavior between clinical supervisors and trainees: Implications for professional standards. *Professional Psychology, 11,* 157–162.

Romeo, S. (1978, June). Dr. Martin Shepard answers his accusers. *Knave*, pp. 14–38.

Ruesch, J. (1961). *Therapeutic communication*. New York: Norton.

Schover, L. R. (1981). Male and female therapists' responses to male and female client sexual material: An analogue study. *Archives of Sexual Behavior, 10,* 477–492.

Schultz, L. G., & McGrath, J. (1978). Developing seduction management skills through the use of video vignettes. *Journal of Humanities, 5,* 70–78.

Searles, H. F. (1965). Oedipal love in the countertransference. In *Collected papers on schizophrenia and related subjects* (pp. 284–303). New York: International Universities Press. (Original work published 1959)

Shepard, M. (1971). *The love treatment: Sexual intimacy between patients and psychotherapists.* New York: Wyden.

Singer, E. (1970). *Key concepts in psychotherapy.* New York: Basic Books.

Singer, J. L., & Pope, K. S. (1978). The use of imagery and fantasy techniques in psychotherapy. In J. L. Singer & K. S. Pope (Eds.), *The power of human imagination: New methods in psychotherapy* (pp. 3–34). New York: Plenum Press.

Tauber, E. S. (1979). Countertransference reexamined. In L. Epstein & A. H. Feiner (Eds.), *Countertransference* (pp. 59–70). New York: Aronson.

Taylor, B. J., & Wagner, N. W. (1976). Sex between therapists and clients: A review and analysis. *Professional Psychology, 7,* 593–601.

Thompson, C. (1950). *Psychoanalysis: Evolution and development.* New York: Hermitage House.

Tower, L. E. (1956). Countertransference. *Journal of the American Psychoanalytic Association, 4,* 224–255.

Turkington, C. (1984, December). Women therapists not immune to sexual involvement suits. *APA Monitor,* p. 15.

VandenBos, G. R., & Stapp, J. (1983). Service providers in psychology: Results of the 1982 APA human resources survey. *American Psychologist, 38,* 1330–1352.

Vinson, J. S. (1984). *Sexual contact with psychotherapists: A study of client reactions and complaint procedures.* Unpublished doctoral dissertation. California School of Professional Psychology, Berkeley, CA.

Weiner, I. B. (1975). *Principles of psychotherapy.* New York: Wiley.

Weiner, M. F. (1978). *Therapist disclosure. The use of self in psychotherapy.* Woburn, MA: Butterworths.

Winnicott, D. (1949). Hate in the countertransference. *International Journal of Psychoanalysis, 30,* 69–75.

Wright, R. W. (1981). Psychologists and professional liability (malpractice) insurance: A retrospective review. *American Psychologist, 36,* 1485–1493.

Zipkin v. Freeman, 436 S. W. 2d 753 (Mo. 1968).

Appendix B

Treating Victims of Therapist– Patient Sexual Involvement

Janet L. Sonne and Kenneth S. Pope

Sexual intimacies with a therapist victimize the patient and tend to cause a variety of acute and chronic sequelae similar to the effects of rape and child sexual abuse. Ten reactions commonly experienced by subsequent therapists are identified and discussed as essential factors to address effectively in the treatment of victims of therapist sex abuse.

Treatment of patients who have been sexually abused by a prior therapist tends to be exceptionally difficult and complex (Sonne, 1987, 1989). Research suggests that about 50% of therapists functioning as therapists will encounter in their practice at least one patient who has been a victim of sexual abuse by a former therapist (Pope & Vetter, 1991).

Such abuse is apparently widespread across *all* mental health professions, forming a major source of ethics, licensing, and malpractice complaints against psychotherapists (e.g., Ethics Committee of the American Psychological Association, 1988; Pope, 1989*a*, *b*). It is exceptionally important to note that the only national research study to include a large, representative sample of each of the three major mental health professions

Reprinted from *Psychotherapy* (1991), *28,* 174–187. Citations that were in press in the original article have been updated.

(i.e., psychiatry, psychology, and social work) found *no significant difference* in the rates at which these three professions engaged in either sexual or nonsexual dual relationships with their patients (Borys & Pope, 1989). However, marriage and family counselors (MFCCs), according to Boatwright (1989), may engage in sexual dual relationships at a *significantly higher rate* than that reported for psychiatrists, psychologists, and social workers. Boatwright (1989) reported recent research conducted by the counseling profession which found that "13% of marriage counselors have admitted having sex with a patient, [and that] 6% said the sex included intercourse" (p. 2), although this research has apparently not yet been published. Although research concerning the incidence and effects of such boundary violations has generally been confined to the United States, more recently studies have been conducted in other countries (e.g., Maruani, Pope & de Verbizier, 1989–1990; Lapierre & Valiquette, 1989).

The effects of therapist–patient sexual intimacies upon the patient—in both acute and chronic aspects—have been illustrated and documented in research employing a variety of methodologies. Studies have examined the effects of abuse on patients who have not returned to a subsequent therapy as well as on those who have, compared patients who have been subjected to abuse by a prior therapist with matched groups of patients who have not been victimized, and explored the sequelae as evaluated variously by the patients themselves, by subsequent therapists, and by independent clinicians through methods including observation, clinical interviews, and standardized psychological testing (Belote, 1974; Bouhoutsos et al., 1983; Brown, 1988; Butler, 1975; Chesler, 1972; Durre, 1980; Feldman-Summers & Jones, 1984; Sonne et al., 1985; L. Stone, 1980; Vinson, 1984). A review of research which has met the important criterion of publication in peer-reviewed professional journals is provided by Pope (1990*b*). Detailed first-person narratives of the sexualization process and its consequences humanize and provide an emotional immediacy which the more systematic studies may fail to capture (Bates & Brodsky, 1988; Freeman & Roy, 1976; Lapierre & Valiquette, 1989; Plaisil, 1985; E. Walker & Young, 1986).

Each approach to sample selection, data collection, and analysis or inference is, of course, limited, and each study can provide only a piece of the puzzle. This observation is by no means original and has been presented in detail in the prior studies and critical reviews. (Readers are referred to the original articles cited above or to critical reviews [e.g., Pope, 1986, 1990a, b] for discussion of the strengths and weaknesses of these methodological approaches, and consequent qualifications and limitations of their findings.) Historically, some have maintained that *all* research concerning sex abuse has been misleading in that only those who have been harmed are motivated to participate in research projects or come to the attention of health care practitioners; thus, according to this view, individuals who have enjoyed and greatly benefited from (or have not been negatively affected by) rape, therapist–patient sex, incest, adult–child sex between nonrelatives, etc., are "invisible"—or at least underrepresented—in the clinical and research literature (for a discussion of this position, see Farrell, 1982; Kinsey et al., 1953; O'Carroll, 1980; and Pomeroy, 1976).[1] Short of an obviously inhumane, unethical, and unacceptable experiment in which patients are randomly assigned to sexualized and nonsexualized treatment conditions and in which each patient is formally evaluated for possible positive, neutral, and/or negative consequences due specifically to the sexualized treatment—a research project that has actually been suggested by Riskin (1979)—there is much that we can never know about how the consequences of sexual victimization by therapists are produced and what factors influence the outcome. Nevertheless, the sequelae of therapist–patient sexual involvement seem to form a distinct Therapist–Patient Sex Syndrome that involves: ambivalence, guilt, emptiness and isolation, sexual confusion, impaired ability to trust, identity and boundary con-

---

[1]We were unable to locate any female authors who have made this claim; all have been male. It is possible that this gender effect is related to the frequently observed (e.g., Borys & Pope, 1989) gender bias of each of these forms of sex abuse: in each, males are significantly over-represented among perpetrators while females are significantly over-represented among the victims.

fusion, emotional lability, suppressed rage, increased suicidal risk, and cognitive dysfunction (Pope, 1985, 1986, 1988, 1989c; Pope & Bouhoutsos, 1986).

The sequelae bear certain similarities both to Rape Response Syndrome and to reaction to incest and other forms of child sexual abuse. This finding should not be surprising in light of the numerous researchers, theorists, and clinicians who have emphasized that while the three phenomena differ from one another in various ways, therapist–patient sexual intimacy shares certain fundamental similarities (e.g., in terms of dynamics, characteristics of perpetrators, use of power, lack of consent, and consequences) with rape and with child sex abuse (e.g., Bailey, 1978; Barnhouse, 1978; Bates & Brodsky, 1988; Borys, 1988; Borys & Pope, 1989; Burgess, 1981; Chesler, 1972; Connel & Wilson, 1974; Dahlberg, 1970; Finkelhor, 1984; Freud, 1915/1983; Gabbard, 1989; Herman et al., 1987; Gilbert & Scher, 1989; Kardener, 1974; Kavoussi & Becker, 1987; Maltz & Holman, 1984; Marmor, 1972; Masters & Johnson, 1976; Pope, 1989b; Pope & Bouhoutsos, 1986; Redlich, 1977; Russell, 1986; Saul, 1962; Searles, 1959; Siassi & Thomas, 1973; L. Stone, 1980; M. Stone, 1976). The shared similarities of therapist–patient sex, rape, and child sex abuse present a variety of scientific, clinical, and practical dilemmas to researchers and therapists (Pope, 1990a).

In addition to the educational materials prepared for patients by the professions (e.g., Committee on Women in Psychology, 1989), state licensing boards (e.g., California Department of Consumer Affairs, 1990), and self-help groups formed by the victims (see Pope & Bouhoutsos, 1986), specific treatment approaches have been developed to help patients who have been sexually victimized by a prior therapist. Such approaches may take the form of individual therapy (Pope & Gabbard, 1989; Pope & Bouhoutsos, 1986; Sonne, 1987), group therapy (Pope & Bouhoutsos, 1986; Sonne, 1989; Sonne et al., 1985), and mediation (Bouhoutsos & Brodsky, 1985; Schoener, Milgrom & Gonsiorek, 1983).

Our purpose in this article is not to review the specific approaches that are readily available in prior publications. Rather, our intent is to identify and discuss ten reactions commonly occurring among clinicians attempting to treat victims of sexual exploitation by a therapist, regardless of the treatment approach—individual, group, or other—they are using. Recognition and constructive utilization of these reactions seem to constitute a fundamental step in helping victims. The ways in which a therapist handles these reactions seems to influence to a great extent whether the subsequent treatment benefits the victim, is useless and a discouraging waste of time, or, in the worst cases, augments the harm and essentially revictimizes the patient.

Indications that a patient has been sexually intimate with a prior therapist can evoke a wide range of reactions, some of them quite intense, from a subsequent therapist. These reactions are normal and understandable. Like countertransference (and many of these reactions *may* be countertransferential), they are not necessarily signs that something is wrong with the subsequent therapy or therapist. As long as the therapist is open and alert to these reactions, and can acknowledge and work with them nondefensively, they can constitute valuable sources of information.

Disbelief and Denial

The new therapist may reflexively reject—without additional data-gathering or genuine reflection—a victim's charges of abuse by a prior therapist. Numerous factors contribute to this bias toward unfounded disbelief or denial. First, the subsequent therapist may hold a naive or idealized view of psychotherapy—that "these things just do not happen." Some respondents to incidence surveys express this point of view quite forcefully (Gechtman, 1989).

Second, the subsequent therapist may be unable to resolve the dissonance experienced when he or she is confronted with the victim's report that a therapist, like him or her, abused the patient. This reaction may be similar to that experienced by a parent at a child's report that the other parent or another relative has been sexually abusing the child. As previously noted, numerous clinicians and researchers have observed the similarity of therapist–patient sexual involvement to incest (in terms of dynamics, consequences, emotional reactions from third parties), and the subsequent therapist may experience the discomfort at having discovered what is analogous to the incest "secret."

Third, some therapists may simply find it hard to believe that a patient—someone who admittedly has "problems" and whose difficulties may involve distortions or dysfunctions in the area of cognition—would be more trustworthy than a colleague. In most cases, after all, the colleague has been initially identified and selected by a graduate training program or medical school as one of the best candidates for filling a sensitive and fiduciary role, numerous professors have evaluated the colleague's work leading to an advanced degree, a variety of clinical supervisors have worked carefully with the individual to ensure that he or she has the requisite judgment, maturity, and character to engage in psychotherapeutic work, the licensing board has determined through their assessment procedures that the individual can be trusted to practice without endangering the public, etc. In some cases, the victimizing therapist is exceptionally respected and prestigious. A famous media psychologist, for example, was accused of engaging in sexual intimacies with a significantly younger female patient for a one-year period. The psychologist maintained that "he was in love with the woman, to the point of considering divorcing his wife and marrying the patient. But he maintained he didn't have sexual relations with her . . . until . . . after she had stopped going to him for treatment. Also, he said he was having impotency problems at the time, and was far too busy to have had an affair with her" (Bloom, 1989, p. B-1). Nevertheless, his license was revoked. Other news accounts have described cases involving the immediate past president of a state professional association, the current president of a state professional association, a prominent researcher and professor at a prestigious university, a psychologist who served both as a university professor and as chair of the ethics committee of a large state psychological association, and a psychologist who served on the state licensing board, (APA's ethics procedures upheld as fair in federal court, 1985; Jalon, 1985; Matheson, 1984, 1985;

Pugh, 1988; The Resignation of ___ ___, 1990; also see Colorado State Board of Psychology Examiners, 1988). The authority, prestige, power, and fame of some perpetrators understandably lead some subsequent clinicians to refuse to believe or even seriously consider a patient's account of abuse.

Fourth, the therapist may erroneously believe that certain factors may legitimize sexual intimacies between therapist and patient. Among such factors are that the intimacies were part of an innovative treatment plan, that the intimacies were initiated by the patient, that the patient "consented" to the intimacies, and that therapist and patient were in love. One of the most frequently mentioned rationales is that the therapist engaged in sex with the patient after termination. However, the aspects of harm associated with intimacies that occur even years after termination can be extensive (Brown, 1988; Ethics Committee of the American Psychological Association, 1988; Gabbard, 1989; Pope & Bouhoutsos, 1986; Vasquez, 1989). Despite the numerous rationales put forth by perpetrators, research has failed to demonstrate any conditions under which therapist–patient sexual intimacies are "safe" for patients, whether the intimacies occur pre- or post-termination (Pope, 1990b).

Fifth, the therapist may find it difficult to give credibility to descriptions of events which are at times extremely bizarre. The patient's narrative may involve such strange and improbable sequences of events, that the story seems almost certainly to be a fabrication. The *documented* cases of therapist–patient sexual involvement, however, *are* bewilderingly varied and many times seem depressingly bizarre. Pope (1989a), for example, reviewed recent licensing disciplinary actions in which therapists were found to have sexually victimized patients who were developmentally disabled teenagers, engaged in sexual intercourse with a patient seen for "marital therapy" while her husband sat unsuspecting in the waiting room, repeatedly whipped the buttocks and extremities of a naked adolescent patient who was 54 years younger than the therapist as part of an "innovative" program to cope with the patient's alcoholism, used vibrators and other sexual equipment on patients who were identified as incest victims, engaged in group sex and masturbation with numerous patients including a 65-year-old nun, manipulated a female patient to stand on her head in the lotus position without her clothes on, took sexual photographs of patients, and engaged in sexual victimization of a ten-year-old female patient. It may be particularly difficult for subsequent therapists to acknowledge the possibility that minor patients have been sexually exploited by prior therapists. Research conducted by Bajt and Pope (1988) suggests that children and adolescents are substantially represented among sexually victimized patients. This study revealed that victimization seemed to involve slightly more female (56%) than male (44%) minor patients. The boys averaged 12 years of age, with a range from 7 to 16. The girls were, on average, 13 years old, with a range from 3 to 17.

Despite the numerous personal tendencies we may have, to dismiss, out of hand, indications that our patients have been sexually exploited by a prior therapist, it is crucially important to maintain alertness and openness to this possibility and to respond with care, sensitivity, and scrupulous professionalism to such indications. While there is some evidence suggesting that the number of false charges is exceptionally small (Pope & Vetter, 1991), it is also important not to assume reflexively that all charges by a patient must necessarily be true. Each case must be assessed carefully and thoroughly on an individual basis.

Minimization of Harm

Subsequent therapists may believe and accept the victim's disclosure of the abuse but may discount or otherwise minimize the short- and long-term damage to the patient caused by the abuse. As with denial of the abuse itself, minimization of the resultant damage may occur as a kind of unconscious or preconscious protection of the profession or of one's colleague (i.e., the perpetrator). It may occur as the therapist's defense against the realization that his or her work with the victim may be arduous and complex. It may occur because the subsequent therapist believes that sexual involvement between therapists and patients is, as a rule, harmless and perhaps even beneficial. Research suggests, for example, that about slightly less than 2% of psychiatrists believe that sexual contact could be appropriate to enhance self-esteem, as a corrective emotional experience, to treat a grief reaction, or to change a patient from one sexual orientation to another; 4.5% believe that it might be useful in treating sexual dysfunction; and 4% believe that it could be appropriate if the therapist were in love with the patient (Herman et al., 1987). Ten percent of clinical social workers believe that such involvement may actually be beneficial for the patient (Gechtman & Bouhoutsos, 1985; see also Gechtman, 1989). Moreover, a national study of instances in which prominent and respected psychologists intentionally broke the law (but were not the subjects of any formal complaint procedure) for the welfare of their patients found that in 9% of the cases, the psychologist maintained that he or she had engaged in sexual relations with a patient for the treatment and welfare of that patient (Pope & Bajt, 1988).

Perhaps obviously, clinicians who have engaged in sexual intimacies with one or more patients tend not to discern any harm from therapist–patient sexual intimacies, even when the patients whom they are examining for harm have been sexually exploited by *other* therapists. Research reported by Holroyd and Bouhoutsos (1985) found that when the subsequent treating therapists (for patients who were sexually abused by prior therapists) were themselves perpetrators, they tended to maintain that the patients had not been harmed by the intimacies. Similarly, Herman and her colleagues (1987) reported that 19% of the perpetrators in their national sample believed that therapist–patient sexual intimacies would benefit patients and 21% believed that such intimacies could be appropriate if the therapist were in love with the patient.

There is yet another reason why some therapists may minimize the harm befalling victims of therapist–patient sexual intimacy. In each of the seven anonymous surveys providing national incidence data about sexually abusive psychiatrists, psychologists, or social workers (see Table 1), the percentage of male clinicians who sexually abuse patients is greater than

Table 1

*Frequency Studies of Therapist–Patient Sex Using National Samples**

Ref. No.	Profession	Sample Size	Return Rate	M	F
1	Psychologists	1,000	70%	12.1	2.6
2	Psychologists	1,000	48%	12.0	3.0
3	Social Workers	1,000	54%	3.8	0.0
4	Psychologists	1,000	59%	9.4	2.5
5	Psychiatrists	5,574	26%	7.1	3.1
6	Psychologists	1,000	46%	3.6	0.5
7	Psychiatrists, Psychologists, and Social Workers[a]	4,800[b]	49%	0.9	0.2

Reference Key: 1) Holroyd & Brodsky, 1977; 2) Pope, Levenson & Schover, 1979; 3) Gechtman & Bouhoutsos, 1985; 4) Pope, Keith-Spiegel & Tabachnick, 1986; 5) Gartrell, Herman, Olarte, Feldstein & Localio, 1986; 6) Pope, Tabachnick & Keith-Spiegel, 1987; 7) Borys and Pope, 1989.
[a]No significant difference among the three professions.
[b]1,600 psychiatrists, 1,600 psychologists, 1,600 social workers.
*Table 1 adapted from Pope & Bouhoutsos (1986, p. 34).

the percentage of female perpetrators (Borys & Pope, 1989; Gartrell et al., 1986 [see also 1989]; Gechtman & Bouhoutsos, 1985; Holroyd & Brodsky, 1977; Pope, Keith-Spiegel & Tabachnick, 1986; Pope, Levenson & Schover, 1979; Pope, Tabachnick & Keith-Spiegel, 1987). Although most of these national studies did not collect data regarding the gender of the victim, those that did as well as studies limited to a specific geographic locale have found the percentage of female victims to be higher than the percentage of male victims (e.g., Bouhoutsos et al., 1983; Gartrell et al., 1986; Holroyd & Brodsky, 1977). Finally, studies that collected information regarding the ages of both the abusing professional and the victimized patient have found that, on average, the therapist tends to be about 12 to 16 years older than the patient (e.g., Bouhoutsos et al., 1983; Holzman, 1984). As one of the studies, which examined a variety of sexualized professional relationships (e.g., student–teacher, supervisor–supervisee) in addition to therapist–patient, observed:

> When sexual contact occurs in the context of psychology training or psychotherapy, the predominant pattern is quite clear and simple: An older, higher status man becomes sexually active with a younger, subordinate woman. (Pope et al., 1979)

These differential percentages of men as perpetrators and women as victims consistently emerge *even* when the overall rates of male and female therapists and of male and female patients are taken into account.

If, as the available research suggests, the modal perpetrator is male and the modal victim is female, the minimization of the harmful consequences may reflect a cultural tendency to discount the victimization of women (Pope, 1990a; L. Walker, 1989). L. Walker (1989) maintains that "sexual and psychological violence against women is . . . pervasive within the institution of psychology" and notes that it is both perpetrated and perpetuated through the sexual victimization of patients (p. 696). The mental health professions have seemed slow to acknowledge the harm, seriousness, and sometimes even the inappropriateness of actions that victimize (e.g., battering), and particularly that sexually victimize (e.g., "date-rape" and other forms of rape, child sexual abuse) women (Courtois, 1988; Finkelhor, 1984; Herman, 1981; Pope, 1990a; Sgroi, 1982; L. Walker, 1979, 1988; C. Walker, Bonner & Kaufman, 1988).

It may be important to clarify that in any of these phenomena there are female perpetrators, advocates, and apologists, just as there are male victims. To point out the differential gender rates among perpetrators and among victims, and the *possible* influence of those rates upon the response of individual treating clinicians or the helping professions more generally is *not* to imply, for example, that the victimization of male patients is somehow less unethical, less harmful, or less important.

Making the Patient Fit the Textbook

The subsequent treating therapist, aware of the modal responses to therapist–patient sexual intimacy, may make assumptions about how the victim is currently responding to the abuse. A therapist, told by the patient that the prior therapist held her down and raped her, may attempt an empathic response such as, "You must have felt terrible." Told by a patient that sexual involvement with a former therapist led to the dissolution of the patient's marriage, the loss of her job, an almost-fatal suicide attempt, and a long-term hospitalization, the subsequent therapist may attempt to offer alliance and support through a comment such as, "You must have hated him."

However well intentioned, such comments may elicit or compound the patient's confusion, shame, and guilt. Many victims remain for long periods in something akin to a state of shock. Their cognitive–affective reactions are numbed. Some have psychologically merged so completely with the exploitive therapist that there is severe boundary disturbance; some are convinced that the prior therapist could read their mind. Moreover, particularly early in the subsequent therapy, some patients may be certain that the sexual abuse was a legitimate and even useful aspect of their therapy, a true manifestation of their therapist's unselfish caring for them. This response is analogous to that of some wives who come to believe that battering is a natural, inevitable, deserved, effective, and even healthy part of their marriage (L. Walker, 1979). Further, as with some children who have been physically or sexually abused by a parent, patients may be ambivalent about their abuser: on one hand they may worship, cling to, and attempt to protect the abuser, and on the other hand they may fear and despise the former therapist.

In addition, like other sexual abuse victims, victims of therapist sex abuse may feel a deep, chronic, and pervasive sense of irrational shame and guilt. It is irrational shame and guilt because it is not abnormal for a patient to experience romantic or sexual transference to the therapist and it is always and without exception the therapist's responsibility to ensure that no sexual involvement with the patient occurs. Despite any cultural views to the contrary, it is never a patient's "fault" that sexual intimacy occurred any more than it is a child's fault that incest occurred or an individual's fault that she or he was raped, *regardless of any other circumstances.* Thus, even if the subsequent therapist's attempts at empathy are technically accurate, the patient may feel at any one time more confused and misunderstood. Like victims of battering, child abuse, or rape, the victim of therapist sexual abuse needs to be allowed to tell his or her own story as it emerges, without feeling intruded upon by the subsequent therapist.

Blaming the Victim

The irrational shame and guilt experienced by many victims of therapist–patient sexual intimacy have a parallel process experienced by many subsequent treating therapists: the tendency to blame the victim (see Ryan, 1971). Just as some may tell a battered woman that in light of the situation she seemed to deserve the beating, or tell an incest victim that she was so sexually precocious and seductive that her lonely father couldn't help himself, or tell a rape victim that by virtue of her clothing (or behavior, etc.) she was just "asking" to be raped, some clinicians may communicate to a victim of therapist–patient sex abuse that she or he was responsible for the abuse. As the previously cited analyses comparing sexual abuse of patients to these other forms of victimization have made clear, perhaps the two beliefs that perpetrators tend to hold most strongly are that the victim was not genuinely harmed and that the victim was not a vulnerable individual but was actually the instigator or at least willing participant (e.g., "she was asking for it"). As one therapist who acknowledged engaging in sexual intimacies with a number of his patients emphasized: "The woman patient is not a helpless, vulnerable individual . . . There had to be cooperation" (Patient–therapist sex in Massachusetts could lead to rape charges, 1989, p. 34). A newspaper quoted an attorney for a therapist in a prominent case outlining a defense in which the patient's *race* as well as her background and alleged eagerness to participate were highlighted: "She [the patient] was not the shy, retiring type that she had portrayed herself to be . . . Our defense was that this was something she voluntarily entered into and he [the therapist] made a judgmental error—he got talked into entering it. . . . She was, you know, free, white, and 21—an adult able to make her own decisions" (A betrayal of trust, 1989, p. F1).

The motivation for blaming may reflect the clinician's conscious or unconscious desire to protect the profession (and thus the perpetrator *and* the subsequent clinician him- or herself)—that the kindly and well-meaning perpetrator acted inappropriately only because he or she was provoked. Or the blaming may be an inaccurate assumption arising from the clinician's accurate interpretation of the victim's intense sexualized transference. The blaming may derive from the clinician's countertransferential collusion with the victim's expressions of shame and guilt regarding the intimacy. Or the blaming may spring from the clinician's own shame and guilt that are elicited by the *clinician's* sexual feelings—a phenomenon discussed in the following section—which have been projected upon the victim. For a review of the literature regarding the issue of the victim's elicitation of, role in, and responsibility for therapist–patient sexual intimacies, see Pope (1990a).

Sexual Reactions to the Victim

Few responses to victims of therapist–patient sex abuse tend to be as surprising and disconcerting as some form of sexual arousal or attraction. Discomfort with sexual arousal or attraction to patients in general appears to be a fundamental problem for many therapists. Research suggests that while an overwhelming majority (87%) of therapists experience sexual attraction to at least some of their patients, over half feel "guilty, anxious, or confused" simply by the occurrence of the attraction (without necessarily experiencing any temptation to act on the attraction). Further, 20% treat this attraction as a completely taboo subject, not mentioning it to anyone else in any professional or personal context (Pope et al., 1986). Clearly, the clinician's experience of sexual arousal or attraction to the victim of a therapist's sexual intimacy could then be particularly upsetting. The subsequent therapist may be alarmed to experience an identification or assumed similarity with the offending therapist and feel actually at risk for acting out sexually with the victim.

In some cases, therapists may also experience sexual fantasies involving victims of therapist–patient sexual intimacies. Sexual fantasies about therapy patients generally are not uncommon either during sex with another person who is not the patient (Pope et al., 1986) or at other times (Pope et al., 1987), but sexual fantasies about patients who have been sexually victimized by a prior therapist may be a specific countertransference reaction as they are in the treatment of incest victims (Ganzarain & Buchele, 1986, 1988) and may be exceptionally difficult to acknowledge, accept, and work through (either privately or with a supervisor or consultant) so that they do not disrupt or distort the therapeutic work with the patient.

Resentment or Discomfort at the Lack of Privacy

When the famous or notorious *Tarasoff v. Regents of the University of California* (1976) case was appealed, both the American Psychological Association and the American Psychiatric Association submitted amicus curiae briefs arguing that confidentiality was necessary to the therapeutic endeavor. As therapists, we tend to value the privacy of our work setting. Victims of therapist sex abuse may decide, at some time during the course of a subsequent therapy or at an even later date, to file a complaint with the civil courts (i.e., a malpractice suit), a licensing board, or an ethics committee. In some states, therapist–patient sex is a felony and the offense may be the cause of criminal proceedings. Thus both patient and subsequent therapist work together knowing that what they discuss may not in fact be confidential, that chart notes may be subpoenaed, that the therapist may be deposed and cross-examined concerning every aspect of the therapeutic discussions, etc. In some cases, attorneys for sexually abusive therapists have maintained that the patient was in no way harmed by the sexual intimacies but that the patient's current difficulties are a result of the incompetence of the subsequent treating therapist. The subsequent clinician may soon find his or her own therapeutic relationship and work with the victim a matter of scrutiny by numerous parties, under sharp attack, and a matter of public record.

Difficulty of "Keeping the Secret"

As the patient reveals the identity of the perpetrator, the subsequent therapist is bound ethically and legally to confidentiality, unless the patient (or the patient's legal representative) gives the therapist informed consent for release of information or unless there is some statutory basis to report (e.g., if the patient is a minor, the therapist must file a formal report of child abuse).

But the secret may be a difficult one to keep. Some subsequent therapists may feel the press of outrage and the desire to rid the profession of the perpetrator. Others may experience the dilemma—similar to other instances of perceived dangerousness to the public—of being legally bound to secrecy but feeling a responsibility to protect the public from further victimization by the sex abuser. Still others may wish to disclose the identity of the perpetrator as a way of psychologically distancing or differentiating themselves from the offending therapist; it is as if they were saying, "Look at what horrible things Dr. X has done, and how different he is from you and me!" Still others may wish to gain the sense of importance from sharing "special knowledge," particularly if the perpetrator is a well-respected and highly influential member of the professional or more general community.

Intrusive Advocacy

In light of the fact that in most instances the patient holds legal control over "the secret," subsequent therapists may feel tempted to guide victims in their decisions regarding whether to take formal action regarding the perpetrator. Some therapists, for example, may desire their victimized patients to file formal complaints because "it is the right thing to do," because it is therapeutic for the victim to "fight back," because it seems imperative to stop the perpetrator from practicing immediately, or a combination of these factors. This desire may be particularly strong if, for example, the subsequent therapist has reason to believe (through the patient's apparently reliable report) that the perpetrator is victimizing other patients. Such a desire, however well-intentioned, may lead subsequent therapists to bring subtle and sometimes not so subtle pressure to bear on patients to report the victimization to a licensing board, an ethics committee, a malpractice lawyer, or, in states in which therapist–patient sexual intimacies are a felony, to a district attorney or law enforcement officer.

On the other hand, some therapists may seek to discourage or prevent victims from taking any formal action. Some may wish to help the victim to "put the abuse in the past" and to "get on with life." Some may want to protect the victim from the uncertain vicissitudes of the complaint process. And some may be convinced that the perpetrator did not really mean any harm and does not deserve to have his or her career disrupted by professional review and possible sanction.

It is crucial to keep in mind that although filing formal complaints seems, as with many rape victims, to be therapeutic and a part of the process of healing and regaining selfhood, some patients may not wish to take formal action and their wishes must be respected. All victims must be allowed to reach their own decisions regarding what formal steps to take, if any, without undue and intrusive influence.

Vicarious Helplessness

When victims attempt to file a complaint, subsequent therapists may find it very difficult to cope with their own feelings of vicarious helplessness as the victim encounters the numerous obstacles, frequent indifference, and a process that is described by many victims as a revictimization. The tendency for some— *but not all*—licensing boards and regulatory organizations for the health care professions to act in a way that protects, allows, or enables professionals engaging in dangerous or questionable practices while paying insufficient attention to the welfare of consumers is well documented (e.g., Barrett, 1990a, b; Bates & Brodsky, 1989; Center for Public Interest Law, 1989; Doctor Discipline Crisis, 1990; Glazer & Glazer, 1989; Hogan, 1979; Levine, 1988; Vinson, 1984; Webber, 1989). A comprehensive study of the medical licensing board in California, for example, concluded: "Physician discipline in California is a code blue emergency. The system can not and does not protect Californians from incompetent medical practice" (Center for Public Interest Law, 1989, p. 1). In one case, a baby died in 1982 related to the actions of a physician, a set of events that would later result in a second-degree murder conviction. In 1983 two more babies died related to the actions of the same physician, and those reviewing matters for the licensing board found merit in the complaints against the physician, but the board itself allowed him to continue to practice. From 1984 to 1986, there were six more deaths, and the physician was convicted in 1989 on nine counts of second degree murder. A recent newspaper account noted that, "Even now, while serving a 56-year sentence . . . , the . . . physician retains his board-issued medical license . . ." (How the system protected a bad doctor, 1990, p. 12). The foreman of the jury that convicted the physician suggested "that the Board of Medical Quality Assurance be prosecuted for negligence in allowing [the physician] to continue practicing" (Webber, 1989, p. 16). The prosecutor heading the District Attorney's medico-legal division observed, "You've got an institution that's not doing its job" (Webber, 1989, p. 1). The physician's own trial attorney stated that the board "should have taken away his license or gotten a temporary restraining order, and saved a few babies' lives" (Barrett, 1990a, p. 12).

The helplessness experienced by many subsequent therapists may focus on three distinct but interrelated areas.

First, the subsequent therapist may be aware—and the patient may become aware—that, as discussed in the section "Disbelief and Denial," perpetrators may hold influential positions on the licensing board or ethics committee, or that prominent perpetrators holding university appointments or high elected office in professional organizations may submit to the board, committee, or malpractice court, untrue or misleading statements defending the therapist against whom the patient is lodging a complaint. The patient may be deprived of a fair and unbiased hearing.

Second, the subsequent therapist or patient may become aware that this particular perpetrator, even if found to have sexually abused the patient, is given a "rehabilitation plan" that in essence enables him or her to continue, after a relatively brief hiatus, abusing patients. Unfortunately, *none* of the vigorous and creative approaches to rehabilitation has demonstrated effectiveness in carefully controlled, independently evaluated research studies (Pope, in 1990*b*). In fact, the executive directors for the licensing boards for psychologists, social workers, marriage and family counselors, etc., in California— which, unfortunately, have encountered the greatest number of perpetrators and have thus had the most extensive experience with the widest variety of rehabilitation approaches—concluded that, in cases involving therapists who became sexually intimate with a patient, "prospects for rehabilitation are minimal and it is doubtful that they should be given the opportunity to ever practice psychotherapy again" (Callanan & O'Connor, 1988, p. 11). Reasons for the failure of various rehabilitation strategies may be due, in part, to the dynamics of individuals who engage in sex abuse (see Table 2). However, ineffectiveness may also be due to the components of the plans themselves. Most rehabilitation methods currently used on a trial or experimental basis seem to utilize a combination of psychotherapy and education/supervision, two factors which have shown no research evidence of decreasing the likelihood of perpetration; in fact, the available research shows a surprising and discouraging tendency for these two factors to be *positively* associated with perpetration (Pope, 1990*a*). The possibility that perpetrators are enabled to return to practice via ineffective rehabilitation programs is notably regrettable in light of indications that "80% of the sexually exploiting therapists have exploited more than one client" (California Dept. of Consumer Affairs, 1990, p. 14) and "the recidivism rate for sexual misconduct is substantial (APA Insurance Trust, 1990, p. 3). Furthermore, in the

Table 2

*Categories of Therapists Who Become Sexually Intimate with a Patient**

POWER AND CONTROL

1. *Sexual Preoccupation:* The therapist views the exploited patient almost solely in terms of the patient's potential to arouse and gratify the therapist sexually. There is an absence of or minimal emotional bonding of the therapist to the patient.

2. *Substitution:* The therapist views the patient as if he or she were (a substitute for) an important figure from the therapist's life (e.g., mother, daughter, former spouse, the therapist's first sexual partner, the object of the therapist's unfilled and idealized childhood infatuation). Therapists may bond intensely to the identity or role into which they attempt to manipulate the patient. In some cases, therapists may become quite regressed and express very primitive impulses.

3. *Attraction to Pathology:* The therapist is attracted to and sexually aroused by the pathological, pathogenic, or abused aspects of the patient's personality, behavior, or history. In a national survey of psychologists, some respondents indicated that they were sexually attracted to such patient characteristics as "paranoia," "narcissism," "hysterical personality style," "severe distur- bance," and "low self-esteem" (Pope, Keith-Spiegel & Tabachnick, 1986, p. 154). Both male and female therapists may experience sexual fantasies or arousal in response to a patient's history of prior sexual abuse (Ganzarin & Buchele, 1986).

4. *Authoritarian Orientation:* The therapist is attracted to or aroused by a relationship in which he or she can maintain authoritarian control over a dependent, less powerful, more vulnerable individual. It is the therapist's ability to bring about submission (rather than any inherent quality of the patient) that is the source of the therapist's attraction to and fulfillment from the relationship. Both therapist and patient focus on the therapist's needs for interpersonal mastery and control. Therapists manifesting this dynamic are often able to maintain such a relationship indefinitely (sometimes resulting in marriage), regardless of whether the formal "therapy" sessions terminate.

5. *Physical Immobilization:* The therapist is attracted to, aroused by, or sat- isfied by sexual activity with a patient who is physically prevented from effective voluntary movement. In some cases, therapists will sexually abuse patients while they are hospitalized and in restraints. In others, therapists will hypnotize patients and, if necessary, tie their hands. In still others, therapists abuse patients who are incapable of effective movement due to impairment from licit or illicit drugs. And sometimes a therapist will simply use superior size or strength to immobilize the patient.

(continued)

Table 2   (continued)

ANGER

6. *Battering:* The therapist's sexualized relationship with the patient includes instances in which the therapist strikes the patient in anger. Such therapists may feel that hitting is justified (as punishment or discipline) by the patient's behavior, or that such physical intervention is an appropriate part of setting limits, or that the attacks (e.g., "aversive behavior") are an integral part of the treatment plan, or that occasional hits are "nothing out of the ordinary." It is also possible for such therapists to feel out of control during an angry episode, and to regret each episode after it occurs.

7. *Emotional Abuse:* The therapist's sexualized relationship with the patient includes angry outbursts during which the therapist screams at and berates the patient. While some therapists seem to regress to the level of a childhood tantrum during these outbursts, patients are often terrified, are frequently devastated, and may become (temporarily) catatonic. It is possible that in a number of cases, such angry abuse follows a pattern of tension building, acute outburst, and kindness or contrition as described by Walker (1979).

8. *Provoking Decompensation:* In an indirect, deceptive, and passive-aggressive manner, the therapist expresses anger by directing the patient to undertake activities ostensibly as part of or in the service of treatment but actually intended to bring about decompensation and harm. Some therapists may, as part of a sexualized relationship with a psychologically fragile and sexually conservative patient, direct the patient to participate in orgies. Other therapists may induce their sexually abused patients to begin using addictive drugs.

SADISM

9. *Pleasure in Causing Pain:* The therapist experiences sexual arousal and pleasure through administering physical pain to the patient. Not infrequently, the therapist asserts that this abuse is a legitimate part of the treatment plan.

10. *Sexualized Humiliation:* The therapist experiences sexual arousal and pleasure through observing the patient in humiliating situations or behaviors.

Note: The three major types (i.e., anger, power, and sadism) of sexually abusive individuals were initially described by Groth & Birnbaum (1979).
*Table 2 adapted from Pope (1989*b*).

absence of rehabilitation techniques that have been adequately validated, professionals conducting experimental rehabilitation procedures on a trial basis may not be obtaining legally or ethically adequate informed consent from the patients treated by perpetrators during the course of rehabilitation; especially in light of the substantial recidivism rate and the failure of clinical supervision to provide adequate protection against a perpetrator re-offending, such patients are being placed at substantial risk for harm and have a right to know that they are participating in an experimental, unvalidated procedure (Pope, 1990a). The Nuremberg Code's well-known first principle is that the "*voluntary* consent" [to participate or withdraw] of those placed at risk by research is "absolutely essential."

Third, patients may react strongly to the professions' policy that allows *any* therapist who has sexually molested patients to return to practice. Whether or not the abusive therapist will actually abuse future patients (i.e., whether an effective method of rehabilitation is possible and has been implemented) is not relevant to these patients; that the professions enable therapists who have engaged—under the guise of providing therapy to those who have come to them for help—in prohibited behaviors that may destroy their patients' lives to continue or resume *therapy* practice as members in good standing seems to such patients to stand as a disincentive to file formal complaints (in that the perpetrator would not be prevented from continuing practice), as a barrier to effective prevention of abuse (e.g., if therapists knew that they were waiving all opportunities to practice therapy by sexually molesting a patient, they might refrain from the initial abuse; furthermore, psychotherapy might not seem to offer such long-term possibilities as a profession for sex abusers), and as actions speaking louder than words concerning the profession's concern for public safety relative to the profession's concern for protecting the interests of its own members. Thus, the subsequent therapist may empathize with or vicariously experience the patient's frustration with a profession that routinely allows sexually abusive therapists— even if such offenders are assumed, for the purposes of argument, to have been completely "rehabilitated" via methods validated through adequate research studies—to return to practice with a very vulnerable and unsuspecting clientele. In most cases, even once a profession has found a therapist to have sexually abused one or more patients, the public is rarely notified. Thus when the therapist returns to practice, new patients of all types (e.g., victims of rape and incest, those who are confused about sexual issues, those whose presenting problems may involve compulsive sexual behavior, those who believe that their only worth is their sexuality) and the parents of minor patients have no information regarding whether the therapist has been found by an ethics committee to have sexually abused patients. Victims of therapist–patient sex abuse cannot be certain whether any subsequent clinician whom they consult has also abused patients and has been allowed by an ethics committee to continue to practice as a member in good standing of the professional organization; that perpetrators are enabled to resume practice may deter many victims from seeking subsequent professional help. Patients who have been abused may point out that if a teacher were found to have sexually abused kindergarten children or if the director of a rape counseling center were found to have sexually abused someone coming for counseling, it is unlikely that the perpetrator would ever be allowed to return—regardless of so-called rehabilitation—to work with the population. And yet mental health professions have allowed perpetrators to resume clinical work with patients and thus continue their sex abuse. [Preventing a sex abuser from seeing patients would *not* end his or her career in the mental health field; there are numerous types of valuable and fulfilling work a psychologist or other mental health professional can perform—e.g., research, writing, administration—that does not put vulnerable and unsuspecting patients at risk.] For example, a prominent APA presentation on the value and effectiveness of rehabilitation of therapists who have engaged in sexual intimacies with their patients as well as a still-mysteriously unpublished study regarding rehabilitation that received media attention were authored by a psychologist who had engaged in sex with several patients, as described by Bates and Brodsky (1989).

The sense of helplessness and frustration which the subsequent therapist may be feeling vicariously may be exacerbated by the patient's identification of the subsequent therapist with the "system" (i.e., the victim is now feeling revictimized by the refusal of the professions to deal effectively with perpetrators and sees both the prior and the subsequent therapists as part of professions declining to act promptly, reasonably, and effectively to enforce the prohibition against sexual victimization of patients).

Serving as the Object of Rage, Neediness, and Ambivalence

The victim of therapist–patient sexual intimacy may vacillate from severe depression to seething anger. The subsequent therapist tends, through the transference and other factors, to serve as a focus of the patient's numerous attempts to work through and heal from the process of victimization. Thus the subsequent therapist may become an object of the victim's frequent and unpredictable periods of rage during which the therapist may feel aggressively criticized and/or pushed away. As a result, the therapist may experience a strong impulse to withdraw from the patient and to avoid both the patient's rage and the therapist's countertransferential guilt and feelings of inadequacy. However, woven through the expressions of rage are often expressions of intense neediness, depression, and loss as the patient struggles with the perpetrator's betrayal of a vital relationship. Suicidal and/or homicidal risk may increase and the therapist must work closely and carefully to assess risk regularly and to address the patient's clinical needs. Hospitalization may be necessary, as it seems to be in about 11% of subsequent treatments (Bouhoutsos et al., 1983; Pope & Vetter, 1991). Caught up in the confusion of the patient's ambivalence (i.e., hating and needing the same object), the subsequent therapist may be inclined to give inadequate attention to two sets of issues. First, *is hospitalization clinically necessary* (e.g., due to the patient's need for constant monitoring to prevent suicide attempts); if not, do the likely benefits of hospitalization (e.g., temporarily decreasing the environmental stresses on the patient) outweigh the likely drawbacks (e.g., increasing the patient's sense of dependence and inability to care for him- or herself)? Second, *does the hospital under consideration provide safe, competent, and experienced care for this patient population*? For example, does the hospital carefully screen its professional and support staff to ensure that sexually abusive candidates are not hired; does hospital administration maintain explicit guidelines regarding appropriate staff–patient relationships; does the hospital offer long-term programs, if clinically indicated for the patient; and are at least some of the staff skilled and experienced in treating this patient population?[2]

Conclusion

The ten therapist reactions noted above seem to occur often in the treatment of victims of therapist–patient sexual intimacy and undoubtedly contribute to the difficulty and complexity of the treatment. By remaining open and sensitive to them, we can use them as a source of information and as a stimulus for reflection and consultation. Thus they become a therapeutic resource rather than a push toward revictimizing the patient.

References

American Psychological Association Insurance Trust (1990). *Bulletin: Sexual misconduct and professional liability claims.* Washington, DC: author.

APA's ethics procedures upheld as fair in federal court. (1985, May 3), *Psychiatric News*, p. 11.

Bailey, K. G. (1978). Psychotherapy or massage parlor technology. *Journal of Consulting and Clinical Psychology, 46,* 1502–1506.

---

[2]The C. F. Menninger Memorial Hospital is an example of a hospital meeting these criteria. Psychologists working in hospital settings who wish to obtain information regarding the creation and implementation of the program may contact the hospital director [G. O. Gabbard, Box 829, Topeka, KS 66601-0829].

Bajt, T. R. & Pope, K. S. (1989). Therapist–patient sexual intimacy involving children and adolescents. *American Psychologist, 44,* 455.

Barnhouse, R. T. (1978). Sex between therapist and patient. *Journal of the American Academy of Psychoanalysis, 6,* 533–546.

Barrett, B. (1990*a*). Bureaucracy impedes action on complaints. *Daily News,* pp. 1, 12–14, May 20.

Barrett, B. (1990*b*). CMA lobby wields power over stricter physician laws. *Daily News,* pp. 1, 14–15, May 20.

Bates, C. R. & Brodsky, A. M. (1989). *Sex in the therapy hour: A case of professional incest,* New York: Guilford.

Belote, B. (1974). *Sexual intimacy between female clients and male psychotherapists.* Unpublished doctoral dissertation, California School of Professional Psychology, San Francisco, CA.

Betrayal of trust (1989). Cedar Springs (Colorado) *Gazette Telegraph,* pp. F1–F2, October 17.

Bloom, D. (1989). Psychologist's license revoked after sex with patient. Riverside (California) *Press Enterprise,* p. B-1, March 22.

Boatwright, D. (1989). Therapist/patient sex legislation sent to governor. Press release from the Office of Senator Dan Boatwright, State Capitol, Sacramento, CA, September 8.

Borys, D. S. (1988). *Dual relationships between therapist and client: A national survey of clinicians' attitudes and practices.* Unpublished doctoral dissertation, University of California, Los Angeles.

Borys, D. S. & Pope, K. S. (1989). Dual relationships between therapists and clients: A national study of psychologists, psychiatrists, and social workers. *Professional Psychology: Research and Practice, 20,* 283–293.

Bouhoutsos, J. & Brodsky, A. M. (1985). Mediation in therapist–client sex: A model. *Psychotherapy, 22,* 189–193.

Bouhoutsos, J., Holroyd, J., Lerman, H., Forer, B. & Greenberg, M. (1983). Sexual intimacy between psychotherapists and patients. *Professional Psychology, 14,* 185–196.

Brigham, R. E. (1989). *Psychotherapy stressors and sexual misconduct: A factor analytic study of the experience of non-offending and offending psychologists in Wisconsin.* Unpublished doctoral dissertation, Wisconsin School of Professional Psychology, Milwaukee, WI.

Brown, L. S. (1988). Harmful effects of posttermination sexual and romantic relationships between therapists and their former clients. *Psychotherapy, 25,* 249–255.

Burgess, A. (1981). Physician sexual misconduct and patients' responses. *American Journal of Psychiatry, 136,* 1335–1342.

Butler, S. (1975). *Sexual contact between therapists and patients.* Unpublished doctoral dissertation. California School of Professional Psychology, Los Angeles.

California Department of Consumer Affairs. (1990). *Professional therapy never includes sex.* (Available from Board of Psychology, 1430 Howe Avenue, Sacramento, CA 95825)

Callanan, K. & O'Connor, T. (1988). *Staff comments and recommendations regarding the report of the Senate Task Force on Psychotherapist and Patients Sexual Relations.* Sacramento: Board of Behavioral Science Examiners and Psychology Examining Committee.

Center for Public Interest Law. (1989). *Physician discipline in California: Report on the physician discipline system of the Board of Medical Quality Assurance.* San Diego, CA: University of San Diego School of Law.

Chesler, P. (1972). *Women and madness.* New York: Avon.

Colorado State Board of Psychology Examiners. (1988). Case No. PY88-01, October 3.

Committee on Women in Psychology (1989). If sex enters into the psychotherapy relationship. *Professional Psychology: Research and Practice, 20,* 112–115.

Connel, N. & Wilson, C. (eds.). (1974). *Rape: The first sourcebook for women.* New York: New American Library.

Courtois, C. A. (1988). *Healing the incest wound.* New York: Norton.

Dahlberg, C. C. (1970). Sexual contact between patient and therapist. *Contemporary Psychoanalysis, 5,* 107–124.

Doctor discipline crisis. (1990). *Los Angeles Times,* p. B-1, May 13.

Durre, L. (1980). Comparing romantic and therapeutic relationships. *In* K. S. Pope (ed.), *On love and loving: Psychological perspectives on the nature and experience of romantic love* (pp. 228–243). San Francisco: Jossey-Bass.

Estrich, S. (1987). *Real rape.* Cambridge, MA: Harvard University Press.

Ethics Committee of the American Psychological Association. (1988). Trends in ethics cases, common pitfalls, and published resources. *American Psychologist, 43,* 564–572.

Farrell, W. (1982). *Myths of incest.* Paper presented to the Conference on Family and Sexuality, Minneapolis.

Feldman-Summers, S. & Jones, G. (1984). Psychological impacts of sexual contact between therapists or other health care professionals and their clients. *Journal of Consulting and Clinical Psychology, 52,* 1054–1061.

Finkelhor, D. (1984). *Child sexual abuse: New theory and research.* New York: Free Press.

Freeman, L. & Roy, J. (1976). *Betrayal.* New York: Stein and Day.

Freud, S. (1915/1983). Further recommendations in the technique of psychoanalysis: Observations on transference-love. *In* P. Rieff (ed.), *Freud: Therapy and technique* (pp. 167–180). New York: Collier Books.

Gabbard, G. O. (ed.). (1989). *Sexual exploitation in professional relationships.* Washington, DC: American Psychiatric Press.

Ganzarain, R. & Buchele, B. (1986). Countertransference when incest is the problem. *International Journal of Group Psychotherapy, 36,* 549–566.

Ganzarain, R. & Buchele, B. (1988). *Fugitives of incest: A perspective from psychoanalysis and groups.* New York: International Universities Press.

Gartrell, N., Herman, J., Olarte, S., Feldstein, M. & Localio, R. (1986). Psychiatrist–patient sexual contact: Results of a national survey, I: Prevalence. *American Journal of Psychiatry, 143,* 1126–1131.

Gartrell, N., Herman, J., Olarte, S., Feldstein, M. & Localio, R. (1989). Prevalence of psychiatrist–patient sexual contact. *In* G. O. Gabbard (ed.), *Sexual exploitation in professional relationships* (pp. 3–14). Washington, DC: American Psychiatric Press.

Gechtman, L. (1989). Sexual contact between social workers and their clients. *In* G. O. Gabbard (ed.), *Sexual exploitation in professional relationships* (pp. 27–38). Washington, DC: American Psychiatric Press.

Gechtman, L. & Bouhoutsos, J. (1985). *Sexual intimacy between social workers and clients.* Paper presented at the annual meeting of the Society for Clinical Social Workers, Universal City, California, October.

Gilbert, L. A. & Scher, M. (1989). The power of an unconscious belief. *Professional Practice of Psychology, 8,* 94–108.

Glazer, M. P. & Glazer, P. M. (1989). *The whistle-blowers.* New York: Basic.

Groth, A. N. & Birnbaum, H. J. (1979). *Men who rape: The psychology of the offender.* New York: Plenum.

Herman, J. L. (1981). *Father–daughter incest.* Cambridge, MA: Harvard University Press.

Herman, J. L., Gartrell, N., Olarte, S., Feldstein, M. & Localio, R. (1987). Psychiatrist–patient sexual contact: Results of a national survey, II: Psychiatrists' Attitudes. *American Journal of Psychiatry, 144,* 164–169.

Hogan, D. B. (1979). *The regulation of psychotherapists, Volumes I–IV.* Cambridge, MA: Ballinger.

Holroyd, J. C. & Bouhoutsos, J. C. (1985). Biased reporting of therapist–client sexual intimacy. *Professional Psychology, 16,* 701–709.

Holroyd, J. C. & Brodsky, A. M. (1977). Psychologists' attitudes and practices regarding erotic and nonerotic physical contact with patients. *American Psychologist, 32,* 843–849.

Holtzman, B. (1984). Who's the Therapist Here? *Smith College Studies in Social Work, 54,* 204–224.

How the system protected a bad doctor. (1990). *Daily News,* p. 12, May 20.

Jalon, A. (1985). Psychologist repentant for having sex with a patient. *Los Angeles Times (Valley Edition),* Part II, p. 6, September 4.

Kardener, S. H. (1974). Sex and the physician–patient relationshp. *American Journal of Psychiatry, 131,* 1134–1136.

Kavoussi, R. J. & Becker, J. V. (1987). Psychiatrist–patient sexual contact. *American Journal of Psychiatry, 144,* 1249–1250.

Kinsey, A. C., Pomeroy, W. B., Martin, C. E. & Gebhard, P. H. (1953). *Sexual behavior in the human female.* Philadelphia: W. B. Saunders.

Lapierre, H. & Valiquette, M. (1989). *J' ai fait l' amour avec mon therapeute: Temoignages sur l' intimite sexuelle en therapie.* Montreal: Les Editions Saint-Martin.

Levine, R. J. (1988). *Ethics and the regulation of clinical research.* New Haven, CT: Yale University Press.

Maltz, W. & Holman, B. (1984). *Incest and sexuality.* Lexington, MA: Lexington Books.

Marmor, J. (1972). Sexual acting out in psychotherapy. *American Journal of Psychoanalysis, 32,* 327–335.

Maruani, G., Pope, K. S. & de Verbizier, J. (1989–1990). Ethics and psychotherapy in France. *Imagination, Cognition, and Personality, 9,* 355–357.

Masters, W. H. & Johnson, V. E. (1976). Principles of the new sex therapy.
American Journal of Psychiatry, 110, 3370–3373.

Matheson, J. (1984). AMI member "whistle-blower" in successful prosecution
of Eau Claire psychiatrist. *AMI of Wisconsin Newsletter,* December, p. 2.

Matheson, J. (1985). Psychiatrist sentenced to prison for five years. *The Milwaukee Journal,* p. 9, July 20.

O'Carroll, T. (1980). *Paedophilia: The radical case.* Boston: Alyson.

Patient–therapist sex in Massachusetts could lead to rape charges. (1989).
Psychiatric News, pp. 1, 34–35, May 9.

Plaisil, E. (1985). *Therapist.* New York: St. Martin's/Marek.

Pomeroy, W. B. (1976). A new look at incest. *Forum,* 9–13, November.

Pope, K. S. (1985). *Diagnosis and treatment of Therapist–Patient Sex Syndrome.*
Paper presented at the annual meeting of the American Psychological
Association, Los Angeles, August.

Pope, K. S. (1986). *Therapist–Patient Sex Syndrome: Research findings.* Paper
presented at the annual meeting of the American Psychiatric Association,
Washington, DC, May.

Pope, K. S. (1988). How clients are harmed by sexual contact with mental
health professionals: The syndrome and its prevalence. *Journal of Counseling and Development, 67,* 222–226.

Pope, K. S. (1989a). Malpractice suits, licensing disciplinary actions, and ethics
cases: Frequencies, causes, and costs. *Independent Practitioner, 9(1),* 22–
26.

Pope, K. S. (1989b). *Identifying and rehabilitating sexually abusive therapists.* Paper
presented at the annual meeting of the American Psychiatric Association,
San Francisco, CA, May.

Pope, K. S. (1989c). Therapist–Patient Sex Syndrome: A guide for attorneys
and subsequent therapists to assessing damage. *In* G. O. Gabbard (ed.),
Sexual exploitation in professional relationships (pp. 39–56). Washington, DC:
American Psychiatric Press.

Pope, K. S. (1990a). Therapist–patient sex as sex abuse: Six scientific, professional, and practical dilemmas in addressing victimization and rehabilitation. *Professional Psychology: Research and Practice, 21,* 227–239.

Pope, K. S. (1990b). Therapist–patient sexual involvement: A review of the
research. *Clinical Psychology Review, 10,* 477–490.

Pope, K. S. & Bajt, T. R. (1988). When laws and values conflict: A dilemma
for psychologists. *American Psychologist, 43,* 828–829.

Pope, K. S. & Bouhoutsos, J. C. (1986). *Sexual intimacy between therapists and
patients.* New York: Praeger.

Pope, K. S. & Gabbard, G. O. (1989). Individual psychotherapy for victims
of therapist–patient sexual intimacy. *In* G. O. Gabbard (ed.), *Sexual exploitation in professional relationships* (pp. 89–100). Washington, DC: American Psychiatric Press.

Pope, K. S. & Vetter, V. A. (1991). Prior therapist–patient sexual involvement
among patients seen by psychologists. *Psychotherapy, 28,* 429–438.

Pope, K. S., Keith-Spiegel, P. & Tabachnick, B. G. (1986). Sexual attraction to clients: The human therapist and the (sometimes) inhuman training system. *American Psychologist, 41*, 147–158.

Pope, K. S., Levenson, H. & Schover, L. S. (1979). Sexual intimacy in psychology training: Results and implications of a national survey. *American Psychologist, 34*, 682–689.

Pope, K. S., Tabachnick, B. G. & Keith-Spiegel, P. (1987). Ethics of practice: The beliefs and behaviors of psychologists as therapists. *American Psychologist, 42*, 993–1006.

Pugh, T. (1988). State charges psychologist with numerous violations. *Rocky Mountain News*, p. 3, March 23.

Redlich, F. C. (1977). The ethics of sex therapy. In W. H. Masters, V. E. Johnson and R. D. Kolodny (eds.), *Ethical issues in sex therapy* (pp. 143–157). Boston: Little, Brown.

The resignation of _____ _____ . (1990, Jan./Feb.). *The California Therapist*, pp. 6–7.

Riskin, L. (1979). Sexual relations between therapists and their patients: Toward research or restrain? *California Law Review, 67*, 1000–1027.

Russell, D. E. H. (1986). *The secret trauma: Incest in the lives of girls and women.* New York: Basic.

Ryan, W. (1971). *Blaming the victim.* New York: Pantheon.

Saul, L. J. (1962). The erotic transference. *Psychoanalytic Quarterly, 31*, 54–61.

Schoener, G. R., Milgrom, J. & Gonsiorek, J. (1983). *Responding therapeutically to clients who have been sexually involved with their psychotherapists.* Monograph, Walk-In Counseling Center, Minneapolis.

Searles, H. F. (1959). Oedipal love in the countertransference. *International Journal of Psychoanalysis, 40*, 180–190.

Sgroi, S. M. (ed.). (1982). *Handbook of clinical intervention in child sexual abuse.* Lexington, MA: Lexington.

Siassi, I. & Thomas M. (1973). Physicians and the new sexual freedom. *American Journal of Psychiatry, 130*, 1256–1257.

Sonne, J. L. (1987). Proscribed sex: Counseling the patient subjected to sexual intimacy by a therapist. *Medical Aspects of Human Sexuality, 16*, 18–23.

Sonne, J. L. (1989). An example of group therapy for victims of therapist–client sexual intimacy. In G. O. Gabbard (ed.), *Sexual exploitation in professional relationships* (pp. 101–127). Washington, DC: American Psychiatric Press.

Sonne, J. L., Meyer, C. B., Borys, D. & Marshall, V. (1985). Clients' reactions to sexual intimacy in therapy. *American Journal of Orthopsychiatry, 55*, 183–189.

Stone, L. G. (1980). *A study of the relationship among anxious attachment, ego functioning, and female patients' vulnerability to sexual involvement with their male psychotherapists.* Unpublished doctoral dissertation, California School of Professional Psychology, Los Angeles.

Stone, M. (1976). Boundary violations between therapist and patient. *Psychiatric Annals, 6*, 670–677.

Tarasoff v. Regents of the University of California (1976), 17 Cal.3d 425, 551 P.d 334.

Vasquez, M. J. T. (1989). *Sexual intimacies with clients after termination: Should the prohibition be explicit?* Paper presented at the annual meeting of the American Psychological Association, New Orleans, August.

Vinson, J. S. (1984). *Sexual contact with psychotherapists: A study of client reactions and complaint procedures.* Unpublished doctoral dissertation, California School of Professional Psychology.

Walker, C. E., Bonner, B. L. & Kaufman, K. L. (1988). *The physically and sexually abused child.* New York: Pergamon.

Walker, E. & Young, T. D. (1986). *A killing cure.* New York: Holt.

Walker, L. E. (1979). *The battered woman.* New York: Harper and Row.

Walker, L. E. (1989). Psychology and violence against women. *American Psychologist, 44,* 695–702.

Walker, L. E. (ed.). (1988). *Handbook on sexual abuse of children.* New York: Springer.

Webber, D. (1989). Prosecutor assails medical probe. *Daily News,* pp. 1, 16, December 26.

Appendix C

Therapist–Patient Sexual Involvement: A Review of the Research

Kenneth S. Pope

Abstract. During the last quarter century, research has begun to provide an empirical basis for testing and refining our conceptions about the occurrence and effects of therapist-patient sexual intimacies. Published reports of research in this area have not only presented intriguing findings but also emphasized the importance of considering the methodological limitations (e.g., selective memory in retrospective studies, reporting biases, unrepresentative samples, and distortions in data obtained from secondary sources) that qualify those findings. Research findings are reviewed suggesting that therapist-patient sexual involvement may be systematically associated with a variety of factors (e.g., gender, age, the use of nonsexual touch in therapy) and may have significantly decreased during the last 12 years.

That our emerging ideas about the occurrence and effects of therapist-patient sexual involvement can be based upon and tested against systematically collected data is due in no small part to the work of Masters and Johnson, who published the first information about the phenomena that was based upon studies of relatively large samples. The data, presented in *Hu-*

Reprinted from *Clinical Psychology Review* (1990), *10*, 477–490. Citations that were in press in the original article have been updated.

man Sexual Response (Masters & Johnson, 1966) and *Human Sexual Inadequacy* (Masters & Johnson, 1970), formed the basis of five major observations.

First, there was a relatively large number (Masters and Johnson do not provide specific figures) of participants in the research who reported sexual involvement with a prior therapist.

Second, most of these reports were judged by the researchers to be valid; a minority were judged to be the participant's fantasy. The researchers examined the possibility that a majority of the reports might be false, but stressed that the problem would still be significant for the profession if only one-fourth of the reports were accurate (Masters & Johnson, 1970).

Third, the reports included every possible combination of male or female therapist with male or female patient (sometimes including group sex).

Fourth, the most frequently reported combination was a male therapist becoming sexually involved with a female patient.

Fifth, because extensive material was collected about each participant's background, development, and sexual history, the authors were able to consider sexual involvement with a therapist in the context of other events in the participant's life. Thus, the effects of sexual involvement with a therapist could be compared to consensual sexual involvement with a spouse, long- and short-term extramarital sexual liaisons, and sexual involvements traditionally considered traumatic (e.g., rape, incest). Masters and Johnson concluded that such involvements, in light of their negative effects, constituted a "tragedy" for the patient (see subsequent section on "Consequences for Patients"). Such extremely negative effects subsequently led Masters and Johnson (1975) to argue that the involvement was tantamount to criminal rape: "We feel that when sexual seduction of patients can be firmly established by due legal process, regardless of whether the seduction was initiated by the patient or the therapist, the therapist should initially be sued for rape rather than malpractice, i.e., the legal process should be criminal rather than civil" (p. 1).

While providing a pioneering research model for the systematic study of therapist-patient sexual involvement, Masters and Johnson made two additional important contributions to this area of study. Their analysis of the imbalance of power in the therapeutic relationship, their emphasis on the necessity of trust, and their characterization of the patient as "essentially defenseless" (Masters and Johnson, 1970) to sexual exploitation by a therapist helped to refocus professional attention upon some of the original factors leading to the prohibition of doctor-patient sexual involvement. Brodsky (1989), for example, points out that the prohibition was formally codified *prior* to the ancient Hippocratic Oath; the diverse reasons (many of which were based upon aspects of harm suffered by the patient) for the prohibition predated and reached far beyond the concept of transference which Freud (1915/1958) stressed in his discussion of the phenomenon.

Research Issues

Masters and Johnson also modeled for subsequent researchers in this area the crucial importance of explicitly noting and seriously considering the limitations and biases inherent in research endeavors. For example, they called attention to the numerous cultural factors that "always have inhibited statistically ideal population sampling. This study proves no exception to the general rule" (Masters & Johnson, 1966, p. 9). The subsequent studies which focused exclusively on the prevalence and effects of therapist-patient sexual involvement are likewise no exception to this general rule, as the investigators themselves have emphasized. A relatively recent research report, for example, summarizes several of the most important limitations:

> As has *often* been observed, there is much that we do not know at this stage about the frequency, nature, and effects of patient abuse; about treatment for victims/survivors; about perpetrators and the process or even possibility of adequate rehabilitative interventions; and about effective prevention of sexual and nonsexual dual relationships. For more detailed discussions of problems in sample selection, the potential similarities and differences between responders

and nonresponders in survey studies, issues in scaling and statistical analysis, the qualified nature of inferences drawn from specific findings, and other research limitations, readers are referred to prior studies of sexual dual relationships, methodological critiques, and relevant review articles. (Borys & Pope, 1989, p. 289)

Two additional sources of potential bias plague many studies of the occurrence and effects of therapist-patient sexual involvement: "the material may be shaped by respondent and patient memory as well as by the usual biases associated with self-report and secondary sources" (Bouhoutsos, Holroyd, Lerman, Forer, & Greenberg, 1983, p. 192). One important aspect of report bias (associated with whether the respondent had or had not engaged in sexual intimacies with a patient) was statistically analyzed by Holroyd and Bouhoutsos (1985); the results are reviewed in a subsequent section. The potential influence of respondent and patient memory may be considerable in any form of survey research, as Pearson, Ross, and Dawes' (1992) review demonstrates. In a study eliciting self-reports of depression, for example, participants were asked whether they had ever been depressed *at any time* during the course of their life (Aneshensel, Estrada, Hansell, & Clark, 1987). This question, as part of a more general survey, was asked four times at intervals from 1979 to 1980, and a fifth time three years later. Only 46% of the participants who had reported having been depressed at some point in their life in one of the first four survey administrations described such a history of depression in the fifth administration. Taylor (1989) reviewed investigations into other forms of memory bias. She found considerable evidence that selective attention and selective memory play influential roles in the ability of individuals to recover from serious trauma. The selectivity of memory must be taken into account in interpreting the data emerging from retrospective studies of therapist-patient sexual involvement.

The premise endorsed by Masters and Johnson—that studies of therapist-patient sexual involvement (as well as other varieties of sexual interaction) utilizing volunteer samples could be useful as long as the sources of possible bias were clearly ac-

knowledged and considered—has not been universally endorsed. The arguments that *all* occurrence and effects research
in this area is so critically flawed that it is at best useless and
at worst destructively misleading seem to fall into three clusters:
(a) cultural bias, (b) volunteer bias, and (c) lack of data based
on experimental manipulation of completely isolated and controlled variables.

First, arguments are framed around the assertion that there
are widely-held cultural myths, beliefs, or biases against any
of a span of sexual activities (e.g., incest, sex between an adult
and an unrelated minor, rape, therapist-patient sex) that can
occur between two individuals, one of whom is in a position
of either trust (e.g., fiduciary relationships) or power vis-à-vis
the other, and that such myths, beliefs, or biases prevent an
objective, research-based assessment of the consequences of
these activities (for a discussion of this argument, see, e.g.,
Kinsey, Pomeroy, Martin, & Gebhard, 1953; Masters & Johnson, 1966; Pomeroy, 1976; Pope, 1990). Thus, McCartney (1966)
argued that his practice of engaging in sex with the many (1500)
female patients for whom this treatment was, in his opinion,
necessary, could never be fairly assessed "because the theoretical and practical application of this treatment is rejected by
the social order and vigorously condemned by most religions"
(p. 234). Similarly, Gross (1977) asserted that it was "conventional morality" that was causing damage to patients by preventing a fair consideration of the uses of erotic contact as an
important aspect of psychotherapy.

> I do not believe that gut sucking righteous indignation, mor-
> alistic appeals for ethical behavior or insulting women by
> regarding them as defenseless victims are going to correct
> the problems created by the current ignorance that we have
> about the sexual nature of psychotherapy. Beating up on
> therapists who reflect our lack of understanding will not
> create new knowledge. (p. 10)

More recently, Benezra (1988) argued that our current conceptions of therapist-patient sexual involvement are hopelessly
biased by "our heavily entrenched values and convictions" that

made it all but impossible to accept views "that are contrary to the Zeitgeist" (p. 5).

Second, arguments are framed around the assertion that research into the potentially negative effects of sexual involvements, such as rape, incest, and so on, is useless and misleading because it is necessarily dependent upon those who volunteer or agree to participate: According to this argument, only those who have been hurt (or believe themselves to have been negatively affected) by incest, rape and so on, are motivated to participate. Thus, the research will erroneously indicate that any such form of sexual involvement (including therapist-patient sexual involvement) produces harm (for a discussion of this argument, see, e.g., Kinsey et al., 1953; Masters, Johnson, & Kolodny, 1977; Pomeroy, 1976; and Pope, 1990). Further, according to this view, it is likely that many if not most of those who volunteer data about being harmed by sexual involvement with a therapist have not actually experienced such involvement. Consistent with this view is a report of malpractice complaints against psychologists over a 10-year period that did not mention even one complaint of therapist-patient sexual involvement considered to be truthful; rather, complaints were attributed to rejected or spurned women:

> [T]he greatest number of [all malpractice] actions are brought by women who lead lives of very quiet desperation, who form close attachments to their therapists, who feel rejected or spurned when they discover that relations are maintained on a formal and professional level, and who then react with allegations of sexual improprieties. (Brownfain, 1971, p. 651)

Similarly, Serban (1981) asserted that female complaints of harm from sexual involvement with a therapist were not related to the treatment or to the patient's clinical condition "but to solving the more pressing problem of finding either a sexual and emotional partner or otherwise to make a handsome financial profit by defrauding the therapist's insurance, if not to victimize him as revenge against men . . ." (p. 81). Thus, according to Serban, those patients who come forward with complaints of harm are only those holding "resentment against the therapist who did not satisfy her dreams of either marrying her or compensating her financially" (p. 82). The nature of such analyses raises the question of what other sorts of cultural biases or stereotypes—distinct from cultural biases against incest, rape, therapist-patient sexual involvement, and so on—might be influencing our approach to these issues (see, for example, Denmark, Russo, Frieze, & Sechzer, 1988; Holroyd, 1983; Walker, 1989). It is also possible that the very human inclination toward "blaming the victim" affects our judgment in this area (Ryan, 1971).

Third, arguments focus on the correlational nature of the data. According to this point of view, absence of controlled experimental manipulation prevents any genuinely scientific inference. Thus, no amount of surveys, retrospective studies of those who have engaged in sexual intimacies in comparison with those who have not, or even prospective studies following those who subsequently become involved with a therapist as well as those who do not can support even tentative inferences regarding consequences of such involvement; the dependent variables may, according to this view, be influenced by unspecified "hidden" variables that were not examined. Riskin (1979) has been one of the chief proponents of this view; he advocates carefully controlled prospective studies in which patients are randomly assigned to either a "sexual involvement" or "no-sexual-involvement" condition. The assertion that only data from experimental research in which subjects are not only randomly selected from the population but also randomly assigned to experimental and control groups are useful tends, as has frequently been observed, to be asserted by organizations or associations who are addressing the question of whether they are engaging in harmful or destructive activities (see Pope, 1990). Thus, Patterson (1987) analyzes the use of such arguments by the tobacco industry, which asserts that there is no valid evidence that smoking causes harm to humans. The argument is based upon the fact that all evidence regarding humans (animal research is discredited because of unknown generalizability to humans) is correlational; in no case have random samples been drawn from the human population and randomly assigned to smoking and no-smoking groups. This position is frequently associated with claims that the (nonexperimental) research produces only one clear effect: harming the organization or association by reducing the trust, respect, or income it receives from consumers and from the public more generally. (For data regarding the view that research in the area of therapist-patient sexual involvement endangers the professional or financial status of therapists, see, e.g., Gartrell, Herman, Olarte, Feldstein, Localio (1987) and Gechtman (1989).)

Although it is possible to adopt an epistemological position that only data produced by one category of experimental research—in which isolated variables are systematically manipulated in a controlled environment—are useful as a basis for knowledge and understanding, the uncritical rejection of all other forms of systematic investigation seems as ill-founded as the uncritical acceptance of one form of investigation. Social psychologist Carol Tavris (1987) addressed the attempt to reject all nonexperimental data in our study of sexual phenomena. In criticizing a survey in the area of sexual involvement that, despite its dismal 4% return rate and numerous design problems, had received favorable attention in the popular press, Tavris nevertheless affirmed the value of survey and other forms of research based upon biased samples:

> Many times social scientists conduct research on unrepresentative samples. . . . Sex researchers, including Grandfather Kinsey, have always had to rely on the kindness of strangers who would be willing to answer impertinent questions . . . [A]ll social scientists appreciate the value of subjective routes to truth . . . Scientists understand that a study is only one fragment of the mosaic; this is why they are at pains to cite other research, both confirming and critical, along with their own. They are aware of the many sources of distortion in research: in the experimenter's own expectations, in the biases of volunteers, in the way instructions and questions are worded. (p. 5)

Research reports bear an important responsibility to describe and discuss aspects (e.g., retrospective, correlational, analogue) of their methodology that affect the nature and strength of the inferences that can be reasonably drawn from the data (Pope, 1990).

Research Findings

Investigations of therapist-patient sexual involvement, based on systematically collected data, have contributed to our emerging—though provisional, qualified, and very incomplete—understanding of the phenomenon. The trends noted below are based upon investigations that have met an important scientific and professional criterion: Each has been published in formally refereed (i.e., manuscripts are assigned by the editor to anonymous peer-reviewers) scientific and professional journals. Research results that survive and benefit from this painstaking process of systematic review created to help ensure the scientific integrity, merit, and trustworthiness of new findings may be less likely (than data communicated *solely* through press-conferences, popular lectures, books, workshops, and television appearances) to contribute to what Tavris (1987) terms "social science fiction."

Gender

As noted above, Masters and Johnson found that, in their samples, the most typical pattern of therapist-patient sexual involvement was a male therapist with a female patient. An attempt to locate all surveys published in peer-reviewed scientific and professional journals indicates that all relevant data reported in these journals are consistent with this predominant pattern. A national survey of psychiatrists (Gartrell, Herman, Olarte, Feldstein, & Localio, 1986), for example, found that 88% of the self-reported instances of therapist-patient sexual intimacies involved male therapists with female patients; 7.6% involved male therapists with male patients; 3.5% involved female therapists with male patients; and 1.4% involved female therapists with female patients.

In the published studies, the differences in the proportions of male and female therapists reporting sexual involvement with their patients are striking. In the first national prevalence study of psychologist-patient sexual intimacies (with a 70% return rate), for example, Holroyd and Brodsky (1977) found that 85% of the therapists (from a sample of 500 male and 500 female psychologists) who reported engaging in erotic contact with patients were male. Similarly, Bouhoutsos and her colleagues (1983) found that 96% of the instances of therapist-patient sexual involvement reported by subsequent therapists involved male therapists. In their review of the published literature, Borys and Pope (1989) noted that all published studies of both sexual and nonsexual dual relationships were consistent (once the overall proportions of male and female professionals and of male and female patients or students were statistically taken into account) with the following premiss: Male professionals, far more than female professionals, tend to engage in both sexual and nonsexual dual relationships and to endorse such relationships (i.e., to indicate that such relationships are ethical, are beneficial to the patient or student, are not harmful); female patients and students, far more than male patients and students, are likely to be involved in such relationships.

One other possible gender difference—possibly artifactual—became apparent during a review of the literature. Without exception, all journal articles reporting studies of the occurrence or effects of therapist-patient sexual involvement included at least one female investigator/author (most articles indicated a collaborative team of both male and female authors; some indicated exclusively female authorship; none indicated exclusively male authorship). In contrast, the literature review found that not only all journal articles but all public presentations (e.g., papers presented to professional associations, books) of the point of view that therapist-patient sexual involvement is not harmful for the patient (and, in some cases, may be beneficial or necessary) were authored by individual (i.e., no collaborative authorship) male therapists.

Discipline

Although national studies of an individual discipline undertaken by professionals belonging to that discipline (e.g., Gartrell et al., 1986; Holroyd & Brodsky, 1977) have produced a wealth of intriguing findings, attempts to determine whether the disciplines differ in their rates of such involvement have been difficult for at least two major reasons. First, the various studies used different forms, sample selection procedures, periods of conducting the research, and so on; thus, apparent differences in rates might be due to such factors. Second, national prevalence studies of therapist-patient sexual involvement involving social workers and marriage and family counselors were not found in the peer-reviewed journals for those disciplines. To date, only one published article has been located that reports a national survey (administering the same instrument during the same time period, etc.) of psychiatrists, psychologists, and social workers. That article, based on an anonymous survey sent to 4800 therapists, reported no significant differences in the rates at which psychiatrists, psychologists, and social workers engaged in sexual intimacies with their patients (Borys & Pope, 1989). (Records of malpractice cases based on allegations of therapist-patient sexual intimacies, however, indicate that approximately three times as many cases involve psychiatrists as involve psychologists, Perr, 1989.)

Theoretical Orientation

No article has reported a significant relationship between theoretical orientation and a therapist's likelihood of becoming sexually involved with a patient. Holroyd and Brodsky (1977), for example, noted that the total number of sexual contact behaviors they studied were statistically unrelated to the therapist orientation.

Age

The research suggests that therapists who become sexually involved with a patient typically do so with a patient who is significantly younger. Gartrell and her colleagues (1986; see also 1989) reported that the average age of the therapists in such relationships was 43 while the average age of the patients was 33. Similarly, Bouhoutsos and her colleagues (1983) reported that the average age of sexually involved therapists in their study was 42 years while the average age of the patient was 30 years.

Patients who become sexually involved with therapists are not exclusively adults. A national study of 81 instances of therapist–patient sexual involvement involving minor patients found male patients ranging in age from 7 through 16 (average age = 12.5) and female patients ranging in age from 3 to 17 (average age = 13.75) (Bajt & Pope, 1989).

Education and Professional Achievement or Recognition

There have been no research data reported in peer-reviewed journals supporting the premise that therapists who become sexually involved with their patients tend to have less formal education or to have received less professional recognition. In fact, the pertinent data, though by no means conclusive, tend to cast doubt on this premise. Gartrell and her colleagues (1986; see also 1989), for example, found that offending psychiatrists were *more* likely than their nonoffending colleagues to have completed an accredited residency. Pope and Bajt (1988) found that a national sample of psychologists who had attained high levels of professional achievement (e.g., diplomate status, APA Fellow status) reported a higher rate of sexual involvement with patients than more general samples of psychologists. Though not a study reporting quantifiable data, Sonne and Pope (1991) review classifications of the various types of offending therapists and provide examples of perpetrators who have held such positions as president of the state professional association, licensing board chair, chair of the ethics committee of a large state psychological association, analytic training institute director, hospital chief of staff, and tenured professor (see also Pope, 1990).

One study reported data suggesting a possible association between therapist-patient sexual involvement and an aspect of training. Individuals who, as students during graduate training, engaged in sexual intimacies with their professors and clinical supervisors were later, as therapists, statistically more likely to engage in sexual intimacies with their patients (Pope, Levenson, & Schover, 1979).

Personal Therapy

No study published in a peer-reviewed journal has found support for the premise that therapists who undergo personal therapy are less likely to become sexually involved with their patients. Gartrell and her colleagues (1986), for example, found that psychiatrists who had completed a personal course of psychotherapy or psychoanalysis were *more* likely to have become sexually involved with a patient. (For a discussion of the failure to find a research basis for the premise that personal therapy reduces the risk of a therapist engaging in sexual intimacies with a patient, see Gechtman, 1989.)

Physical Contact with Patients

There are no published data supporting the premise that therapists who engage in nonsexual physical contact with their patients are more likely to become sexually involved with their patients. There is, however, some evidence that differential (nonsexual) touching of patients based upon the patients' gender is associated with sexual involvement.

> Erotic contact not leading to intercourse is associated with older, more experienced therapists who do not otherwise typically touch their patients at a rate different from other therapists (except when mutually initiated). Sexual intercourse with patients is associated with the touching of opposite-sex patients but not same-sex patients. It is the differential application of touching—rather than touching per se—that is related to intercourse. (Holroyd & Brodsky, 1980, p. 810)

Patient Risk Factors

Although various clinical (e.g., borderline personality disorder) and historical (e.g., history of incest) factors have been suggested as placing a patient at greater risk for sexual involvement with a therapist (see previous section on "blaming the victim"), no research published in peer-reviewed journals has provided support for this notion. (Pertinent research would need to evaluate such variables in light of the base-rate of their occurrence in the relevant patient population.) Bates and Brodsky (1989) reviewed the accumulated data and concluded: "The best single predictor of exploitation in therapy is a therapist who has exploited another patient in the past" (p. 141).

Consequences for Patients

Various approaches have been attempted to learn something of the ways in which intimacies with a therapist may affect a patient (e.g., Bouhoutsos et al., 1983; Brown, 1988; Butler & Zelen, 1977; Feldman-Summers & Jones, 1984; Herman, Gartrell, Olarte, Feldstein, & Localio, 1987; Sonne, Meyer, Borys, & Marshall, 1985; Vinson, 1987). The pioneering research by Masters and Johnson has led to diverse subsequent studies conducted by other investigators. These studies have evaluated patients who have sought help from a subsequent therapist as well as those who have not. They have evaluated groups of patients who have engaged in sexual intimacies with a psychotherapist in contrast with matched groups of patients who have not engaged in such intimacies and of patients who have engaged in intimacies with physicians who were not psychotherapists. They have also examined the possible effects of such intimacies as assessed by the patients themselves, by subsequent therapists treating the individual, and by independent clinicians utilizing such methods as clinical interview, observation, and standard psychological test instruments (for reviews of such investigations, see Gabbard, 1989; Pope & Bouhoutsos, 1986). They also have examined the possible effects of such intimacies as assessed by the patients themselves, by subsequent therapists treating the individual, and by independent clinicians utilizing such methods as clinical interview, observation, and standardized psychological test instruments (for reviews of such investigations, see Gabbard, 1989; Pope & Bouhoutsos, 1986). Pope (1988) suggested that the negative effects identified by such studies tended to cluster into 10 general categories: (a) ambivalence, (b) guilt, (c) emptiness and isolation, (d) sexual confusion, (e) impaired ability to trust, (f) boundary disturbance and diffusion of identity, (g) emotional lability, (h) suppressed rage, (i) increased suicidal risk, and (j) cognitive dysfunction, particularly in the area of attention and concentration, frequently involving intrusive thoughts, unbidden images, flashbacks, and nightmares.

Subsequent Therapists

As previously noted, research findings consistently support the premise that male therapists are more likely than female therapists to engage in sexual intimacies with their patients (even when the overall proportions of male and female therapists are taken into account). One study suggests not only that the subsequent treating therapists of such patients are more likely to be male but also another intriguing trend: "A comparison of repeaters, one-time offenders, and nonoffenders on this variable revealed highly significant differences, with repeat offenders the most likely to have treated previously involved patients and nonoffenders the least" (Gartrell et al., 1987, p. 289). Research reported by Holroyd and Bouhoutsos (1985) found that offenders serving as subsequent treating therapists were much less likely (than nonoffending colleagues serving as subsequent treating therapists) to find that patients were harmed in any way as a result of sexual intimacies with a prior therapist. Similarly, offending therapists are more likely to believe that sexual intimacies with a patient can be beneficial for the patient (Herman et al., 1987).

Are Fewer Therapists Becoming Sexually Involved With Their Patients?

Some therapists who have studied therapist-patient sexual involvement maintain that the rate of such involvement is currently quite high. . . . Lapierre and Valiquette (1989, p. 19) estimated that the percentage was approximately 15%. Such high estimates, whether or not accurate, are not supported by research data published in peer-reviewed journals. An analysis of the six national surveys of the rates of therapist-patient sexual involvement published in peer-reviewed journals (i.e., Borys & Pope, 1989; Gartrell et al., 1986; Holroyd & Brodsky, 1977; Pope, Keith-Spiegel, & Tabachnick, 1986; Pope et al., 1979; Pope, Tabachnick, & Keith-Spiegel, 1987) indicates an intriguing and hopeful trend. There is a reasonably steady decline in the self-reported rates of such involvement from the earliest figures of 12.0–12.1% for male therapists and 2.6–3.0% for female therapists in the earliest two studies to 0.9–3.6% for male therapists and 0.2–0.5% for female therapists in the two most recent studies. Although alternative explanations for this trend must be considered (see, e.g., Borys & Pope, 1989), it is possible that these studies, spanning a dozen years, reflect an actual decline in the rate of sexual involvement with patients.

We cannot be certain what factors are—or could be—effective in decreasing the rate. Pending future research that could shed light on this process, the following possibilities are worth considering. The professions have publicized a variety of efforts at prevention, which may be producing useful results (see Gabbard, 1989; Pope & Bouhoutsos, 1986). An increasing number of states have termed therapist-patient sexual intimacy a felony; criminalization of the act may have a deterrent effect. A number of highly-publicized multimillion dollar malpractice awards may also be serving a deterrent function (e.g., Perr, 1989; Pope, 1989; The Resignation of _____ , 1990; Shearer, 1981; Torry, 1989; Walker & Young, 1986; Zane, 1990). Such suits may also, by rejecting defenses by which perpetrators may have attempted to rationalize their behavior, have helped eliminate the belief— especially among potential offenders—that sexual involvement with someone the therapist has agreed to treat can ever be justified. For example, Cummings and Sobel (1985) reviewed cases handled by the APA Insurance Trust and noted:

> A number of cases have been filed where treatment has been terminated, a sexual relationship has been started, and a malpractice suit has been filed subsequently. The courts have ruled that the emotional transference is still extant even though the termination has taken place. (p. 187)

A more recent case illustrates this point vividly; a plaintiff was awarded $1 million despite the psychologist's defense that he had waited until after termination to engage in sexual relations and that he had then married his former patient and remained married to her for five years (Torry, 1989). An increasing number of potential offenders may be accepting (or at least conforming their behavior to) the conclusion that sexual relationships with patients after termination appear no less harmful or more ethical than pretermination relationships (see, e.g., Brown, 1988; Ethics Committee of the American Psychological Association, 1988; Gabbard & Pope, 1989; Vasquez, 1989). Yet another factor that may reduce the rate of sexual involvement with patients has been an increased recognition of the problems with many of the initial rehabilitation efforts that unintentionally enabled perpetrators to continue to engage in intimacies. It is clear, for example, that evaluations of experimental approaches to rehabilitation must take into account such factors as the low base rate of discovery of subsequent abuse and the rights of patients treated by perpetrators during and after rehabilitation attempts (Pope, 1990).

In light of the severe damage that can result from therapist-patient sexual involvement, the apparent decline in occurrence can serve the profession better as motivation for more intense efforts at understanding and prevention than as occasion for complacency and self-congratulation. Attempts by our profession to highlight indications that the prevalence of such intimacies is relatively small and conceivably declining may remind our patients and the public of White House Chief of Staff John Sununu's defensive reaction to the publicity surrounding the Alaskan oil spill by the Exxon Valdez: "Three quarters of [the oil] was contained within the ship. There's been very little reporting on that" (Dubious Achievement Awards, 1990, p. 82).

Research in this area is a healthy and hopeful sign of our profession's developing sense of responsibility and willingness to examine, scientifically and nondefensively, an unethical and iatrogenic act perpetrated by therapists. Research may also be playing an important role in the (apparently) declining rate of occurrence: The diversity of published research by which we expand and test our understanding of therapist-patient sexual involvement may be leading a wider variety of clinicians to take this issue seriously, to confront more immediately the possibility that it places patients at risk for harm, and to cooperate more vigorously in the scientific, clinical, and professional attempts to address this phenomenon effectively.

References

Aneshensel, C. S., Estrada, A. L., Hansell, M. J., & Clark, V. A. (1987). Social psychological aspects of reporting behavior: Lifetime depressive episode reports. *Journal of Health and Social Behavior, 28,* 232–246.

Bajt, T. R., & Pope, K. S. (1989). Therapist–patient sexual intimacy involving children and adolescents. *American Psychologist, 44,* 455.

Bates, C. R., & Brodsky, A. M. (1989). *Sex in the therapy hour: A case of professional incest.* New York: Guilford.

Benezra, E. E. (1988, March). *Psychiatrist–patient sexual involvement: Retrospective and prospective implications.* Paper presented at the meeting of the Illinois Psychiatric Society, Chicago.

Bouhoutsos, J., Holroyd, J., Lerman, H., Forer, B., & Greenberg, M. (1983). Sexual intimacy between psychotherapists and patients. *Professional Psychology, 14,* 185–196.

Borys, D. S., & Pope, K. S. (1989). Dual relationships between therapist and client: A national study of psychologists, psychiatrists, and social workers. *Professional Psychology: Research and Practice, 20,* 283–293.

Brodsky, A. M. (1989). Sex between patient and therapist: Psychology's data and response. In G. O. Gabbard (Ed.), *Sexual exploitation in professional relationships* (pp. 15–25). Washington, DC: American Psychiatric Press.

Brown, L. S. (1988). Harmful effects of posttermination sexual and romantic relationships with former clients. *Psychotherapy, 25,* 249–255.

Brownfain, J. J. (1971). The APA professional liability insurance program. *American Psychologist, 26,* 648–652.

Butler, S. E., & Zelen, S. L. (1977). Sexual intimacies between therapists and patients. *Psychotherapy, 14,* 139–145.

Cummings, N. A., & Sobel, S. B. (1985). Malpractice insurance: Update on sex claims. *Psychotherapy, 22,* 186–188.

Denmark, F., Russo, N. F., Frieze, I. H., & Sechzer, J. A. (1988). Guidelines for avoiding sexism in research: A report of the Ad Hoc Committee on Nonsexist Research. *American Psychologist, 43,* 582–585.

Dubious Achievement Awards. (1990, January). *Esquire,* pp. 79–92.

Ethics Committee of the American Psychological Association. (1988). Trends in ethics cases, common pitfalls, and published resources. *American Psychologist, 43,* 564–572.

Feldman-Summers, S., & Jones, G. (1984). Psychological impacts of sexual contact between therapists or other health care professionals and their clients. *Journal of Consulting and Clinical Psychology, 52,* 1054–1061.

Freud, S. (1958). Observations on the transference-love. In S. Strachey (Ed.), *Complete psychological works of Sigmund Freud* (pp. 157–173). London: Hogarth. (Translated by J. Strachey. Originally published 1915.)

Gabbard, G. O. (Ed.). (1989). *Sexual exploitation in professional relationships.* Washington, DC: American Psychiatric Press.

Gabbard, G. O., & Pope, K. S. (1989). Sexual intimacies after termination: Clinical, ethical, and legal aspects. In G. O. Gabbard (Ed.), *Sexual exploitation in professional relationships* (pp. 115–128). Washington, DC: American Psychiatric Press.

Gartrell, N., Herman, J., Olarte, S., Feldstein, M. & Localio, R. (1986). Psychiatrist-patient sexual contact: Results of a national survey. *American Journal of Psychiatry, 143,* 112–131.

Gartrell, N., Herman, J., Olarte, S., Feldstein, M. & Localio, R. (1987). Reporting practices of psychiatrists who knew of sexual misconduct by colleagues. *American Journal of Orthopsychiatry, 57,* 287–295.

Gartrell, N., Herman, J., Olarte, S., Feldstein, M. & Localio, R. (1989). Prevalence of psychiatrist-patient sexual contact. In G. O. Gabbard (Ed.), *Sexual exploitation in professional relationships* (pp. 3–13). Washington, DC: American Psychiatric Press.

Gechtman, L. (1989). Sexual contact between social workers and their clients. In G. O. Gabbard (Ed.), *Sexual exploitation in professional relationships* (pp. 27–38). Washington, DC: American Psychiatric Press.

Gross, Z. (1977, August). *Erotic contact as a source of emotional learning in psychotherapy.* Paper presented at the annual meeting of the American Psychological Association, San Francisco.

Herman, J., Gartrell, N., Olarte, S., Feldstein, M. & Localio, R. (1987). Psychiatrist-patient sexual contact: Results of a national survey, II: Psychiatrists' attitudes. *American Journal of Psychiatry, 144,* 164–169.

Holroyd, J. C. (1983). Erotic contact as an instance of sex-biased therapy. In J. Murray & P. R. Abramson (Eds.), *Handbook of bias in psychotherapy* (pp. 285–308). New York: Praeger.

Holroyd, J. C., & Bouhoutsos, J. C. (1985). Sources of bias in reporting effects of sexual contact with patients. *Professional Psychology: Research and Practice, 16,* 701–709.

Holroyd, J. C., & Brodsky, A. M. (1977). Psychologists' attitudes and practices regarding erotic and nonerotic physical contact with clients. *American Psychologist, 32,* 843–849.

Holroyd, J. C., & Brodsky, A. M. (1980). Does touching patients lead to sexual intercourse? *Professional Psychology, 11,* 807–811.

Kinsey, A. C., Pomeroy, W. B., Martin, C. E., & Gebhard, P. H. (1953). *Sexual behavior in the human female.* Philadelphia: W. B. Saunders.

Lapierre, H., & Valiquette, M. (1989). *J'ai fait l'amour avec mon therapeute: Temoignages sur l'intimite sexuelle en therapie.* Montreal, Canada: Les Editions Saint-Martin.

Masters, W. H., & Johnson, V. E. (1966). *Human sexual response.* New York: Bantam.

Masters, W. H., & Johnson, V. E. (1970). *Human sexual inadequacy*. New York: Bantam.

Masters, W. H., & Johnson, V. E. (1975, May). *Principles of the new sex therapy*. Paper presented at the annual meeting of the American Psychiatric Association, Anaheim, CA.

Masters, W. H., Johnson, V. E., & Kolodny, R. D. (Eds.). (1977). *Ethical issues in sex therapy*. Boston: Little, Brown.

McCartney, J. (1966). Overt transference. *Journal of Sex Research, 2*, 227–237.

Patterson, J. Y. (1987). *The dread disease: Cancer and modern American culture*. Cambridge, MA: Harvard University Press.

Pearson, R. W., Ross, M. & Dawes, R. M. (1992). Personal recall and the limits of retrospective questions in surveys. In J. Tanur (Ed.), *Questions about questions: Inquiries into the cognitive bases of surveys*. Beverly Hills, CA: Sage.

Perr, I. N. (1989). Medicolegal aspects of professional sexual exploitation. In G. O. Gabbard (Ed.), *Sexual exploitation in professional relationships* (pp. 211–227). Washington, DC: American Psychiatric Press.

Pomeroy, W. B. (1976, November). A new look at incest. *Forum*, 9–13.

Pope, K. S. (1988). How clients are harmed by sexual contact with mental health professionals. *Journal of Counseling and Development, 67*, 222–226.

Pope, K. S. (1989). Malpractice suits, licensing disciplinary actions, and ethics cases: Frequencies, causes, and costs. *Independent Practitioner, 9*(1), 22–26.

Pope, K. S. (1990). Therapist-patient sex as sex abuse: Six scientific and professional dilemmas in addressing victimization and rehabilitation. *Professional Psychology: Research and Practice, 21*, 227–239.

Pope, K. S., & Bajt, T. R. (1988). When laws and values conflict: A dilemma for psychologists. *American Psychologist, 43*, 828–829.

Pope, K. S., & Bouhoutsos, J. C. (1986). *Sexual intimacies between therapists and patients*. New York: Praeger.

Pope, K. S., Keith-Spiegel, P., & Tabachnick, B. G. (1986). Sexual attraction to clients: The human therapist and the (sometimes) inhuman training system. *American Psychologist, 41*, 147–158.

Pope, K. S., Levenson, H., & Schover, L. R. (1979). Sexual intimacy in psychology training: Results and implications of a national survey. *American Psychologist, 34*, 682–689.

Pope, K. S., Tabachnick, B. G., & Keith-Spiegel, P. (1987). Ethics of practice: The beliefs and behaviors of psychologists as therapists. *American Psychologist, 42*, 993–1006.

The resignation of _____. (1990, Jan/Feb). *The California Therapist*, pp. 6–7.

Riskin, L. (1979). Sexual relations between psychotherapists and their patients: Toward research or restraint? *California Law Review, 67*, 1000–1027.

Ryan, W. (1971). *Blaming the victim*. New York: Pantheon Books.

Serban, G. (1981). Sexual activity in therapy: Legal and ethical issues. *American Journal of Psychotherapy, 35*, 76–85.

Shearer, L. (1981, August 23). Sex between patient and physician. *Los Angeles Times Parade*, p. 8.

Sonne, J. L., & Pope, K. S. (1991). Treating victims of therapist-patient sexual involvement. *Psychotherapy, 28,* 174–187.

Sonne, J. L., Meyer, C. B., Borys, D., & Marshall, V. (1985). Clients' reactions to sexual intimacy in therapy. *American Journal of Orthopsychiatry, 55,* 183–189.

Tavris, C. (1987, November 1). Method is all but lost in the imagery of social-science fiction. *Los Angeles Times,* Section V, p. 5.

Taylor, S. E. (1989). *Positive illusions: Creative self-deception and the healthy mind.* New York: Basic Books.

Torry, S. (1989, October 22). Divorce-malpractice suit won by heiress: Judgment against psychologist is $1 million. *Washington Post,* pp. B1, B9.

Vasquez, M. J. T. (1989, August). *Sexual intimacies with clients after termination: Should the prohibition be explicit?* Paper presented at the annual meeting of the American Psychological Association, New Orleans.

Vinson, J. S. (1987). Use of complaint procedures in cases of therapist-patient sexual contact. *Professional Psychology: Research and Practice, 18,* 159–164.

Walker, E., & Young, P. D. (1986). *A killing cure.* New York: Holt, Rinehart, & Winston.

Walker, L. E. A. (1989). Psychology and violence against women. *American Psychologist, 44,* 695–702.

Zane, M. (1990, January 27). $1.5 million verdict against doctor who seduced patient. *San Francisco Chronicle,* p. 4.

Index

Abrahams, D., 73
Abramowitz, C. V., 215
Abramowitz, S. I., 66, 74, 215
Acceptance of content, 43–44
Actions. *See also* Therapist–client
   intimacies
  beating as intervention, 148–151
  of client, misperception of, 96–98
  consent of client, 184–185
  risk for sexual intimacies, 180–182
  uncharacteristic behaviors, 187–
   189
Age
  of client, 10, 58–59, 246–247,
   279–280
  of therapist, 279–280
Altruism, 31
American Psychiatric Association,
  28–29
American Psychological Association
  (APA), 20, 186–187, 206
  Insurance Trust, 28, 284
  Task Force on Bias in
   Psychotherapy With Lesbians
   and Gay Men, 61, 62
Anal intercourse, therapy goal
  involving, 175
Anger
  of client, at therapist's voyeurism,
   144–145
  as reaction to sexual feelings, 98–
   99
  sexually abusive therapists and,
   257
"Anna O." *See* Pappenheim, Bertha
Anxiety
  about unresolved personal issues,
   84–85
  countertransference, 123–124,
   214–215

APA. *See* American Psychological
  Association
Arizmendi, T. G., 57
Aronson, V., 73
Avoidance
  avoidance of, 8–9
  as clue to sexual feelings, 105–106
  materials available on sexual
   feelings and, 23–24
  of movement toward termination,
   94–95
  sources of, 24–30

Bajt, T. R., 244, 280
Ballou, M. B., 69
Banquer, M., 72
Bates, C., 186n, 191, 238, 240, 254,
  259, 262, 282, 286
Barber, T., 143–144
Beating
  as intervention, 148–151
  in marital relationship, 175
Benezra, E. E., 273–274
Berek, J. S., 72
Bergin, A. E., 59, 60
Berland, D., 58
Berscheid, E., 97
Beutler, L. E., 57, 58, 191
Bias
  gender, 62–67, 239n
  against homosexuality, 60–61
  research limitations and, 271–277
"Blaming the victim," 249–250, 275
"Blank screen" approach, 122–124
Bloomfield, H. H., 72
Boatwright, D., 238
Body awareness exercises, 72, 75–
  76
Boredom, 115–116
Borenzweig, H., 59

About the Authors

Kenneth S. Pope, PhD, received graduate degrees from Harvard and Yale, is a Diplomate in Clinical Psychology, and is a Fellow of the American Psychological Association (APA) and the American Psychological Society. Having previously served as clinical director and psychology director in both private hospital and community mental health center settings, he is currently in independent practice. He taught courses in abnormal psychology, psychological and neuropsychological assessment, and related areas at the University of California, Los Angeles (UCLA), where he served as a psychotherapy supervisor in the UCLA Psychology Clinic. He served as chair of the Ethics Committees of the APA and of the American Board of Professional Psychology. His books include *Sexual Intimacies Between Therapists and Patients* (with J. C. Bouhoutsos), *Ethics in Psychotherapy and Counseling* (with M. J. T. Vasquez), *The MMPI, MMPI-2, and MMPI-A in Court: A Practical Guide for Expert Witnesses and Attorneys* (with J. N. Butcher and J. Seelen), *The Stream of Consciousness: Scientific Investigations Into the Flow of Human Experience*, and *The Power of Human Imagination: New Methods of Psychotherapy* (the latter two with J. L. Singer).

Janet L. Sonne, PhD, is currently on the faculty of the Department of Psychiatry at the Loma Linda University of Medicine, where she supervises and teaches psychiatry residents and medical students. She conducts an independent practice that includes assessment and psychotherapy, serves as a consultant to the Medical Board of California, and testifies as an expert witness in civil and administrative cases.

She completed her undergraduate work at Stanford University and received her doctorate from UCLA. She completed her clinical internship at the UCLA Neuropsychiatric Institute. Following graduate school, she supervised therapists-in-training in the UCLA Psychology Clinic and was on the staff of Patton Hospital, providing assessment and therapeutic services to people with sexual difficulties and supervision to psychology interns.

She helped establish and served as the first group therapist for the UCLA Post-Therapy Support Project, providing consultation, support, assessment, and therapy for patients who had been sexually abused by their former therapists. The Project also created a teaching model in which therapists were trained to provide such services. Dr. Sonne has published a number of works addressing the topic of sexual intimacies between therapists and patients, and has served on the Ethics Committees of the California Psychological Association and of the APA.

Jean Holroyd, PhD, is Director of the Clinical Psychology Internship program at the UCLA Department of Psychiatry and Biobehavioral Sciences, where she has taught since 1969. A diplomate in clinical psychology, she is a fellow of the APA and of the Society for Clinical and Experimental Hypnosis. She completed her undergraduate work at the University of Maryland and received her doctorate from the University of Minnesota, where she completed her clinical internship. After graduation, Dr. Holroyd was assistant to the staff at the Mayo Clinic and later served as chief psychologist at a community mental health center. She has also conducted an independent practice. Dr. Holroyd is a recipient of the Crasilneck and the Roy Dorcas Awards for research from the Society for Clinical and Experimental Hypnosis, and a special citation from the APA Board of Ethnic Minority Affairs for Dedicated Services Toward Minority Concerns.

She was coauthor of the first national study of psychologists' attitudes and practices regarding erotic and nonerotic physical contact with patients, published in *American Psychologist* (1977), and other works on this topic. She served on the committees that developed APA's *General Guidelines for Providers of Psychological Services*, clinical standards of care for women, and clinical standards of care for ethnic minorities; on APA's Education and Training Board; and on the California Psychological Association's Ethics Committee. She also served as co-chair of the APA Task Force on Sex Bias and Sex Role Stereotyping in Psychotherapeutic Practice. She published the Questionnaire on Resources and Stress, a test that is used with families of chronically ill or handicapped individuals.